UNSUNG
HEROES OF
ANIMATION

UNSUNG
HEROES OF
ANIMATION

Chris Robinson

British Library Cataloguing in Publication Data

Unsung Heroes of Animation
A catalogue entry for this book is available from the British Library

ISBN: 0 86196 665 1 (Paperback)

Published by
John Libbey Publishing, Box 276, Eastleigh SO50 5YS, UK
e-mail: libbeyj@asianet.co.th; web site: www.johnlibbey.com

Orders: **Book Representation & Distribution Ltd**. info@bookreps.com

Distributed in North America by **Indiana University Press**, 601 North Morton St, Bloomington, IN 47404, USA. www.iupress.indiana.edu

Distributed in Australasia by **Elsevier Australia**, 30–52 Smidmore Street, Marrickville NSW 2204, Australia. www.elsevier.com.au

Distributed in Japan by **United Publishers Services Ltd**, 1-32-5 Higashi-shinagawa, Shinagawa-ku, Tokyo 140-0002, Japan. info@ups.co.jp

Printed in Malaysia by Vivar Printing Sdn. Bhd., 48000 Rawang, Selangor Darul Ehsan.

Contents

For Otto Alder and Gerben Schermer, who were celebrating animation's unsung long before I came around.

They are called biographies but to me they are something else – a biography of a mystery, a biography of a time. There has to be something about that character that I felt an empathy for and it was maybe a mystery in me that I tried to solve. I always thought of them as a central character in the foreground of a bigger story.
Nick Tosches

Introduction

A few words about the title of this book. It is an homage to Nick Tosches' 1984 book, *Unsung Heroes of Rock and Roll*. Tosches is a writer I admire enormously. His style and tone influenced a lot of animator profiles found in this book. Tosches' book is an introduction to a variety of forgotten pre-Elvis rock and roll musicians. It was Tosches' contention that Elvis triggered, not the birth of rock n' roll, but it's death. For Tosches, these early rock and rollers were the real soul and spirit of rock music before Elvis turned it into a soulless manufactured industry for teens and twits.

Unlike Tosches, I don't contend that there is a similar defining moment in animation. Throughout its history, animation has been primarily defined as cartoons that make people laugh, a medium of gags, caricatures, animals and fart jokes. Most people have no idea that there also exists a more personal, provocative and poetic side of animation, one that is not made for money and mass audiences. *Unsung Heroes of Animation* is an introduction to those faces and voices that remain largely unseen and unappreciated.

This is by no means a complete survey of independent or personal animation. Because of time, energy, and a lousy memory, there are many worthy animators (Gerd Gockell, Kirsten Winter, Jerzy Kucia, Chris Hinton, Paul Driessen, Taku Furukawa, and many more) who are not included here. The independent animation community is small and intimate. At times, it's like living in a village. Everyone seems to know what everyone else is doing. During my fourteen years with the Ottawa International Animation Festival, I have gotten to know many of these people. In many cases, I consider them friends more than colleagues. In fact, the main reason I got into this strange little world of animation was because of the people. I simply found them, for the most part, very warm, humble and outgoing human beings. For a shy, insecure, and feckless mid-twenties man, this was heaven, a place I wanted to be.

In this world I have tried to find myself and figure out just what it is that I'm supposed to be doing with my life. As such, the pieces in this book are highly subjective and often personal. Many of these writings say more about my own concerns, fears and obsessions than they perhaps do about the subjects. As the Tosches' epitaph says, 'there has to be something about that character that I felt an empathy for and it was maybe a mystery in me that I tried to solve'. In short, through these people and films, I have, I guess, been trying to find myself.

These pieces were written over a nine-year period, for a variety of publications, and as much as some of the writing makes me cringe a bit (I sometimes see lazy, repetitious ideas. In fact, it's amazing how much I rip myself off), I've decided to leave the older texts (pre-2005) as they were when I originally wrote them. Some of these animators have made new films, but rather than muck with the rhythm and tone of the original piece, I felt it was better to just leave them as they were written.

I'd like to thank: all the subjects for their time and trust; the incredible and generous Genevieve Willis for taking time during her stay in Japan to provide feedback and proofing; my publisher, John Libbey; past and present colleagues at the Ottawa International Animation Festival and beyond including Tom Knott, Tom McSorley, John Connolly, Mark Langer, Alyson Carty, Hayden Mindell, David Ehrlich, Linda Simensky, Marc Glassman, Ellen Besen, Melissa Wheeler and Claude Lord of the National Film Board of Canada, Toril Simonsen of the Norwegian Film, Heather Kenyon, Ron Diamond, Dan Sarto and everyone at Animation World Network for permission to re-print some articles originally written for them, Wyndam Wise at *Take One Magazine*, Mark Peranson at *Cinemascope Magazine*, Andre Coutu, and Maral Mohammadian; and Kelly, Betty and Jarvis Neall, as always, for enduring all this obsessive behaviour.

Chris Robinson

July 2005
Ottawa, Canada

Chapter 1

Raimund Krumme:
The Powers That Be (1996)

The Message

Given the increasing obsession with technology in animation, it's refreshing to discover the work of Raimund Krumme. Somewhere between Buster Keaton, Samuel Beckett and Chuck Jones, Krumme turns minimalist line drawings into complex, imaginative, and often humorous meditations on class, power, mass media, and, with an ironic twist, animation itself. Structured around an allegorical journey, Krumme's exiled Keatonesque 'everymen' travel through barren, absurd, and often cruel landscapes in a quest for self-knowledge. And in Krumme's work, like that of fellow countryman, Wim Wenders, the landscape also functions as an equation of a character's state of mind, often reflecting a deeper torment.

The key to stabilizing the characters' torments is through power. But power itself is an ever-changing and often superficial entity. In *Rope Dance* (1986) and *The Magic Flute* (1993), power comes through knowledge and love. In *Spectators* (1989), power is illusory, seemingly achieved through the mass media, while *Passage* (1994) comments on the absurd resiliency of hierarchical power. Finally, power is reflected through Krumme himself, who, through a series of Brechtian self-reflexive strategies (e.g. using his materials as an active part of the fiction), attempts to keep the audience at an emotional yet meditative distance, while playfully reminding his characters that they are just that: characters.

What makes Krumme's work so special is not his existential queries, but rather his ability to treat these issues in an often comic and imaginative fashion. Watching Krumme's creative manipulation of space is not unlike viewing the films of Buster Keaton, Jackie Chan or Gene Kelly, whose physical manoeuvres and astonishing use of space as a supporting character, defy all reason. While academics can ponder over the sociological and philosophical implications of each scene, there is an emotional element at work, contrary to Krumme's Brechtian ambitions, that is quite simply hypnotic.

Born in Cologne in 1950, Krumme spent his post-student years dabbling in a variety of activities. In addition to teaching, Krumme also illustrated, and produced radio plays for children.

Raimund Krumme

Krumme's entrance into animation was, he notes, 'quite by accident'. A company approached him to do drawings for a children's film. He did the drawings, went to the set, and ended up directing the film, a cut-out piece entitled, *Phantômes des Châteaux* (1980). Krumme would go on to direct three more films for children:

5

Spaghetti (1981) (about a boy who, forced to eat his spaghetti, instead attempts to build his own world out of the food), *Puzzle* (1982), and *And The Chair Flew Through The Window* (1984).

Puzzle, produced in the Netherlands, was initially inspired by a photo of handicapped children. In it were kids who, despite their disabilities (some couldn't see or walk), helped each other get around. The second inspiration came from the memory of the actions of a group of children. According to Krumme, the children had formed a group, leaving one child out. A second child, the schoolyard 'henchman', was responsible for keeping other children out of the group. In the end, the rejected child formed a second and more popular group, and even the 'henchman' wanted to be part of the new group.

At the beginning of the film, five puzzle pieces move about rather aimlessly. A sixth puzzle piece attempts to join but is rejected. Eventually the group becomes four, then three, then two, etc. In the meantime, the rejected pieces form a group of their own. Finally, realizing that they can accomplish more together, all six pieces come together and become a self-sufficient globe.

The success of Krumme's work stems from his ability to merge the personal and the universal in a playful environment. However, *Puzzle's* straightforward style leaves little to the imagination and consequently reduces its subject to a cliché.

Krumme's fourth and final children's film, *And The Chair Flew Through The Window,* is a startling contrast to the rest of his work.

The Message

The film was based on an unpublished book of illustrations by Krumme about three pieces of furniture who flee from their house and travel the city streets. *And The Chair ...* is an imaginative, at times surreal film that, despite being aimed at children, seems more along the lines of Martin Scorcese's *After Hours*.

Rope Dance was the first film that enabled Krumme to shift from making films for children towards a more personalized style. In the film, two characters (based on Krumme's relationship with his father) struggle for control of a rope within a continually shifting rectangular plane. While some have viewed the film, in its seemingly negative view towards the father, as cruel, *Rope Dance* is an innovative and tender meditation on the transference of knowledge, and with it power, from generation to generation. What elevates the film beyond Krumme's previous work is his marvelous use of the rope and rectangle. The rope, a symbol of knowledge, undergoes continual shifts in the film as the characters develop. Initially, the rope is a series of tracks that the father lays for the son, then, just as quickly, the rope becomes a means of control as the son becomes a puppet under the unbearable control of the father. For a moment there is peace as the two swing the rope in unison over the rectangle which has now become a well. Later, the son attempts to break free of the rope in order to join the crowd, but the father is unwilling, indeed unable, to let go. Eventually the son assumes control of the rope, and in the film's most tender moment, the son returns to lead the now blind father.

The Message

7

Despite Krumme's initial insecurity with *Rope Dance* (according to Krumme, a friend who had only seen his early films, thought that *Rope Dance* was 'very bad'), it went on to critical and popular acclaim at numerous festivals, including Annecy and Hiroshima.

Because of *Rope Dance's* success, Krumme attended many festivals and became interested in audiences, specifically in their emotional responses to the images and sounds before them. The result of Krumme's fascination was *Spectators*, a biting parable about public reaction using the relationship between a film and its audience. Krumme, who admits to finding the power of the masses, 'quite frightening', was also motivated by the importance in Germany at the time of possessing uniform opinions. Krumme adds that while things have changed now, there was a time, following unification, where anyone who expressed doubts about the new state was viewed as a traitor.

In *Spectators*, the cinema becomes a repressive environment where people lose themselves in a series of images and sounds. This over-reliance on mass media is nowhere better illustrated than when the film breaks down, causing the crowd to go into a state of panic and frenzy. The audience becomes a uniform pattern of repressed emotion where all reactions must correspond to those of the majority.

Spectators reveals, like Fritz Lang's *Fury*, a fear of the often reactionary and over-emotional power of the masses. Krumme's frantic, dizzying camera reflects the ever-changing moods of the audience, while the refusal of a central character reflects, not only the lack of individuality in contemporary society, but also the need to be led (which is nicely illustrated through Krumme's nod to *Animal Farm*, where the audience turns into rows of clucking chickens). And again, space plays a pivotal role in the film. In contrast to the open spaces of Krumme's other films, *Spectators* offers a constricting, claustrophobic landscape that at once bears a close resemblance to a prison, while emphasizing the almost hyper-repressive nature of the characters.

During this time, Krumme was living in Paris and Berlin. The transient state left Krumme in what one might call a mid-mid-life crisis. The feeling of uncertainty about his direction, says Krumme, led to an increasingly fragile existence, where dimensions changed and things were not what they seemed to be. Out of this in-between, surreal state came *Crossroads*, Krumme's most Beckett-inspired work.

Like *Rope Dance*, *Crossroads* features a basic symbol, in this case, an intersection. A man crosses the screen and walks along the frame of the film. The frame soon becomes a tightrope, then a road which leads to an intersection. Now the man must decide which path to take. In deciding his course of action, he must confront the advice of his shadow and three other men. But the man soon finds that each path only leads him back to the centre. Soon, all four characters (echoing the brilliant scene in Keaton's *Sherlock Jr.* that finds Buster trapped within the frame and at the mercy of the editor), enter spaces which suddenly change from corridors into walls. What appears to be hopeful one moment turns into entrapment the next. It soon becomes apparent that no matter how hard the characters try, they simply aren't going anywhere. But inexplicably, Krumme's characters, in spite of the impossibility of their actions, do go on.

Passage merges elements of Leo Tolstoy's story, *Master and Man* with a dash of Tex Avery, Fred Astaire and Jerry Lewis, to create one of his most explicit and absurd political commentaries. Two men, a porter and his master, have to cross a frozen pond. Fearing the danger ahead of them, each tries to follow the other, leaving their social roles behind. But once the danger is over, everything returns to its original state.

The most inspired moments of the film come during the sequence on the ice, where the characters, having broken free of their social roles, become part-Jerry Lewis, part-Fred Astaire. Using the very materials (lines and paper) with which they were created, the duo

The Message

9

engages in ice skating, dismemberment and snowball fights as they frantically attempt to cross the frozen pond.

Despite the Tex Avery-inspired lunacy of *Passage*, we should not overlook the value of the message underlying the film: hierarchy is culturally, not naturally conceived.

Following *Passage*, Krumme explored a new avenue: computer animation. He was asked to contribute to the animated-opera series, 'Opera Imaginaire'. Appreciating the playful and expressive quality of Mozart, Krumme selected a scene from *The Magic Flute* in which an imprisoned Pamina, thinking she has been abandoned by her lover, considers suicide. Fortunately, three wise boys save Pamina from her torments.

Aside from the new technical approach, *The Magic Flute* still possesses basic Krumme traits. Once again, Krumme structures the film around a journey (albeit an internal one) to reflect the character's wandering state. The surrounding landscape again plays a pivotal role, in its mirroring of the character's state of mind. Throughout the film, Pamina moves through a maze of spaces which, echoing *Crossroads*, initially simulate freedom, but quickly resume the form of prison walls.

The most striking feature of the film is Krumme's character design. Replacing the black stick-figures are geometrically shaped characters made out of triangles and circles. Krumme says that, as this was his first computer venture, he not only wanted to keep the characters simple using basic geometric shapes, but he also wanted their design to reflect the very ordered and rational behaviour of the characters, especially the three wise boys.

The Magic Flute is technically unlike anything Krumme has done before. Working on a computer for the first time using TOON-BOX, a 2D animation palette, Krumme, like his characters, entered a new, and at times frustrating, creative environment. While TOONBOX enabled Krumme to do things he couldn't do by hand (e.g. changing colours) and relieved him from tedious work (e.g. inbetweening), it was not an entirely happy experience. Krumme found that he had to compromise a great deal and that he was often forced into a subservient role with the computer. But despite his overall unhappiness with the final product, he admits that he would like to work with computers again.

In 1994 Krumme was approached by producer Ron Diamond to do a commercial for Acme Filmworks in Los Angeles. And while Krumme is the first to acknowledge the financial rewards of doing advertisements, he says that the offer also gave him a chance to work in a new creative environment. Unlike his independent work, an often long and arduous task, commercial work is short and intense. But perhaps more importantly, commercial work enabled Krumme to move to a new geographical environment, the United States. Krumme had come to a stage where he felt it was time to leave Germany. The desire was not motivated by any bitterness, just a need to explore, like his character in *Crossroads*, a new avenue. Krumme has since completed a number of commercials and continues to work for Diamond and live in California for most of the year, returning to Germany for a few weeks every summer.

One of the common criticisms of Krumme's work is that 'it's all the same'. Not only does this criticism imply that an individual aesthetic is defined solely by its technique, it denies story and plot its rightful place within the artist's style. And while Krumme's films from *Rope Dance* to *Passage* certainly bear an unmistakable 'Krumme-look', it is wrong to reduce these complex and varied works to a single style. To paraphrase Samuel Beckett, danger lies in the neatness of identification. At the same time, given Krumme's on-going desire to experiment formally (ranging from fictional and children's films to commercials, operas, and computer animation), it is simply wrong to reduce Krumme's work to such a narrow definition.

But perhaps the most important aspect of Krumme's work is his craftsmanship. Unlike today's technological dynamos who view craftsmanship solely in terms of technique with scant attention to story, Krumme's work is inspiring because he merges a deceptively simple story and technique into a creative and complex imagining of contemporary society. And, in what is perhaps his ultimate irony, Krumme's basic black and white drawings allow us to see that the reality we take for granted is not in fact black and white.

Filmography of Raimund Krumme

1980	*Phantomes des Chateaux*
1981	*Spaghetti*
1982	*Puzzle*
1983	Production of animated scenes for the feature film *Realtime* by Hellmuth Costard
1984	*And The Chair Flew Through the Window*
1986	*Rope Dance*
1989	*Spectators*
1991	*Crossroads*
1993	*The Magic Flute*
1994	*Passage*
2002	*The Message*

Chapter 2

Angst for the Memories: Stefan Schabenbeck (1998)

'Schabenbeck is one of the greatest but least known authors of contemporary Polish animation'
Giannalberto Bendazzi, *Cartoons*

Top: *Everything is a Number*

Bottom: *Stairs*

Upon first glance, the films of Stefan Schabenbeck appear as reactionary polarizations of issues that warrant more elaboration. They are. But they are also clever, passionate, and often humourous condemnations of the on-going dehumanization of humanity. What dissuades us from rejecting Schabenbeck as a 60s reactionary is the universality and timelessness of his work. On one hand, his films reflect a specific time and culture as they are blunt critiques of bureaucracy within 1960s Poland; on the other, the themes of dehumanization that he expresses are as relevant today as they were thirty years ago. Although he only made six independent films, Stefan Schabenbeck's career certainly warrants more notice than it has been given. Not unlike the work of Samuel Beckett, Buster Keaton, and German animator, Raimund Krumme, his films are tragicomic pieces about the human condition.

Stefan Schabenbeck was born in 1940 in Zakopane, Poland. He graduated from the Secondary School of Fine Arts in Warsaw and was trained as a cameraman in the Lodz Filmschool. His introduction to animation was quite strange, 'I made my first film when I was studying – a teacher told me during my studies that the Semafor studio needed one more film to fulfill their production plan. So I wrote a script and sent it and they accepted. That was cut-out animation with parts of drawn animation (*Everything is A Number*) – that was on the whole my very first film. It wasn't exactly as it should be, but I did win a prize at Oberhausen with it.' Due to Schabenbeck's initial success, he was given more creative freedom.

At that time, Polish animation studios were state owned, and as such were forced to adhere to a bureaucratic process which included the preparation of monthly and yearly strategies for the approval of a Cinematographic office. 'Studio Semafor', says Schabenbeck, 'produced primarily children's and experimental films because this meant good publicity at international festivals. The production schedule offered an average time for production of three months. One had to send in a script or a storyboard and a motivation telling them why a film was useful for the "education of the people".'

Despite the bureaucracy, the environment was not entirely unfavourable. Funding was consistent and the studios were pretty much left alone. Each studio had an arts council consisting of their best directors, who had a say in the production plans. The system, whatever its faults, enabled creative diversity and expression to continue on a fairly consistent basis. On the other hand, the system was not without its absurdities. *The Draught*, which for Schabenbeck was simply about human relations and the wall between people, was not allowed to be sent to foreign festivals because the censors saw the 'wall' as the iron curtain. 'There was a note of

13

protest', says Schabenbeck, 'from the DDR and so the Polish side was forced to withdraw the film. And I went to Oberhausen with another film-it was quite an affair-but I didn't care to talk to the Press about the real reasons-but everybody knew why. And I had some trouble in the studio and then I wrote a letter to the Ministry of Culture and I complained. I never got an answer, but they transferred me to another studio in Warsaw.'

A combination of political and economic reasons led Schabenbeck to not only stop making personal films, but also to leave Poland. 'I felt trapped in Poland', says Schabenbeck, 'there were no personal liberties, although it appears like there were. For example, I was invited to the Annecy festival, but wasn't allowed to go.' Finally, when his mother found an opportunity to go to Germany, Schabenbeck followed.

But in Germany, Schabenbeck found that it was difficult to continue making personal films. 'When I came to Germany, I had to nourish my family and there was no possibility to make my own films. I had to make money so I did some commercials and I worked a bit for the German *Sesame Street*. Then I got quite lucky, when I was in Hamburg for two weeks I got a commercial assignment. I did that as a freelance. Then I rented a studio and I started, although I didn't speak any German. Actually the company ordered a commercial with actors and it was quite a surprise for them to discover that I actually made animated films. But the commissioner found that to be a good thing. And then I made six short TV spots. That was for welfare markets for the postal office. I did that very fast, because the deadline was the day before yesterday and I did it in two weeks mostly with cut-outs.' Since then, Schabenbeck has continued to make commercial films in Germany, and, since 1990, has also being teaching at an Art College in Lodz.

When asked if he was happy with his films, Schabenbeck said that he didn't like his films initially, but has since developed a fondness for them. And given the sudden appearance of Schabenbeck's films at international festivals, it seems many share this fondness.

In *Everything is a Number* (1966) a man attempts to survive in a world of numbers and geometric shapes. But in the end, the man is cloned and ultimately becomes just another number. Schabenbeck's graduate film is a smart and comic critique of bureaucracy and technology. The film is almost comically anti-*Sesame Street* in its attack on our increased reliance on numbers. Ironically, Schabenbeck would go on to work for *Sesame Street* in Germany.

Exclamanation Mark (1967): A society of ant-like creatures constructs a ball. Once the ball is created, they attempt to move it up a hill, but it rolls down and crushes them into shape of an exclamation mark. The beauty of the film is Schabenbeck's ability to turn a simple idea into a smart critique.

Schabenbeck's poetic masterpiece, *The Stairs* (1968), involves a man climbing an endless set of stairs. When he reaches the last stair, he dies and takes the form of a new stair. A solemn work that is, with the exception of the humourous self-reflexive opening, unrelenting in its allegorical depiction of life's journey.

In *The Drought* (1969), we see the image of a series of cracks or islands. We then see two groups trying to fill in the cracks in order to come together, but each attempt is met with failure. Finally the camera pulls back to reveal many cracks that need to be filled. Then, in a moment of supreme nihilism, it rains. Is this a call to God for a great flood to fill in the cracks of a system that will soon drown? *The Drought* is a scream of frustration with both the world and, more specifically, the repression of cultures in a Communist system.

Wind (1969), Schabenbeck's first colour film is, ironically, not very colourful. This is the first film with an identifiable landscape, this time a city. But within it, we see the same dull clouds and faceless people. An envelope falls on the top of a building. The people race to the top to get the envelope. However, it falls to the ground and is picked up by someone. Upon picking it up he turns green. Suddenly, the crowd chases after the man and his information. No one knows what the envelope contains, but they assume it to be important information or knowledge.

With echoes of Buster Keaton's *Cops*, the crowd pursues the man. He eventually loses them and opens the envelope. As he does, the wind blows the letter away. The film ends with the man frantically chasing the letter. He too believes that he carried something valuable. *Wind* is a brilliant interpretation of the power of the modern media and its ability to make the most irrelevant issue monumental.

Schabenbeck's final film, *Invasion* (1970) addresses the threat of technology. A series of alien ships land on a planet. After a series of explorations, diggings, and a brief combat scene with a group of white globs, the alien machines move deeper into the planet, where we discover that they are inside a human eye.

Filmography of Stefan Schabenbeck

1966	*Everthing is a Number*
1967	*Exclamation Mark*
1968	*Stairs*
1969	*The Drought*
1969	*Wind*
1970	*Invasion*

Chapter 3

George Griffin's Complicated Cartoons
(1999)

'The denial of lower, coarse, vulgar, venal, servile-in a word, natural-enjoyment, which constitutes the sacred sphere of culture, implies an affirmation of the superiority of those who can be satisfied with the sublimated, refined, disinterested, gratuitous, distinguished pleasures forever closed to the profane. That is why art and cultural consumption are predisposed, consciously and deliberately or not, to fulfill a social function of legitimating social differences.'
Pierre Bourdieu

Flying Fur

Since the arrival of cultural studies onto the academic scene, questions of taste and issues of high and low culture have become more prominent. Where it was once acceptable in film studies (itself a field that was once thought of as unfit for academics) to discuss 'high' artists like Jean-Luc Godard, Chantal Akerman, or Ingmar Bergman, cultural studies paved the way for studies of Ed Wood, Keanu Reeves, George Lucas, and animation.

However, while animation's acceptance into the ivory tower initially suggests a uniting of the 'vulgar' and 'refined', it has instead furthered the gap. In animation, we often use the labels, 'cartoon' and 'animation' film to define our viewing experience. 'Cartoons,' of course, suggest either satirical films by the old studios like Warner Bros., Disney, etc. or a numbing merchandising entertainment product of entertainment. In general, 'cartoon' suggests an inferior product of entertainment. Conversely, an animation film suggests a work of art that is more intellectual than sensual. We rarely hear anyone say that they saw a Norman McLaren or Priit Parn cartoon; just as we don't say, 'I saw an animation film by Tex Avery or Chuck Jones'. Perhaps more than any other animator, American George Griffin has rigorously deliberated over the issue of entertainment and art in his films, teachings and writings. Like Godard and Wim Wenders, Griffin, while often holding his nose at all things popular, cannot escape his own fascination with and enjoyment of consumer culture.

In *Koko* (1988), based on the Charlie Parker song, Griffin greets us with a dizzying dance of torn Pop Art images. Shreds of consumer culture flash before us, swayed and absorbed by the tempo and power of Parker's horn. Parker's be-bop emphasized spontaneity, fragmentation, anger, and general explosiveness. His music mirrored the mood of a schizoid post-war period. Parker's music also rejects the conformist sounds of assembly line big band jazz, in favour of a more personal and intimate form of expression. During

that time animation was also undergoing a similar shift in expression. The assembly line animation work of Walt Disney, Warner Bros. and Walter Lantz spawned a new style of animation by the likes of U.P.A. studio, Norman McLaren, Robert Breer, and others, that was more experimental and personal. By quoting both Parker's music (which itself quotes from both Woody Woodpecker and a tepid swing standard by Charlie Burnett called *Cheroke*) and post-war advertising images, Griffin not only acknowledges

George Griffin

17

the shift from pop to personal, but, by removing – and, in effect, killing – the images from their original commercial context, he re-creates them (as Parker has done) as something more intensely personal.

Facing page, top:
New Fangled
bottom: *Viewmaster*

This page:
Lineage (both images)

19

From his early anti-cartoons and writings of the 1970s through to his more accessible work of the 1990s (specifically *A Little Routine*), New York animator, George Griffin, has relentlessly explored the relationship between supposed high and low culture. In films, Griffin negotiates personal and animation history within a self-re-flexive landscape that strives to re-claim cartoons as an adult medium.

The son of a political cartoonist, it is surprising, given his preoccu-pation with the early traditions of animation, that Griffin's roots are not in animation: 'I wasn't allowed to have comic books or coloring books as a child. I saw the Disney films, but it wasn't until late in my twenties that I decided to do it. I always drew, but I never had any orientation towards animation or cartoons.' After working briefly in a government office, Griffin found a job as an apprentice for a live-action director and eventually ended up at a commercial animation studio called Focus Design: 'I got that job and I worked there for one year. I did all the studio cel animation work that everyone does short of animating'. Working under a variety of old animators, including Phil Kemmelman and former Disney animator, Jack Schnirk, Griffin learned 'the old fashioned way' to draw and sequence. Griffin entered animation at a fairly active time: 'Commercial production was really open. *Yellow Sub-marine* pushed a certain button. There were a lot of madmen making commercials. A lot of people who were otherwise conven-tional were wild and took drugs and made funny drawings. All of that turned up in the commercial world. R.O. Blechman, while maybe not one of those people, was certainly very much a part of the pop sensibility of minimalism with an experimental attitude towards design.'

While freelancing at a variety of studios and even landing a teaching job at New York University, Griffin began making his own films in 1969, including a political film called *One Man's Laundry*. 'It was a script a friend of mine wrote as a live action film. We translated it to a cartoon and there were a lot of compromises made along the way.

The Anti-Cartoons

The early part of Griffin's career is dominated by a series of films investigating the illusory nature of animation. Throughout these films, which include *Trik Film 3*, *Head*, *Viewmaster*, and finally *Lineage*, Griffin repeatedly investigates the material roots of the medium while incorporating his own personal history.

By the early 1970s, Griffin had made a number of short, experi-mental films, but he considers *Trik Film 3* (1973) to be the first of

20

these 'anti-cartoons'. *Trik Film 3* begins with the frame-by-frame image of a hand sitting at what initially appears to be a restaurant table. After finishing a coffee, the hand begins to doodle in a notebook. We see the title, '*Trik Film 3*'. The scene then cuts to the animated film version of the flipbook. The remainder of the film interplays between the notebook doodles and the animated film. *Trik Film 3* ends with the artist's hand flipping the notebook images. The camera then pulls back to reveal that what we thought was a restaurant, was in fact a film studio.

At once a documentary on the making of a flipbook, *Trik Film 3* also shows the beginnings of Griffin's obsession with breaking cinematic illusions. The weaving of the two scenes reveals both the materiality and physical labour required to compose the drawings. Of course, ironically, these revelatory scenes are in fact animated themselves, so in the end the illusion remains to some degree intact.

Head (initially called *Trick Film 4*) carries on the 'investigation' started in *Trick Film 3*, but in a more fragmented and varied manner: 'Head was made at the Mcdowell Colony, which is an arts colony in New Hampshire. What I was doing was not making drawings for a film, I was just making drawings. A lot of large scale drawings of this square head, that's where they started happening.' Appropriately, the only connecting images in *Head* are heads; whether a head of film, the head of the artist, or the head of various drawings. The film plays with various facial expressions and is linked by a live action shot of Griffin addressing the camera and talking about his change from youth to middle age. He explains that while his aging face shows a well-defined character, his drawings have on the other hand reverted from complicated pictures of his youth to very simple, childlike drawings. This regression is a reference to Emile Cohl, who began his career creating detailed caricatures and drawings before turning to an almost stick-figure style in animation. *Head* rejects the notion of style in favour of a more primitive anti-style, and alongside Griffin's ongoing reminder of the material nature of the medium (e.g. seeing the paper that is being drawn on), *Head* becomes a celebration of the artist, not as a great magician, but as a labourer.

Head is also notable for the debut of Griffin's Saul Steinberg-influenced 'square guy' alter ego. Aside from the character's relationship to Griffin ('it's a reflection of my self-image as a kind of square guy'), 'square guy' is also representative of Griffin's anti-style ambitions of the time. Not only is the square guy a diversion from the primarily circular characters of modern animation, but he also reflects Griffin's desire to 'reduce the idea of what a portrait is to just the bare essentials and to make a style of drawing that anybody could do'.

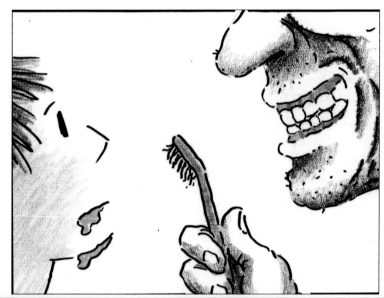

Top: *A Little Routine*.

Bottom: *The Club*

During this time, Griffin's activities were not limited to making films. He was deeply involved in 'para-cinema,' specifically flip books, art installations and, maybe most significantly, his book, *Frames*, 'a selection of drawings and statements by independent American animators' that was assembled by Griffin and New York artists, Kathy Rose, Al Jarnow, Anita Thacher, and Victor Faccinto: 'Frames came out of this little clique that sprang in New York, that was kind of the anti-ASIFA group; a group of people who were making independent films which were much more experimental and who felt that ASIFA was not serving the interests of the true film family'.

Griffin and company sent a letter to animators across America inviting them to contribute to the book. In the letter, animation is defined as both a 'frame-by-frame technique and a frame-by-frame awareness'. Participants were asked to 'submit 1 or 2 pages containing drawings, diagrams, photographs, or text'. While the final intent of the book was 'to stimulate dialogue among a wide range of artists and their audiences', Griffin admits that there may have been more self-serving motivations: 'It was really a reaction to Cecile Starr's book, *Experimental Animation* where she included some of us and left others of us out and we felt we were a much bigger more important thing than just Cecile's book that had just one chapter devoted to our generation. We felt like young turks, and we had a bunch of meetings and we had projects. Looking back on it, it really deteriorated into a party time. Then I went to go off to teach at Harvard.'

Prior to his Harvard venture, Griffin produced *Viewmaster*, a film that originally began as eight drawings made for what was to be a circular book. Initially, the film, which was made to show at galleries, appears to be a running race between an odd assortment of characters and creatures. The camera eventually pulls back to reveal that what we've been watching is merely a cycle of the same action. Minimalist tricks aside, what is most interesting about *Viewmaster* is Griffin's rejection of a consistent style of animation. Each frame consists of drastically different characterizations ranging from classical animation to scribbly lines. Here, Griffin refuses homogeneity. Our shells never honestly reflect the internal mess lurking beneath. *Viewmaster* provides snapshots of those internal beasts.

The anti-cartoon period culminates with *Lineage,* which is a summary of Griffin's work to date: 'It was a way to say good bye to a certain kind of work. I had made these experimental or gallery films. They were fairly extreme and I felt I had to go on to something else.' *Lineage* also evolved out of Griffin's period at Harvard where he became irritated with the tenured eggheads who argued that

Sketch from *Flying Fur*

artistic validity came through the cold hands of abstraction and formalism.

Lineage is philosophical, but spiced with a playful self-awareness of its ambitions. Despite its thirty-minute length, *Lineage* can, in many ways, be summed up in the opening minutes of the film. As a line crosses the screen, Griffin's voice explains the intended meaning of the image. The central theme is a line. A line that links Griffin to his artist father and to animation's past (Griffin tells us that his father saw Winsor McCay 'perform' in Atlanta). The solitary line also extends to Griffin's own life as an artist living in New York for many years. From there, we see more lines as Griffin's voice begins to count the drawings necessary to make up each image. Eventually the lines increase until what we are seeing is an abstract film. The counting reminds us of both the labour and mundane nature of the process of creating. Extending this theme of the artist as labourer, we next see Square Head hand cranking the images we have seen. Bored with the images, the 'projectionist' falls asleep. In just a few minutes, with limited images, Griffin manages to bring personal and collective histories into musings on the material nature and hidden class structures of the medium. The remainder of the film expands on this investigation as Griffin parodies museum texts (in the recreation of an archival film featuring, we assume, Griffin as a live Square Head acting as a sketch artist) and academics, always with a keen awareness of his own implication. In the end, there is no absolute solution to the investigation. Instead, we are presented with a series of scattered musings on the nature of being(s).

Out of the Closet: Re-Claiming the Cartoon

Lineage marked the end of Griffin's overtly formalist experiments and signaled a turn towards more audience friendly 'cartoons'. This is not to say that the depth of Griffin's work minimized; instead one could argue that Griffin has merely re-claimed the cartoon as an adult medium: 'I wanted to expand the agenda for the cartoon, a word whose root connotation of drawing or sketch had been seriously compromised by the saccharin, infantile, Disney sensibility'.

Although his next film, *It's An Ok Life* was something of a departure in terms of it being a narrative driven, commissioned film, it was not the first time Griffin had attempted to make a 'cartoon'. In 1975, during what was Griffin's most productive artistic period, he produced the notorious film, *The Club*. The film consists of a long, sweeping tracking shot inside an elite men's club. In place of humans are cocks. Dickheads. Literally. Heh heh heh. Enough said.

It's an OK Life (1980) was a commissioned film for PBS about the life and death of a 21st century everyman. Again, like *The Club* and later, *New Fangled*, *It's An OK Life* is a fairly one-dimensional film. Nevertheless, the film is well animated with a definite Griffin touch (ranging from the simple graphic style to the self-deprecating humour, enhanced by the neurotic narrator). The most astonishing thing about the film is how accurate Griffin's vision of the future, with references to cloning, computer crimes and, most appropriately, a life that is generally 'quick and painless', has turned out to be. Not surprisingly, the rather ominous ending of *Life*, with its implication of suicide, was cut out of the television version: 'They thought it would be too dark a proposal for public television. Instead, it ends with the typical couple embracing looking at the sunset (with a question mark at least).'

The frantic, madcap, stream-of-consciousness *Flying Fur* (1981), is at once Griffin's *Bimbo's Initiation* (Fleischer) and an interrogation of political and social violence. The images and tempo are based on the soundtrack for an old *Tom and Jerry* cartoon called *Putting On The Dog*. The resemblance ends there. The chase scenes and anarchic violence are far removed from a *Tom and Jerry* film. Griffin ingeniously subverts the cartoon genre into a commentary of violence, hatred and racism. The wolf vs. mouse vs. cat scenario is expressed as being racially motivated. There is no logic to this hatred or violence. It is unharnessed and manic. Characters are going so fast that they never stop to consider the implications of their actions. Complicating things further is the lack of clear identities. Characters change identities and allegiances throughout the film. In the end, there is no good or evil, just an incoherent world of fragmented identities, surviving on exploitation and violence.

Following *Koko* Griffin made the anti-advertising film, *New Fangled*. A series of voices in the background sputter on in advertising jargon as the animator tries to accommodate their needs visually. At its core, *New Fangled* is about double-speak and the manipulation of semantics. Unfortunately, *New Fangled* fails to convince; it focuses more on outlandish lingo than on the more subtle and dangerous psychological strategies of the advertising world.

New Fangled is also a surprising film from an artist who reluctantly gave in to the world of commercials. Throughout the 1970s, Griffin was often an arrogant and uncompromising opponent of all things commercial. In the mid-1980s, Griffin bought a house, had a kid, and paid bills. The winds of the family defeated the aimless storms of bohemian morality.

Speaking of domestic realities, *A Little Routine* (1994), Griffin's most recent film, is a tender portrait of the family. It contains a number of Griffin preoccupations (family, animation history, and power). Made with his then six-year-old daughter, *A Little Routine* is a night in the life of a daughter and father and the power struggle between child and parent: 'It's kind of a war that goes on to determine who knows what is best to determine decisions for the group or for the child. So the film is about that political struggle.'

The importance of family has been present in virtually all of Griffin's films, but no more movingly than in *A Little Routine*. As George prepares Nora for bed, he sings a song (*Ol' Man River*) that his father sang to him. Initially, we travel back to hear the grandfather singing to a young George. For a moment, past and present unite.

While Griffin has arguably failed to radicalize anyone other than academics, he has provided a forum for interested viewers to re-think a number of terms that have been taken for granted. Stylistically, Griffin has rejected a consistent and 'proper' or 'complex' style. In doing so he has sought a more democratic style that encourages simplicity, while ass-slapping socialized notions of taste. At the same time, Griffin's use of diverse styles and techniques reflects a larger personal and universal investigation into the fragmented, isolated self of the late 20th century.

Through an on-going discourse with animation's past and its roots in drawing, Griffin has maintained an open dialogue between past and present and tried to alter the very standard notion of 'cartoon'.

We often lose sight of the fact that the earliest animation films were made for adults and were minimalist (pencil and paper) in approach. These early artists worked directly and intimately with their medium. Today, technology has increasingly become a mediator between creator and material. Through this, Griffin has also attempted to shift cartoons from their infantile persona to their previous incarnation as satirical, often surrealist forms of expression made primarily for an adult audience.

George Griffin's work offers no certainties and this is their greatest strength. The refusal of a cohesive, ordered universe elevates Griffin's work into a shared experience that entertains, educates, and provokes. In Griffin's world, the questions are the answers.

Filmography of George Griffin

1969	*Displacement*
1969	*Rapid Transit*
1971	*One Man's Laundry* (co-director)
1972	*The Candy Machine*
1973	*Trikfilm 3*
1973	*Trikfilm 1*
1975	*L'Age Door*
1975	*Head*
1975	*The Club*
1975	*The Meadow's Green* (co-director)
1976	*Step Print*
1976	*Hand Collations*
1976	*Viewmaster*
1977	*Thumbnail Sketches*
1977	*Space*
1977	*Block Print*
1979	*Lineage*
1979	*Pulse, 8:00*
1980	*It's an OK Life*
1981	*Flying Fur*
1982	*Aquaducks*
1984	*Thicket*
1988	*Ko-Ko*
1990	*New Fangled*
1994	*A Little Routine*
1995	*Festival*

Chapter 4

René Jodoin:
Philosopher Functionaire
(1999)

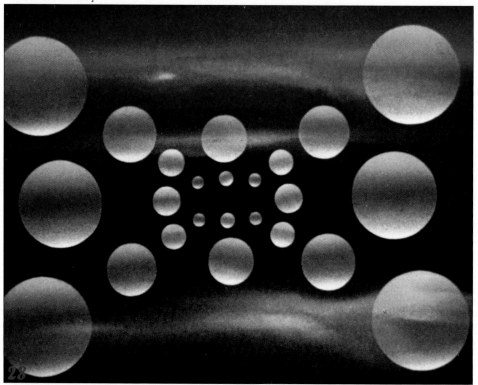

You could win a trivia contest by asking the following question: Who made films in the 1940s with Norman McLaren, started the National Film Board's French animation studio and shepherded the development of computer animation in this country? René Jodoin, the artist who accomplished these and many other things, is a figure who clearly deserves rescuing from the anonymity of abandoned NFB catalogues and newsletters. Like Colin Low, Wolf Koenig and Tom Daly, Jodoin allowed his natural humility and love of the early ideals of the Film Board to obscure his genuine contributions to Canadian film. And like many of his filmmaking colleagues, Jodoin deliberately downplayed his own reputation in order to work better as a fonctionnaire, a civil servant, who could produce artistic films for educational purposes.

Jodoin's willingness to experiment, inherited from his days working with McLaren, revolutionized the NFB in the 1960s and solidified its reputation as the leading producer of intelligent, challenging and diverse animation films. During those years, he discovered or nurtured such talents as Pierre Hebert, Co Hoedeman, Jacques Drouin and Paul Driessen. Fighting the good fight for sexual equality, Jodoin gave directorial jobs to many female animators including Caroline Leaf, Suzanne Gervais and Francine Desbiens. Jodoin also brought computer systems into the Film Board, allowing Peter Foldes to start the process that has changed animation in the past two decades. And, through it all, Jodoin remained an animation director who always enjoyed creating his own abstract and complex films.

Jodoin's initial work for the NFB in the 1940s involved the designing of titles, maps and diagrams for a variety of documentary and war films. For a while Jodoin was in charge of the title department, but was soon pulled away to produce a series of folk songs called *Let's Sing Together*. Jodoin's contributions to *Let's Sing Together* included 'Home on the Range' (which features a slow pan across a prairie landscape), 'Square Dance' (featuring very simple

figures dancing) and 'Alouette', which was codirected with Norman McLaren. This cutout film consists of two parts. In the chorus, a bird 'bounces' back and forth to the music. During the verses, the text of the song appears in various corners of the frame. 'I always thought that part of the game was to use the text in an interesting way', notes Jodoin. By highlighting the text, the films actually encouraged active participation from the audience. On the whole, *Alouette* is awk-

René Jodoin

29

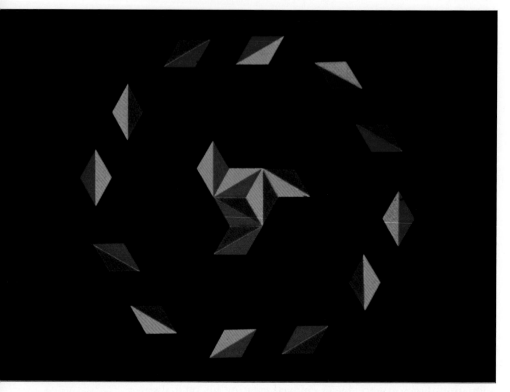

ward and primitive, however the experimental choreography of the lyrics remains quite striking and provides a momentary hint of Jodoin's later, more accomplished work

Following the war, all or most of the people Jodoin admired and learned from were gone. John Grierson was in the United States, McLaren was in China and after failing to get a scholarship to attend a film school in France, Jodoin and Grant Munro decided to travel to Mexico. Jodoin and Munro had met a man named Castro Leal who was setting up a Mexican film board in the NFB's mould, and he invited the two to Mexico to help him get things started. However, when it came time to work at the Mexican film board, the two found it was largely occupied by business types who were not totally convinced of the NFB's artistic ways. Things didn't quite pan out. So after turning down a job to do live-action editing, Jodoin and Munro spent another year travelling around Mexico painting before Jodoin returned to Ottawa.

While Jodoin did not officially return to the Board, he did begin making a film with McLaren. 'Norman and I met and discussed ideas many times', says Jodoin. 'We came up with a simple but attractive idea. If the two of us were doing motion, what would be

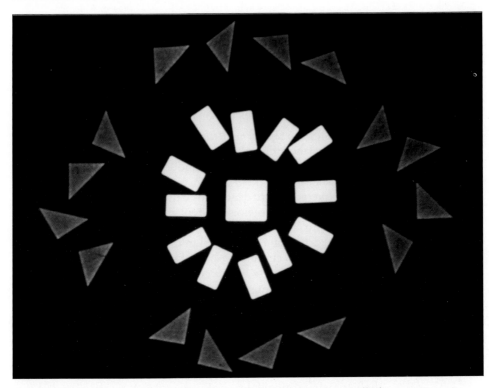

the natural next move? It was a bit like a mime and then we applied this to the structure. We were shooting under very primitive conditions. It was an old building, even the old title stand was shaking. We found it rather boring. The song was to be done directly on the film. We worked on that for a while, but decided to leave it.' Some years later McLaren finished the film, which was called *Spheres*, to the accompaniment of Glenn Gould.

Dance Squared [©1961 The National Film Board of Canada.]

After *Spheres*, Jodoin moved to Toronto where he freelanced for various production houses (Audio Pictures and for a time he worked out of Graphic Associates, owned by former NFB colleagues George Dunning and Jim MacKay) before finding a permanent job as the art director for Current Publications, a publishing firm that put out medicine and health journals. In 1954, Jodoin, bored by his work at Current Publications, accepted an invitation to return to the NFB, this time as a director in the NFB-sponsored film division. Jodoin's first works were a series of training films for the Royal Canadian Air Force. Taken as a whole, these films, with such lively titles as *Introduction to Jet Engines* and *Antenna Fundamentals*, are quite dull. Nevertheless, there are some striking scenes that seem more tailored to an abstract film than an industrial film. In Jet Engines, for example, a scene demonstrating the interaction

31

between gases and blades resembles a bizarre Busby Berkeley sequence as interpreted by Oscar Fischinger. In *Antenna Fundamentals*, radiation wave patterns are demonstrated through a dance of blue and red circles which expand and interact. In both films, the use of colour, shape and movement is quite extraordinary and lays the groundwork for Jodoin's more detailed explorations of geometrical figures in his personal films.

In 1961, Jodoin finally had the chance to make his own film. 'I wanted to make a film about something that didn't have pictures. I jumped onto it. I needed sound and square dance music was ideal. I asked Maurice Blackburn if he would find me something. He found some old square dance music that was recorded at a party in Ottawa with all sorts of noise. He cut all of that out and restructured it for the film. I had to do this in a basement with a kind of Rube Goldberg arrangement. I couldn't move the camera for any changes. I had to cut huge copies of the square. It was in the same room where Universe was being shot.' The result was *Dance Squared*, an intriguing, albeit primitive, film that explores the geometrical possibilities of a square. The film is at times too slow and deliberate; nevertheless, *Dance Squared* is unique in its attempt to integrate the pedagogical into an abstract field of expression.

Notes on a Triangle is considered by many to be Jodoin's masterpiece. An extension of *Dance Squared*, *Notes on a Triangle* examines the geometrical possibilities of a triangle. A single triangle splits and rotates into a variety of different shapes and colours. As with *Dance Squared*, the music plays a pivotal role in extending Jodoin's work beyond the pedagogical. The waltz-inspired fiddle music of Maurice Blackburn adds a lightness to the film which lures the viewer far from the very precise and logical constructs and into a world of seemingly random bursts of colour and shapes. It is this ability to display delicate morsels of complexity under the guise of visual and aural candy that makes Jodoin's work so magnificent.

One of the lauded moments of *Notes on a Triangle* is a brief zoom that occurs midway through the film. During this zoom, the shapes continue to expand and move about. 'With computers today that would be trivial', notes animator Pierre Hebert, 'but doing this with cutouts on an old camera is really an accomplishment'. Says Jodoin, 'There was a notion of something going on forever. There were maybe two zooms, but you are conscious of one. The whole thing was designed exponentially so that you compensate for the fact that you are approaching a flat thing. You are actually moving in space.'

After the Film Board moved to Montreal in 1956 and set up a French-production division, there was pressure to establish a French-animation unit. 'A few years after the move to Montreal',

A Matter of Form
[©1984 The National Film Board of Canada.]

says Jodoin, 'there was an influx of young people who wanted to do animation. I wasn't particularly keen on it, but you had to put yourself in the position of all these younger people and that's how we all got together and proposed the idea. The whole of French production were enthusiastic about it, so when I presented it to the director of production he said, "Yes, on one condition, that you do it".' So in 1965, Jodoin became the director of the French-animation unit.

'It was primitive to begin with. There was very little money and no locale. Everyone (many of the new animators were already working at the Board in other departments) stayed where they were, and we rented a bus for people to work out of.' In order to get both respect and money, Jodoin turned to his very roots as an NFB animator and proposed the series, Contemporary Songs of French Canada. The seed of the idea evolved out of McLaren's initial *Let's Sing Together* series, and it was a brilliant stroke. At once, the series enabled Jodoin to get more money for the department and, like *Let's Sing Together*, provided an ideal training exercise for a number of young animators. '[The series] made it easier to get to the next step, which was getting a room to work in.' 'He knew', says Pierre Hebert, 'that he had to prove something and knew he had to make

33

something. He delivered the films with a limited budget and it allowed the studio to save money.'

There is no denying Norman McLaren's immense role in establishing the Film Board's international reputation; however, it is foolish to underestimate the impact of Jodoin. While the English studio languished in producing narrative-driven cel animation, the French studio, in part because of a low budget, explored diverse avenues of expression. Under Jodoin's lead, the French unit attracted the likes of Co Hoedeman, Ishu Patel, Paul Driessen, Caroline Leaf, Pierre Hebert, Francine Desbiens, Andre Leduc and Jacques Drouin. The result was some of the most strikingly original films that the Board had ever produced. In achieving this, Jodoin consciously avoided hiring experienced animators. Instead, he encouraged young talent who were not yet formed as artists, let alone as animators. It was Jodoin's goal to train them on the job. Even more remarkable was Jodoin's openness to women artists. It is a well-known fact that animation, especially cel animation, has traditionally been a male-dominated medium. It is a little known fact that Francine Desbiens was the first French-Canadian woman to direct an animation film. 'At one time', says Desbiens, 'there were more women than men. After Jodoin left the department, there were 10 years where not one woman was employed as a freelancer or as a permanent. He was way out in front of everybody.' Jodoin's liberal attitudes also extended to an interest in developing computer animation as an artistic tool. 'The National Research Council came around to visit and discuss their problems. They were working on a project with CBC and Radio-Canada', says Jodoin. 'I wasn't too impressed with all that, but finally they asked the Film Board to cooperate. We went down to see what they were doing and we realized that we could animate line drawing.' Unfortunately, the Film Board was never really in a position to follow through on its early computer exploration. 'Things changed', notes Hebert, 'because the NFB couldn't afford to keep up and the people doing the same in the US were better funded'. Indeed, Jodoin was not in total agreement with the NFB's aim to be at the forefront of computer animation development. 'Rene favoured lighter equipment that would be put in the hands of the animators', notes Hebert. 'This is what he had in mind and of course, this is the way it is today. Rene was seeing things differently.'

In 1979, Jodoin resigned from his position to work on his own films. 'When Rene left', notes Paul Driessen, 'I think it was a heavy blow to the department. After that the people in charge of the department were much more commercial and didn't really stand for anything.' Between 1979 and his retirement from the board in 1985, Jodoin completed two films, *A Matter of Form* (1984) and

34

Rectangle and Rectangles (1985). A Matter of Form is an intriguing and clever film, but is really just a variation on ideas previously explored. Three dots interact to form a line that expands from different points to create various shapes and colours. Echoing the thoughts of Heraclitus, *Matter of Form* presents a world in a constant state of change. More interesting is *Rectangle and Rectangles*, an almost violent film that assaults the viewer with an onslaught of colours, shapes and an incessant, disturbing flickering (the video comes with a warning that it may trigger epileptic seizures). 'The aim was to show time. I tried to make a film with the absence of almost everything so that you could see time move and visually you can become interested through the play of colour and motion.' It is a film that leaves one with impressions, not absolutes. There are traces of movement and colour, but nothing definitive.

Remarkably, Jodoin remains hard at work in his basement on a computer film he has tentatively titled *Traces*. The goal of the film, scheduled to be released in late 1999, is to try to evoke people's experience of music. It's like traces of things past and present. 'I find it extraordinary', says Hebert, who is currently producing a video series to celebrate Jodoin's work, 'that this man of 79 is still looking for things he had in mind in the 1940s. There is a strong sense of necessity in him that has a lot of continuity in what he did. I would like to be like that.' It was Heraclitus who believed that the universe is in a constant state of change and that 'the beginning and end are the same', but like the words of all great philosophers, they are little more than abstract musings. Jodoin has applied these words both artistically and institutionally throughout his life.

Oddly enough, Jodoin's determined exploration of the infinite is deeply rooted in a traditional belief (inherited from McLaren and ultimately Grierson) in the active function of the civil servant. In an age where we view the institutional as 'dead weight', the work of Rene Jodoin, a man of the institution, suggests that perhaps we, not our institutions, have become stagnant and unchanging.

Filmography of René Jodoin

1944	*Alouette* (with Norman McLaren)
1959	*An Introduction to Jet Engines*
1961	*Dance Squared*
1966	*Notes on a Triangle*
1969	*Spheres* (with Norman McLaren)
1984	*Rectangle and Rectangles*
1984	*A Matter of Form*
1999	*Between Time and Space*

Chapter 5

Being Igor Kovalyov (2000)

Image from
Kovalyov's latest film,
Milch (2005)

Where the dead walk with open eyes/Where the dead walk with open eyes/Where the dead walk with open eyes

I wonder if my dog thinks about dying. I doubt it. Too busy licking her ass. My son definitely doesn't think about it. He's so busy trying to figure this damn world out, while trying not to shit in his pants. I don't think about it so much anymore. I wonder more about time. Time is all around me. It's always different. Icons of time. Clocks. Televisions. Computers. Cars. Watches. Video machines. Always reminding you. Invisible. Slow like the hushed flow of a stream, then an unacknowledged blur. Always moving. Silence. Quietly ticking. A blank screen. A portion of space. You anticipate time visible. The time of memory. A timeless, spaceless time drifting between memories and landscapes while you sit, stand, live in a physical time you are not living. Alongside the memories, dreams, hopes, and lusts lurk beneath and carry your imaginings to another space and time. Time surrounds us, swallows us, defines us, drips off us, then fucks us. And really that is the key: betrayal. We are betrayed by time. William Faulkner once wrote that it was foolish to fight time. You always lose. Yet we can't help it. We embark on a journey that entices and teases us before leading us to the dirt, snakes and worms. We betray ourselves before we've even started. We believe we are something. Milch

In this we remain in a constant state of limbo, neither one thing nor the other; living for the moment rather than in the moment. Too busy looking forward to enjoy any moment. In always looking forward, we destroy the very thing we seek: freedom. The fool believes that freedom comes through rewarding the self. Liberation is born out of giving oneself over first to self, then to other. I'm not talking about butt plugs, vibrators, or basic carnal desires. I'm referring to something deeper, knotted within the minds and hearts of all of us. And it is these very themes that are the roots of the work of Igor Kovalyov.

There was a time when Igor Kovalyov was born. Father and Grandfather were army men. Igor didn't like guns. Didn't wanna play war games with the other kids. He played with his dolls and drew pictures. He loved his parents, but loved his grandma even more. He trusted her. Shared his libidinous secrets with her. He played with dolls until he discovered his pud. The explosive stream of spasmodic exhilaration flushed young Igor on a new journey into a world where the dolls talked back and the seed turned momentary eruptions into little tit sucking shitters. Papa passed, but Igor stayed sheltered within his comfortable middle class home. Igor wanted to be a leader just like General Grandpa, but deep down he knew he was a mama's boy. A mama's boy who stayed snuggly within her comforting arms until he was 26 years old. Then the journey began, as it has for all of us, alone.

Kiev is a provincial town. Igor made primitive, bland little drawings. The Kiev studio said, 'we can try'.

Kovalyov worked as an in-betweener and an ink and painter, but it wasn't until he applied for the Kiev animation studio class that he really began animating. 'I had this class at the Kiev studio and it was very hard to get into. We had to take special tests. I got in and started working as an animator.' During this time in Kiev, where Kovalyov was also studying with his life-long friend, Alexander Tatarsky, a new cinema school opened in Moscow. Kovalyov was invited to attend the school. The teachers included legendary Russian animators, Yuri Norstein, Fedor Chitruk, and for eight hours in Kovalyov's life, Andrei Tarkovsky. 'Khitruk was an amazing teacher. He always wanted to give us everything. I was never crazy about his films, but I was crazy about how he was feeling animation.' Norstein, on the other hand, was not such an enthusiastic teacher. He was more protective and jealous. The period was monumental in the development and shaping of Kovalyov's artistic path. Within the booming cultural life of Moscow, Kovalyov discovered the world. First there was Borivoj Dovnikovic and the Zagreb school. There was Bergman, Dreyer, Tarkovsky. But more than any other artists, there were Priit Pärn and Robert Bresson. While Bresson clearly influenced Kovalyov's cinematic style and the

ongoing dialogue between dream and reality, Pärn shaped Kovalyov's graphic style (you should see the shit Kovalyov was drawing
before he discovered Mr. Pärn). He saw Pärn's film, *Triangle*, in a
movie theatre in Kiev. It was playing in front of a crummy little
live action feature. Kovalyov was so taken with the film, he bought
tickets for the next screening just to see *Triangle again*. Initially it
was the bold, chaotic graphic style that attracted Kovalyov, but
soon he realized that it was also the animation. An excited Kovalyov
left the cinema and started calling everyone to find who this
Estonian was. Pärn was the first of many teachers.

After three years of study, Kovalyov worked in Kiev for a year
before joining Alexander Tatarsky in Moscow. Initially, they
worked for the Moscow TV studio, and hated every minute of it.
'We hated clients and we always had problems with Moscow TV
studio. There were lots of revisions: "this is for kids", "this is not
funny", "this is a dirty joke". We always dreamed of complete
freedom.' Freedom finally stumbled upon the duo when a representative from Goskino studio offered Kovalyov and Tatarsky a
chance to open their own studio. 'We were shocked. Nobody had
ever said anything like that to us before. Of course this occurred
during the first or second year of perestroika, so things where easing   *Flying Nansen*

39

Bird in The Window
(both images)

up a little.' Kovalyov and Tatarsky were provided with an old orthodox church for their studio. 'When we came there it was very strange to work in the church.' Within these sacred walls, Pilot Studios was born.

Tatarsky and Kovalyov worked on many films together including the award-winning, *The Dark Side of the Moon* (Kovalyov provided the script and design, but Tatarsky directed the film because Kovalyov was still in Kiev). But at the same time, it became apparent that this was not the perfect environment for Kovalyov. 'Alexander was more like a producer. I was always more on the artistic side. I was drawing always. I had ideas. During this time, I told Alexander that I cannot do funny films anymore. It's enough. I really want to do something different. He said that he was upset but of course I could do anything.'

While bedridden with an ulcer for a month in a Moscow hospital, Kovalyov began working on an old idea. Taken from a dream that he had, Kovalyov envisioned a couple living in an apartment. The big difference was that that the woman was a big hen. Kovalyov used his bedridden time to create a detailed storyboard (the only time he would use a storyboard). When he finished it he showed it to Tatarsky and Pilot producer, Anatoly Prokhorov. 'They were shocked. You should have seen their faces.' Both men felt the film was ready to shoot.

Igor was once a hockey goalie. I've always like goalies. They wear really cool masks with crazy artwork on them. Goalies are always a little different from the rest of the players. Imagine, they are the last line of defense. Padded from head to toe, they are asked to stop a piece of rubber, often travelling at 100 mph, from getting through them. It's fucking crazy really. And yet through it all, they express no emotion. The portrait of serenity. It's unique to goalies because for the rest of us masks serve many functions. They can do many things: smiles, laughs, tears, groans and grins. But you never know what lies beneath those artifices. You think you know. You assume you know. In the deepest regions of your naïve heart you don't want to know what lies beneath these strange surfaces we encounter on a daily basis. This is very much the world that Igor Kovalyov's films depict. His characters smile politely while betraying, sneaking. Lecherous beasts existing for themselves. No one able to truly communicate with another. No one knowing the other. The result is a world of loneliness, alienation and imprisonment. Imagine a world where you think your friend might be fucking your lover. While the dead sleep in one room, life goes on unbeknownst to them. This is the kind of world that Kovalyov has created. A dark landscape of paranoia. Selfish, alienated beings desperate for any kind of contact at any kind of price. To contact is to live. To live is to feel the warmth of a woven cloth sheltering them from their fears.

Hen, His Wife is set in a small apartment. There is a blue man, his hen wife, and a human-worm pet. Life is fine. A visitor arrives. He reveals the hen to the man. The man freaks out. Tosses the chicken out. Hallucinates. In the end, facing a life of loneliness, changes to accommodate her. The hen returns momentarily. Upon discovering his change, she flees in horror. This is not what she wanted. This is not the man she married. Just another fugged up family. The visitor exists only within the conscience of this blue man who cannot see the world around him for what it is. But while the ensuing awakening breaks the circular monotony of the couple's life (as symbolized by the bus circling atop the record player), the man, though physically altered, remains the same blind being he was before, but now alone.

The reaction to the film was varied. Colleagues Zhenia Delioussine and Andrei Svislotsky (who would follow Kovalyov to Hollywood) didn't understand it. Yuri Norstein saw it and said he would like to see it again. For Kovalyov this was a big compliment coming from the guarded Norstein. For Khitruk, *Hen, His Wife* was a prime example of an independent film made not for money but for the self. On the festival circuit, *Hen, His Wife* surprised many and pissed off even more when it won the Grand Prize at the Ottawa '90 International Animation Festival.

Kovalyov's next film, *Andrei Svislotski (named after Kovalyov's friend and colleague)* is his most Bressonian to date. *Andrei Svislotsky* provides a glimpse into the paranoid relationship between two men and, briefly, a woman. We are not clear what the relationship is between these characters. One man appears to be the master of the other two characters. Kovalyov presents the story through a series of fragmented and faded polaroids of human activity. The film is dominated by dirty, blurred, brown colours. The home is near a cliff and surrounded by trees, a crumbling wall, bars and an electric generator. With echoes of film noir, Kovalyov provides momentary clues that suggest there is something lurking beneath the surface of their mundane actions. Even the end is left open. We know the man has jumped from a cliff. We assume that he has been betrayed. The quick shots of letters being written, read and hidden tell us as much. But does the man die? Was he escaping? Was he in fact a prisoner of this servant? Nothing is clear. We are just granted a momentary glimpse into the lives of strangers.

Kovalyov didn't even have a title for the film until the end. 'My friend had an amazing idea. "You should create another character, but don't show the character. He should serve as a witness to the story." I wanted the rhythm of a Polish name ... ski ... ski ... Tarkovsky ... or maybe it was my family's Polish blood.' Colleague Andrei Svislotski provided the missing link.

The witness throughout the film is in fact the boy Igor Kovalyov. *Andrei Svislotski* is set in Kovalyov's summer home of Bucha. He would spend many summers there with his grandparents. The film is an ode to the sights and sounds of childhood. This is a mysterious adult world seen through the eyes of an uncomprehending child and an adult trying to collect and direct those memories. We observe people everyday. Assumptions, thoughts, feelings, reactions appear and fade every minute. We assume relationships based on body language and gestures. Movements. It solidifies our own existence. We give them names to understand our own complexities. It gives us order, wholeness, temporary peace.

> *'Look there at Dis! And see the place where you must arm yourself with fortitude'* (Dante)

The Faust Years

In 1991, Kovalyov sold his soul. After capturing the Grand Prize at Ottawa '90, Kovalyov was invited to the US to screen his work. Hungarian artist, Gabor Csupo was at one those screenings. Csupo had recently formed an animation studio with his then wife, Arlene Klasky. 'I showed my film for an audience and Gabor was there. He asked me to come to the studio so he could show my film to his friends.' Following the screening, Csupo offered Kovalyov a job at the studio. But Kovalyov refused, 'I said that I can't because I am starting the second film (Andrei Svislotsky) of my trilogy. I have to finish that film.' Csupo offered to fund the film, but Kovalyov felt that the film must be finished in Russia. Upon finishing *Svislotsky*, Kovalyov accepted Csupo's offer to work at Klasky-Csupo. 'I figured that I only live once', says Kovalyov, 'so why not'. The creative differences with Tatarsky seemed to ease Kovalyov's decision. 'While Alexander and I were never fighting, we were absolutely different people. I thought that he was planning to do more commercial work.' So in late 1991, Kovalyov headed for Hollywood. Kovalyov has since lived a dream life. In exchange for directing drivel like *Real Monsters* and *The Rugrats Movie*, Kovalyov was given free reign to continue making his own personal films.

Bird in the Window (1996) was the first film Kovalyov made at Klasky-Csupo and the final part of the informal trilogy. *Bird in The Window* rivals both Ingmar Bergman's *Wild Strawberries* (1958) and Tarkovsky's *Mirror* (1975) for the quality and depth of its nostalgic and dreamlike merging of past and present, and, within that, the on-going tensions between childhood and adulthood. In the film, a man returns to visit a woman who lives with a gardener, two Chinese men, and a small child (whose repeated attempts to communicate with the man are frustrated by the mother). Following a flurry of strange events where reality and dream overlap, the man, frustrated by his inability to see what is being hidden from him, leaves. As he approaches the front gate of the house, the child

43

comes running from the balcony and jumps to his death. The man lowers his hat and carries on. The final image sees the man near a lighthouse with a statue of a bird that he had removed from the house.

Bird in The Window is Kovalyov's attempt to summarize and incorporate the tensions from *Hen* and *Svislotsky* into a final confrontation with identity and betrayal. The man, upon arrival, emits an air of machismo and self-assurance. But gradually we witness the crumbling of this masculine exterior as the man confronts a series of internal doors behind which lie the child, the woman (at once maternal and sexual), and the Chinese men (simultaneously signifying 'other' as foreigners and homosexuals). In the end, the death of the child symbolizes the death of the past and with it the death of innocence and freedom. The final image of the trilogy shows the resulting evolution turn into a suddenly humbled man sitting alone with nothing but a stagnant memento from the past. Fear of the unknown has led to his betrayal of them.

Like all of Kovalyov's work, *Bird in The Window* is extremely personal. The house is based on the home Kovalyov lived in with his third wife and daughter. The father/husband is a stranger in his own home and he sees that he no longer belongs there. He is as much a stranger as the Chinese borders. He did not understand the people he was supposed to love and protect. He does not understand himself. The child, who needs him most, is abandoned and left to die. By the time *Bird in The Window* was complete, Kovalyov had left his wife.

Flying Nansen

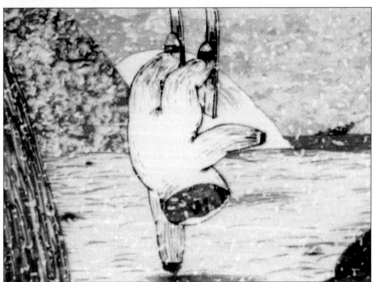

Kovalyov is very particular about the use of sound and music in his work. The soundtracks are mostly functional. Occasionally, we will hear a piece of music, as in *Hen, His Wife* or *Bird in The Window*. *Andrei Svislotski* is essentially a silent film. 'Sound is very important. When I have a rough idea I always imagine the sound. I am always listening separately.' Like Bresson and Dreyer, Kovalyov uses music for an emotional resonance. 'I don't like it in the background. I can imagine bits in my films playing stronger without music.'

Kovalyov's most recent film, *Flying Nansen*, is slightly different in tone from the other works. In addition to a slight increase in the use of music, *Nansen* is at times a very funny film (e.g. Nansen spends two days trying to do a handstand with skis on). Indeed, the original idea was to make it into a gag-orientated comedy. However, Kovalyov didn't feel that it worked with this film.

As a child, Kovalyov had read the diary of Norway's most famous explorer. It was written in journal form and filled with adventures. Later, Kovalyov made a number of sketches based on Nansen. When he discovered the drawings, he decided he didn't need the book. In the end, the film had nothing to do with the life of Nansen.

Nansen was also Kovalyov's first computer film. Kovalyov's designer, Dima Malanitchev, convinced him that the film could be done faster and easier on the computer. Kovalyov was not so sure. 'I didn't believe it. I used brown ink on wet paper, blurred. It takes

Andrei Svislotski

Milch a long time by hand but this was achieved on the computer. But we still didn't have texture. It was very hard. Our amazing technical director said it's not possible, but he worked for two days and he got it.' Kovalyov was initially worried about people recognizing the computer, but his concerns proved unfounded. *Nansen* has a similar rhythm to the early films and doesn't feel weighted down in any way by the computer. Kovalyov's thick graphic style with its muted browns remains intact. In fact, most people are surprised to discover that *Nansen* was a computer film.

Like the other films, we have no idea where or when we are. The days on the inter-titles mean nothing. Nansen meets bears, hunters and finally a woman before continuing his journey. It is almost a parody of the macho male adventurer braving the arctic regions. And for what? What motivates such journeys? It is almost Kovalyov's acceptance of his own solitude and isolation. Families come. Families go. He remains alone. *Flying Nansen* is Kovalyov's swinging bachelor pad film.

Flying Nansen greets us like a moving fresco. Near the end of the film, Kovalyov re-creates a Giotto fresco and one is immediately struck by the similarity of expression between the characters in both works. Indeed, one would not be out of place viewing all of Kovalyov's work as moving frescos. The camera slides along effortlessly in most of his films and yet, ironically, his characters are always limited in their movement. They have borders, limitations, walls. They are like characters within a fresco. Like many of Giotto's frescos, we see frozen faces filled with emotions we cannot fully understand.

At the moment, Kovalyov is nearing the completion of the film, *Milk*, a story of three generations of a family: a boy, father, mother and grandparents, 'They live in the same house, but you don't need to understand how they are related'.

While Kovalyov has had great success with his Faustian period films, he does not feel he has made his best film yet. Despite suggestions that maybe he cannot make this film in Hollywood, he thinks he can. He actually enjoys his life in Hollywood and admits that he is spoiled. And, certainly, when we look at the scenario, why shouldn't he enjoy it? You can say he sold out or betrayed the spirit of independence, but that's nonsense. In Russia, Kovalyov had to endure Tatarsky's desire to make funny films. In Hollywood, he has to do the same, but unlike Pilot (especially under current Moscow conditions), he is assured of the opportunity to make his own films. Russia did not provide that kind of security.

I've done everything I said I wouldn't do. I've embraced all that I've despised. A bloated, twisted mind, lying to itself. Domesticity claws at my flesh. Romance has become empty. Woven lies now split. What do I want? Nothing. Art and purity are gone. All has rotted. Gone. Erased. Faded. Stifled and suffocated. Eyes now dead. But I stumble on.

Filmography of Igor Kovalyov

1983   *The Other Side of the Moon* (with Alexander Tatarsky)
1984   *Cubic-Rubic*
1985   *Wings, Legs and Tails*
1986   *The Investigation is carried out by Kolobocks*
1989   *Hen, His Wife*
1991   *Andrei Svislotski*
1992   *Here Comes the Cat*
1994   *Aaahh!!! Real Monsters* (TV series)
1996   *Bird in the Window*
1998   *The Rugrats* (feature)
2000   *Flying Nansen*
2002   *The Way the Dead Love* (internet series)
2005   *Milch*

Chapter 6

Fat Chicks and Imbeciles:
The Films of Priit Pärn

Karl and Marilyn
Facing: Priit Pärn

(2000/2005)

ook behind the billboards for *Finding Nemo* and *Brother Bear* and you'll find a secret world of animation hidden from the general population. It's a world where there are no ducks, bears, rabbits (well, ok, there are some rabbits) or other assorted 'cute' big-eyed anthropomorphic perversions of humanity. Instead it's populated with artists whose creations rival those of any musician, painter, poet, or hockey player. One of those treasures is Estonian Priit Pärn. Pärn's animated films are bitingly funny, often complex explorations of the effects of structures on human beings.

In addition to being an animator, Pärn is also a noted graphic artist, teacher and lecturer whose influence is so far-reaching that students from Finland, Japan, Switzerland and America travel to Estonia to work with him. In 2001, he received the prestigious ASIFA award,

which is given to an individual who has made significant contributions to the art of animation.

For those who've come to know animation only through Hollywood films and American television, Pärn's work is as refreshing as it is startling. The rounded, pristinely-drawn characters and landscapes that dominate traditional animation are replaced in Pärn's work with a primitive style that rejects comfortable, eye-soothing tints and classical drawing technique. His bold colours and sketchy, childlike drawing leap out at the viewer, loudly announcing, 'This ain't no Disney cartoon!'

The first Pärn film I saw was *1895*. It's 30 minutes long; typically, an animation short of more than 9 minutes worries an audience – they prepare to suffer. But at that screening of *1895* I, and everyone else in the cinema, sat dumbfounded. It was like watching an animated version of *Monty Python* meets Beckett. 'What the hell was that?' I said aloud to no one in particular. It shook my senses. It baffled my brains. I wanted more.

Triangle

The Night of the Carrots

Priit Pärn was born in the summer of 1946, in the Danish-named Estonian capital of Tallinn. As an adult, he worked as a biologist and stuntman (he is not the basis for the Estonian midget stuntman on 'The Simpsons'), then turned to animation in the mid-1970s. A designer on three films, he was given the chance to direct his own production, 'Is the Earth Round', in 1977. Taking Heraclitus' line that you can never step into the same river twice, Pärn's debut featured a man who decides to walk in one direction to prove that the Earth is round.

'It was like my own problem', says Pärn, 'because until a certain year my main interest was to go as far as you can traveling. It seemed to me that this was real life. This man leaves but comes back poor. His friends have stayed, have nice houses, but he has seen the whole world.'

While one can see the roots of Pärn's design, colour and playful use of symbolism in *Is the Earth Round*, it has all the problems of a first film, including a poorly recorded soundtrack and awkward pacing. 'At this time I didn't know anything about filmmaking', he says. 'When we made sound I had to think how it would be – if it's OK to make some breaks between sound or if it's a bad mistake. It was like inventing a bicycle.'

Following his 1979 children's film, *And Plays Tricks* (his first international success), and *Exercises for an Independent Life*, he made *Triangle*. Released in 1982, *Triangle* remains a landmark in Estonian animation for its examination of modern relations between a man and a woman; it fuses the personal and political into a witty observation of contemporary domestic politics.

Triangle deals with a twisted love triangle between a married couple (Victor and Julia) and a little man who lives under their stove (Eduard). Victor and Julia lead a static life. She cooks. He reads the paper. Lurking beneath this sterile relationship are Julia's fantasies of being loved and caressed. When Victor walks out on Julia, little Eduard emerges from beneath the stove to fulfill, Julia's hopes of passion and escape. But soon the passion passes and Eduard settles comfortably, paper in hand, into Victor's old chair. When Victor returns, there is a brief joyous moment of reconciliation with Julia, but lust once again turns to sterility and silence. In the meantime, Eduard returns to the stove and his own empty relationship with Veronica, the woman he left behind. Foreshadowing virtually all of Pärn's later films, the characters in *Triangle* are too busy imagining who they are not rather than being who they are. Pärn has a simpler explanation: 'My wife was in the hospital and I was learning how to cook. There is an old Estonian folk tale about a small man who comes out from under the stove and asks for food and eats everything. I just wanted to make a film about cooking.'

His blunt portrait of domestic life in the Soviet Union was far removed from the typical children's animation films that were being tossed out in both Estonia and Russia, and it was a shock to many who saw it. Igor Kovalyov, (*Flying Nansen, Hen, His Wife*) one of the transplanted Ukrainians who brought Pärn's style to Hollywood, saw *Triangle* in a movie theatre in Kiev in 1982: 'It was playing in front of a live-action feature. I was so amazed that I bought tickets for the next screening just to see *Triangle* again ... I had never seen anything like this. I was so excited I called all my friends to find out who this Pärn was.'

'No one wanted to allow the film onto the Soviet screens', recalls Estonian film critic Jaan Ruus. 'It was a controversy among Soviet animators who were used to either drawing like Disney or drawing very exact and precise pictures.'

Pärn's *Breakfast on the Grass* (1988) is considered by many to be one of the masterpieces of animation. In examining a few moments in the daily lives of four Estonians, Pärn trenchantly critiques life in the Soviet Union by giving viewers a rare glimpse of the absurdities of Communist society and what people endure on a daily basis just to survive. As with *Triangle*, *Breakfast on the Grass* astonished Russian audiences with its frank portrait of modern Soviet life.

'I think the general audience was not prepared for this kind of animation', recalls Pärn. 'It is a description of a very concrete society told in a realistic way using a dramatic structure that is closer to a live-action feature. But the story is performed using the tools of animation – visual gags, metamorphosis and different drawing styles. Usually so-called serious stories are dark, heavy, slow and boring. I try to make my serious film funny, multileveled and ironic. I think this fusing of the serious and comic confused people.'

In 1992, the year after Estonia became independent, Pärn completed *Hotel E*, a bitter and sometimes myopic critique of the hypocrisy of both the East and the West. While the East represses art and language, he contends, the West, for all its freedom, lacks art and language and, with that, individuality. Playing with stereotypes, Pärn paints the East as a dark, grey world while he fills the West with bright colours and friendly, smiling faces. Beneath this

Hotel E

1985 (both images)

pop art sugarcoating, he seems to be saying that the West is a culture of sterility and illusion. No one does anything, no ones says anything, yet everything is 'just great'.

'I had been traveling a lot between East and West', says Pärn. 'I was between two systems. This is my own story, up to a certain point. This is not a film about two systems, about East and West; for me it is a story about this person.' While Estonia's independence afforded Pärn more freedom, it came with a price: 'In the Soviet time everything which was not permitted was forbidden. So there were an endless number of restrictions that were political, but just insane. Now all the limits are connected with money. The final result is very often the same as before, sometimes worse.'

Breakfast on the Grass (both images)

A major weakness in *Hotel E* is Pärn's criticism of the West, and Americans in particular. He lumps Americans into a group of staid, hollow shells who have nothing to do and nothing to say. Now, yes, Pärn is exaggerating Western lifestyle to a degree in order to caution Estonian and Soviet viewers not to be too hopeful about the dissolution of the Soviet Union. Still, Pärn's caricature of the West is extreme and relentless. In doing so, he ends up mirroring the perceived hateful and superficial tendencies attitudes he accuses Americans of possessing.

Pärn's post-independence films still contain healthy doses of

absurdism and symbolism, but their tone is significantly lighter and wittier. His most recent films, *1895* (co-directed with Janno Poldma in 1995), *Night of the Carrots* (1998) and *Karl and Marilyn*, move beyond examinations of individuals within specific ideological systems toward larger cultural and technological infrastructures.

In *1895*, Pärn used the centenary of cinema as an opportunity to deconstruct it. (The film opens with the statement 'The cinema, it is a lie'.) The structure of the film is straightforward: The protagonist, Jean-Paul, does not know who he is and decides to travel around the world in search of his identity. (It turns out he's the co-creator of cinema, Louis Lumière.)

Pärn uses Jean-Paul's journey to analyze the cinema and its influence on our perceptions of the world. He argues that our ideas of nationality and history are constructed by cinema. (For example, footage from Sergei Eisenstein's fictional film, *October,* was often used as documentary footage of the Russian Revolution.) During Jean-Paul's travels, each country is reduced to a stereotype – Italy is red wine and the Mafia; Switzerland is clocks and Swiss Army knives.

Cinema, Pärn seems to argue, has become so ingrained in our lives that we often allow it to replace our own perspective of the past. In a sense, *1895* is an anti-cinema film. It reminds us that there was a time when motion pictures did not exist and suggests that perhaps a movieless world was not such a bad thing. In a world without films, cinema aficionados might have done something more beneficial for humanity. (At one point we learn that François Truffaut was working on an invention for synthetic rain clouds before giving it all up to become a film critic and director.) As with all of Pärn's work, there is an autobiographical element to the films. In *1895* he acknowledges his own complicity in propagating the evils of cinema through the character of Louis' brother Auguste Lumière, who disappears at the beginning of the film to become a biologist (like Pärn) before returning at the end to invent cinema with Louis/Jean-Paul. Pärn reverses cinema's role as an instigator of a generic memory and instead uses it to explore his personal memories of both his life and his films.

Night of the Carrots examines the effect of computers and the Internet on contemporary society, as well as the cult of celebrity. The story finds crowds of people, led by the protagonist, Diego, trying to get into a sanitarium-like institution called 'PGI'. It's not clear why these people want into PGI; as the narrator says, 'Being contenders was their real aim because once they were in they would have nothing to do'. In each of PGI's rooms we meet a variety of bizarre characters who want only to escape. The occupants each have a personal dream that, they soon discover, they cannot realize because they are literally plugged into their rooms.

Escape from PGI is possible only during one night when all the rabbits (who control the world through computers) turn into carrots. Contrary to the ominous warnings about a Y2K cataclysm that preceded the new millennium, Pärn instead saw the period during which he was making *Night of the Carrots* as a moment of temporary liberation. For one evening, Pärn suggests, we could step outside of our rooms, away from our computers and embrace the natural world and, with it, ourselves.

Pärn used his main characters in *Night* – each based on a famous individual – to examine the cult of celebrity. Just as the Internet offers virtual interaction and experience, within PGI's seemingly glamorous world of fame, there is nothing but loneliness and longing. Not surprisingly, while the film resonates as a fable for our time about the plight of Everyman, it also poignantly echoes aspects of Pärn's own life.

Pärn's most recent film, *Karl and Marilyn*, is a story about a man and a woman. Karl wants to flee from the pressures of fame. Marilyn, a rural girl, is tired of her boring country life and wants fame. Karl (Marx?) has his beard shaved off, murders the barber, and goes underground. Marilyn (Monroe) kills her grandmother, and goes to the city in search of fame. She achieves it when a gust of wind from the sewer lifts her skirt up. The masses are enthralled. After a while, though, they tire of her skirt antics. During a *Karl and Marilyn*

performance, Karl inadvertently rises out of the sewer. The people are relieved that Karl has returned. Is this a cautionary tale about the return of communism? Are young Estonians rejecting their roots (in one scene, Marilyn is shown knitting with her grandmother in a distinctly Estonian style) for the glitter and glam of capitalism? What happens when they realize just how empty it all is? Will communism (as we're beginning to see hints of in Russia) return to power?

For the record, Pärn thinks this interpretation is ridiculous: 'It's a story about a man and woman and how men are always pressured to be someone, while women are simply supposed to "be" '.

Karl and Marilyn is strikingly designed and features some funny moments, but overall the film feels rushed and unsatisfactory.

Beyond his personal films, Pärn has also made a handful of unique commercials over the years and is currently co-creating an animated series called *Frank and Wendy*. The commercials, all featuring the Pärn 'look' and his sexually-tinged humour, allowed Pärn to be a bit more playful. They include the cider commercial *Oiva* (2000), *Remix* (1999), and a social awareness short for MTV Europe's *Free Action* series (1999). But the best of the bunch remain the controversial *Absolut Pärn* (1996) and the award-winning *Switch off The Lights* (1989).

Influential as he is, not everyone loves Pärn's work. Some find his films repetitive, sexist, ugly, and illogical ('It is not my problem what some people call my works', Pärn responds.). It is easy to understand some of the criticisms. Because of the lack of accessibility to independent or personal animation, a healthy percentage of North American animation professionals continue to foolishly believe that Disney animation is the standard, the 'norm', the Bible. In that context, Pärn's drawings appear sloppy, fed directly by the devil. But these are also folks who like their art like they like their food: cheap, simple, and fast. They seek answers, not questions.

Pärn's design style has also become so heavily imitated in Estonia and other parts of the world that it is becoming a bit tiresome and Parn's resounding influence on the design styles of many other Estonian animators (Ulo Pikkov, Janno Põldma, Priit Tender, Kasper Jancis) has led a few folks to complain that the apparent complexity of Estonian animation is nothing more than a shell game run by dilettantes. Of course, people often forget that the Estonians, with their relatively unique language and roots, often have a different way of processing the world around them.

Easily the biggest charge against Pärn is that his work is sexist. Women, these critics suggest, are little more than superficial, man-abiding creatures who like nothing more than to cook, clean,

Frank and Wendy

and fuck. Perhaps these same critics need to take a look at the men in Pärn's films. They are not exactly paragons of wisdom, beauty and truth either. But, hey, I'm a man so I'm probably the wrong person to ask.

One thing is certain; Priit Pärn has fashioned a body of work that, through its very uncertainty, irony and rejection of accessible solutions, succinctly reflects our own complex, absurd and trivial condition. Each of his films asks us to consider how these systems are subtly (and not so subtly) shifting and molding our actions, thoughts and beliefs. As we become lost in an ever-expanding maze of technology that is turning us away from the outside world, Pärn aspires to show us who we are and where we've come from – while reminding us that it doesn't have to be this way. In so doing, he escapes the constrictions of conventional animation and cartoon storytelling and takes his place as an international citizen in the kingdom of art.

Filmography of Priit Pärn

1977	*Is the Earth Round?*
1979	*And Plays Tricks*
1982	*Triangle*
1983	*Exercises for an Independent Life*
1984	*Time Out*
1988	*Breakfast on The Grass*
1991	*Hotel E*
1995	*1895*
1998	*The Night of the Carrots*
2003	*Karl and Marilyn*
2003	*Frank and Wendy* (TV Series)

Chapter 7

There Once Was A Man
Called Pjotr Sapegin (2000)

The Saltmill

Once upon a time there was a man named Pjotr Sapegin. He came from a far away Eastern or Western, depending on your point of view, country of Russia before moving to the Nordic regions where he became an internationally successful maker of animation films (*Mons the Cat, One Day A Man Bought A House, The Saltmill*). He evolved out of generations of circus acrobats, poets, painters and writers. He lived in a big court of brick buildings which belonged to the art union. The courtyard provided a world of discovery for young Pjotr. An enormous backyard contained hips, heads and noses of revolutionary heroes which lay scattered beside moulds for marble statues. The landscape continually changed as the severed limbs of marble were transformed one by one into gigantic odes to Lenin.

Pjotr was born in Moscow. Moscow was dirty. Sure it was green, there were trees and parks and even grass, but it was dirty and ugly. But for Pjotr, the ugliness smelled good. The aroma of dust, snow, marble was the stuff of dreams. 'The landscape is one of the strongest memories from my childhood. My parents did not participate in the production of Lenin's head, so they were as poor as rats.' Pjotr's parents were painters, but this was no Bohemian Mecca. 'Art was work and it was nothing much to talk about; just do it.' While they may not have spoken of art, Sapegin and his young mates did indeed talk. 'We definitely were talking too much. We all were in the conspiracy against the stupidity of the state, and that was deliciously dangerous.' During long vodka sessions at the kitchen table, politics, flying saucers, urban legends, adventures in the dark, mysterious mountains of Tibet were all topics of conversation. 'I knew at least five people who personally saw the abominable snowman. One lady was even carrying his child.'

Sapegin enjoyed his years as a young man in the Soviet Union, and what life of youth is complete without physical yearnings? While never the most athletically gifted of beings, he did embrace the sports passion of the 1970s: slalom skiing. Of course there were no hills in Moscow, but there were deep valleys. 'It was absolutely breathtaking and just imagine, most of our equipment was self-made, and often self-constructed.' Karate replaced slalom in the 80s. 'It was like in Japan in 1800, we had rival schools and secret societies.' Oh, and of course, there was that other youthful pleasure: sex. Flirting, looking for adventures in odd circumstances, and generally dreaming of conquering the milky bosom of any girl acknow-

Pjotr Sapegin

ledging them, erotic games were the bane of Sapegin and his friends' existence.

Time passed.
Scents, secrets and desires lay scattered
among the cluttered compartments
of conspicuous memories

Privileged Pjotr grew and grew and not surprisingly he became an artist. First, he studied with a painter and then he attended a school of theatre. Five years passed and one day Pjotr awoke a state theatre designer. 'I got my first artistic job as a theatre designer at the age of 18. It was great to build a world, which is different, and live there separated from the rest of life by the parimeter of the stage.'

A beautiful island paradise nestled within the walls of a dirty,
hostile sea.

He found success over the years and produced work for many performances. As Pjotr matured and came to understand his soul, he sought change. The strange power of desire carried him to the shores of Norway and her alluring landscape. At first, the harsh Nordic climate greeted the Russian with indifference. He began by cleansing the chewed remains left scattered on cheap china by the palettes of the people. Eventually Pjotr climbed the sweet thighs of fame to bare his soul and small – or big depending on your perspective – genitals before all who cared to see. Soon the call of the soul grew louder than the cries of the women and Pjotr found himself immersed in the manual, creating art for magazines, theatre and whatever would enable his family to eat. On this new road, Pjotr met the celluloid poets of the soul and turned toward the chemicals of sound and light to learn new means of finding life's

In the Corner of the World

cure. Realizing that the Norwegians, aside from Ivo Caprino, had relatively little experience making animation films, Pjotr the Virtuous, Honest, and Pious, who had never animated in his life, spun that tangled web and next found himself standing with a stop motion camera among the new voices of Norwegian moving images.

Art, the eternal expression of the soul, key to life's mysteries.

The dark chaos beneath the shimmering sheath of banausic sobriety.

That's what generations of poets, painters, writers and charlatans would have you believe.

Humans all of them and all of them lie, equivocate, and spin.

Security, stability, and comfort sheltered behind the facade of currency, the roots of these gestures of the grandeur.

Sapegin had a new home, a new career, but no money. Fortunately for Sapegin, the Olympics were in town. Realizing that there was now a pot of gold in the Norwegian cultural programme, the hungry Sapegin and a friend licked their lips and began dreaming of an animation series made with the fat bucks of the Olympics. The idea was to have a parallel Olympics with different creatures coming from all kinds of countries. Inspired by the oceanside aroma of a nearby seafood restaurant, the famished duo based their character on a 'pink, shapeless, flexible, fresh, tasty' shrimp. Then they dumped the idea as it was too close to the paralympics (for special people) and insteadtook their delicious shrimp and turned him into Edvard. Edvard took his name from the composer Edvard Grieg, who, while lacking the qualities of a genius, could compose some scintillating film scores. With its melodramatic reflections of Chaplin, Keaton and the other silent shadows from cinema's birth, Greig's music was perfectly suited to Sapegin's animation,

The premise of *Edvard* is simple. A Chaplinesque 'shrimp' wanders around the Nordic seascape adapting to the strange environment around him. Sapegin made five *Edvard* films and they all combine live action and clay animation. Even in the first film, *Edvard* (1992), Sapegin's talents are apparent. Edvard meets a young woman and subsequently turns into everything he is feeling (heart, flowers, sculpture) for her. In the rather strange, *The Naked Truth* (1993), Edvard is introduced to the bare essentials of humanity as he encounters a group of nudists on the beach. During hisventure, Edvard assumes the form of all the body parts he sees, and also that of a hot dog ... *Unbearable Lightness of Longing* is the most technically accomplished of the Edvard series and foreshadows later films with Sapegin's detailed, multi-textured backgrounds. The backgrounds were created by painting on a mirror and leaving parts of

63

the surface open to reflect a second background. Edvard sees a beautiful woman fall asleep on the beach. Lonely horny Edvard falls immediately in love and imagines ways to wow his sleeping beauty. Finally, he builds a boat for the woman. She awakens, smiles and waves, but alas, it is not Edvard she acknowledges but a beau in another boat. Once again Edvard is left alone.

Seemingly taken from Sapegin's Russian backyard, *Stand In* (1995) has Edvard jumping into action as he reads a story about the statue of a baby being stolen. With echoes of Starewich's *The Mascot*, Edvard takes to the streets and tries to replace the statue. He assumes various forms until he hears the roar of the audience. But we soon see the applause is for the return of the statue ... which subsequently leaves Edvard crushed ... literally. In the final film, *The Cruise Ship*, Edvard dreams that he is on a passing ocean liner and chasing the dame of his dreams. Unfortunately, the lass is too busy fleeing the perverted come-ons of a hapless old timer to notice Edvard. Seeing that his dream girl is being bothered by the half-soused tourist, he sabotages the man's libidinous plans and sends him fleeing. Just as Edvard seeks to comfort the woman, a handsome stranger comes to take his dream away. From here the director inflicts the utmost cruelty on the shrimp by attaching him to the drunk's ass, where he is slammed against walls before being flushed down the toilet. Fortunately, it was all a dream.

Silent comedy served as a major influence in the construction of the Edvard series, although at times Edvard's randiness seems more attuned to the primal antics of English comedian, Benny Hill. Like Chaplin and Keaton's characters, Edvard is a perceived unsung hero or loser. Of course, Edvard is additionally handicapped by the reality that he is a clay sea creature who is about the size of my middle finger. Like the great silent comics, Edvard wants desperately to fit in with the surrounding society. He wants nothing more than to be loved and accepted for what and who he is. Unfortunately, no one can even see him. Sharing more with Chaplin's tramp, Edvard is even willing, unlike Keaton's character, to shed his identity in order to gain acceptance.

One can't help but think back to Sapegin's rocky landscapes and the discombobulated stones of his youth. Just as the yard was continually transforming, with body parts appearing and reappearing, Edvard is a constantly shifting figure in search of a stable centre of being. As in Keaton's films, landscapes are ever-present in the *Edvard* series and play a pivotal role secondary character, dictating the direction of Edvard. At the same time, Edvard shares many characteristics with his creator, notably the fact that both were new to their environment and learning to adapt to and understand the surrounding culture. Edvard's story is very much Pjotr's; although, to my knowledge, Pjotr was never flushed or crushed...well not literally anyway.

Despite Edvard's modest popularity in Norway, it becomes rapidly apparent by the second or third film that he is a one-dimensional character. Edvard's chameleon transformations and Benny Hill hard-ons could only carry the films so far. Tired of being mocked and tortured by his creator, Edvard finally flashed the finger to his creator. And so Edvard now rests, we hope, in peace.

Edvard served Sapegin well. He worked on the series from 1992-1996 and the films afforded Sapegin the opportunity to develop and hone his animation skills. More importantly, the sacrifices of poor Edvard temporarily fed and clothed the Sapegin family.

Given Sapegin's inexperience, it is no surprise that his work environment was rather primitive. Working on 16mm for his first film, Sapegin constructed his own glass table. 'I had window frames, you know winter window frames, so I just piled up twelve layers and it was great. It was the only time I didn't get any reflections on those window frames. It was so easy and actually fast. So I thought, yep, that's probably my thing to do.' Sapegin first began experimenting with the glass table for his film, *Ippolita the Little Amazon*.

Ippolita emerged out of a failed Hercules project. With a stream of rejections and a 'god knows how I needed money then' reality, Sapegin divided the Greek hero into a girl (Ippolita) and a goat

Snails

(Esmeralda). What is instantly striking about *Ippolita* is the influence of Sapegin's stage design. Using a combination of cut-outs and clay, the wild, roaring backgrounds explode within the frame, lending an expressive theatrical element to the film. Having been abandoned by their tribe (which is visually represented through a jolting fusion of blacks and reds), Ippolita and Esmeralda journey through ancient Greece. Along the way they encounter a variety of Herculean-like labours. A chameleon-like bull, who, despite being killed by calm Esmeralda's arrow, pursues the duo in different forms. They are saved by the mighty hand of Appolon, the god of light and music. After being forced from Hesperide's garden, they encounter Atlas who offers to get the golden apples if they will hold the world up. After ditching the worm-infested pommes, they repay Appolon's favour by saving him from a beast. The duo then carry on, what Appolon calls, the beginning of their journey. Their journey ends as it begins.

Sapegin's work is casual and sober. We wonder whether we wander through a life in progress. Ippolita and Esmeralda walk through life unaware. Heroism arrives serenely. A serendipitous greeting unrecognized.

Ippolita is a keen inversion and parody of a masculine, virile, world. Sapegin re-constructs the masculine world of Greece through the unassuming, assured eyes of a woman, Ippolita remains an important film for Sapegin because it was his first experience with a female character. 'It was the first time I tried to work with a female main character and I absolutely loved it.' Not really knowing women by definition, Sapegin found himself less in control of his character than usual. Sapegin found this manner of working exciting and liberating in the ways that it led him towards new ideas and storylines.

Nestled beside his window frames with eyes scanning for greener pastures, Sapegin's inner bulb lit: he would become rich by making commercials. Using some leftover film, he made the hilarious *Fishballs*. The film was shot in 1 1/2 days on 35mm and was to be part of Sapegin's new commercial portfolio. *Fishballs* is a dramatic departure in style from *Edvard* and clearly foreshadows the crisp clay animation and stylish, colourful flowing backgrounds of *Mons The Cat*. In *Fishballs*, a young Mons the Cat (making his first appearance) sits by the water eagerly seeking out food. He rejects a female fish and then a male fish appears, but, rather than taking the whole fish, the cat grabs at his pearly white genitals. Sapegin received no commercial offers. While Sapegin expresses surprise that he did not get jobs, there is no doubt that the sly, transplanted Russian was well aware (Sapegin's voice is heard at the end asking 'How was it?') that he was making an anti-commercial. Sapegin simply could not go gentle without first biting the hand...or in this case, the balls that feed.

Distribution and funding, those tired, repetitive refrains, remain a problem for Sapegin. Funding comes primarily from the Norwegian Film Institute who also distributes the films. There is a competition for project funding a couple of times a year. Short Animation and Documentary proposals are lumped into one bin and if the idea is worthy enough to be among the top ten, you get financing. Films are shown in theatres but no money is paid to the filmmakers. TV channels buy films, sometimes even show them, but there is very little money for a short film. So, for independent animators like Sapegin, he must rely primarily on international festivals to find an audience and a buyer.

The animation 'boom' has found its way to Norway, however the problem remains the same: most of the money is going to 'big companies who just found out where the money is in our humanistic bad conscience towards children's time'.

In Sapegin's eyes, the Norwegian animation community is quite different from other countries' because of the gap between generations of animators. Most of the people in the industry are quite young and have never had any role models. While this can be an overwhelming situation, it removes many pressures and allows the animators to be more liberal and adventurous. Of course, with this freedom and their staunch refusal to work for the 'bad guys', most of the animators are opening and closing studios and fighting to find funding. With age comes fatigue and with fatigue comes compromise. 'Young people don't really know all those things which we know already because we have families and sick parents. We have to pay bills, the house and the car and god knows what. And they must have Sundays and they must have holidays off, and they don't hear anything. Despite the uncertainty, Sapegin likens this younger generation to the early days of the National Film Board of Canada and believes that many of today's artists 'will become the masters for a new generation'.

Following *Fishballs*, Sapegin made *Mons the Cat*, his first international 'hit'. *Mons the Cat* is based on a Norwegian folk tale. After refusing to eat his catfish, Mons in turn chews up the entire village community until he explodes à la Monty Python and everything returns to normal ... a dream. Mons now enjoys his catfish without complaints.

A haunting, nightmarish tale of a hyper-consumer living on overdrive within a wild, free-flowing capitalist marketplace? Maybe, but Sapegin was more interested in the cat. 'The cat as an animal is the perfect anti-hero because it is basically a nasty character. He kills,

One Day a Man Bought a House

he steals, he isn't really faithful, he never served, but at the same time he's so loveable. If you see a cat eating a mouse, that's when the cat is at his best, he's nice, he's smiling, he looks very, very cute.' Just like a tycoon as he is taking down another country.

Mons was shot in only four weeks, but Sapegin spent about two months just trying to figure out how to end the story: 'In *Mons the Cat* I used the actual media of animation as an expressive tool, as a storytelling tool. And then I said, "Ah, ha, that's where a lot of things are hidden in animation, so you have to see why you are making this film not in live action but in animation, what possibilities it gives you, how you can play with an environment within the reality of animation'.'

With *Mons*, we see Sapegin's most concerted use of mobile, multi-coloured backgrounds that sweep in and out of each scene. Originally, Sapegin had intended to make the backgrounds entirely in clay, but his 'rotten clay' was too soft and would not hold a solid form. So Sapegin heated the clay sticks with a lighter and used them like crayons on a glass surface. He would use this technique again in *The Saltmill*.

As might be expected, Sapegin works with very few people. 'The ideal set is that I have one more person working with me, and this person is some kind of orchestra leader.' At the moment, Sapegin's main team consists of Janne Hansen, a Volda College graduate. Sapegin also works with Lisa Fearnley, who shot *One Day A Man Bought A House*. 'She is an exceptional, exceptional photographer.'

What is perhaps most remarkable about *Mons The Cat* is the quality of the clay animation. It seems incredible that an artist with no previous animation experience could master the medium so quickly. But, as always there is a little secret. A former colleague in Moscow used to work with clay and while Sapegin never saw her work, he did see her puppets at home. 'We'd been making some toys for kids also and I sort of stole a lot of her aesthetic in a way. But I also thought that if I will work with animation ever I will try to make it as close to live action as possible. When you look at real people out in the street they are made out of different material which by definition is different from environment they live in, so I thought I will probably try to find an environment which is contradictory to the physical substance of the characters. That's why I went for clay, because also of my theatre modeling experience. That's where my backgrounds actually came from, from theatre models.'

One Day A Man Bought A House is a twisted tale about a man who moves into a house only to discover another occupant: a rat. Unwilling to share his new home, the man embarks on a series of methods to exterminate the rat. However, each murderous gesture (including the use of the infamous Malaysian pitbull cat) is mistaken for a sign of affection. The rat, a woman, soon believes that the man loves her. She dolls herself up, approaches the man and they marry and live happily ever after.

Ippolita, the Little Amazon

Sapegin wrote the original story and his wife re-wrote it for the film. The story was actually made in 1995 and was in production for almost three years. This perverse, bestial fairytale is actually based on a true story ... well sort of. 'The story came out of an accident when I had to kill a rat, and I tried to persuade her with a sausage and she ate the sausage then I couldn't kill her because I thought she now thinks that I'm a nice guy.'

Adapting his stage experience, Sapegin creates some stunning noirish chiaroscuro-lit backgrounds that seem taken from a Hitchcock or Orson Welles film. Combined with Randall Myers noir-tinged score, the backgrounds add a playful and ironic atmosphere of tension and uncertainty.

Perversity aside, *One Day A Man Bought A House* is a tale of misunderstanding. Sapegin slams conventions and expectations, turning the inappropriate or unnatural into new possibilities. Not that I suggest that we all run out and start humping animals, but instead we should look beneath the surface and embrace the film as a light tale that questions our perceptions of the so-called natural. Things we take for granted should not be taken for granted. Nothing is natural.

Sapegin worked on *One Day* and *The Salt Mill* concurrently. Once again, bills were outstanding. 'It was such a bad day and I said, "fuck a duck, we have to do once more like we did on *Mons*", for weeks everybody got paid, and we just kept rolling.' So that's how it started, as usual. Once again, Sapegin returned to a folk tale for his story source. The script was written by Studio Magica colleague, Lars Tommerbakke and both he and Sapegin worked on the story together. On one level, *The Salt Mill* is a tale about how the sea became salted, but deeper still it is about the accidental discovery of independence and identity. In a small town, all the salt is owned by a greedy old man. The Sea has no salt. The town has no salt. A young man digs for salt everyday. He is a 'yes' man who works only for a sandwich ... unsalted of course. While digging, the man discovers a cave and within it a salt troll. The man trades his sandwich to the troll for control of the salt. The man hastens immediately to the local tavern and offers the patrons salt for their fish and chips. Still the 'yes' man, the idiot-savant gives the rich man all of the salt and tells him the secret to owning the mill. The greedy man sets sail in a boat, says the magic words and drowns in the sea as the salt pours into his boat.

Sapegin finds folk tales a challenge to work with because they are constructed on different moral issues, so they must be twisted around. 'If you really look at the folk tales, they are completely pre-Christian, they came from pre-moral time, and to tell the story which will communicate with our society, you cannot just tell folk tale because people will get absolutely confused with what you are actually saying.' By altering the ending of the film, *The Salt Mill*, like *One Day*, became a tale based on misunderstanding. The young man in *Salt Mill* finds his independence completely by accident and in spite of his utter stupidity. In Sapegin's surreal fairytale world, there are no grand gestures, no mythical heroes, no profound logic, only everymen who, like Beckett characters inadvertently bump into solutions.

Sapegin recently left Studio Magica, a studio he co-founded upon arriving in Norway, to form Zoofilm. 'It became a little boring and I felt we were moving towards different cities. We had a big studio and you always have to paint. It became a bit heavy and I also want to work with experimental things and they want me to do television series. Zoofilm was formed in May 1999 with two other partners who, surprisingly, are not animation people. 'I have to prove to them that this genre can exist next to live action. I have to prove that I'm capable of doing things and it's basically great.'

The first Zoofilm project, *In The Corner of the World*, is a short

The man and the rat from *One Day a Man Bought a House*

71

Shakespeare 'pick-up' film. *In the Corner* returns to the style of *Edvard* using clay characters on a manipulated live action background. The concept behind *In the Corner* was to restore the original meaning of Shakespeare's poetry which, for all its high brow interpretations, was basically written to score with chicks. '*In the Corner of the World* was an extreme experiment. It came from the idea after I saw *Shakespeare In Love* which I liked very much and everybody else hated it absolutely, my partners hated it, my son hated it, also because it was wimpy. I thought it was great.'

Currently, Sapegin is working on a variety of projects including an interpretation of *Hamlet* and *Bernard Bityourtongue*. 'It's a book which was written by a very famous crime novelist and me. It's a crime story with two murders, for children. So this book is going to be an animation film, it's a half live action. The story takes place inside a puppet theatre. The marionettes have a life of their own and one of them is a killer, basically.' Sapegin has also approached Canada's National Film Board about co-producing a top secret project involving Puccini.

Despite a prosperous 1997, where Sapegin made four commercials for the National Lottery and four for a radio station, recent financial frustrations forced him to re-consider his artistic direction. 'I thought, "Ok", let's just give up and make a straightforward

Mons the Cat

animation silly for children.' But poor Pjotr still couldn't get it right. 'We made the film and sent it to some Danish consultants and they said, "What kind of film is this? It's no action and the main character is a well behaved girl".' Nevertheless, *Snails,* recently won a top prize at the Montreal Children's Film Festival.

Given Sapegin's highly stylized backgrounds, it would seem natural that he look the other way and perhaps try more abstract, non-narrative animations. However, Pjotr has a very good theory on this. 'I absolutely refuse to accept the definition of art on these two sections, figurative and non-figurative, because abstract art is one of the components in figurative art, it's a part in figurative art and by working in abstract media you are cheating yourself in a way because you will end up with a story which is maybe not on the screen but you hear it in back of your head anyway. So, if you develop abstract things up to a certain point, it will start to become figurative, if you just keep to developing the thing and so that is what I am doing, always using abstract things in a composition in storytelling also. It's kind of hidden inside in the paintings in the figurative paintings.'

For now, this life in progress carries on beyond these pages and our slanted tale of one life must come to an end. Young Pjotr is now older Pjotr. He has grown far from the acrobats, karate experts, snowmen, and marble landscapes of his youth. His new Nordic life is one of rats, cats, salt, and seas. Financial insecurities aside, Pjotr is happy, busy and Norwegian. 'I am a Norwegian filmmaker, and I am planted absolutely thoroughly. I just don't wanna go back to Russia – it's a really hectic place.'

Filmography of Pjotr Sapegin

1991	*Herkules*
1992	*Edvard*
1993	*Edvard – The Naked Truth*
1993	*Fish Balls*
1993	*Edvard – The Unbearable Lightness of Longing*
1994	*Ippolita – The Little Amazon*
1995	*Edvard – The Stand-in*
1995	*Mons the Cat*
1996	*Edvard – The Cruise Tripper*
1998	*One Day a Man Bought a House*
1998	*The Salt Mill*
1999	*Snails*
1999	*In a Corner of the World*
2001	*Aria*
2003	*Through my Thick Glasses*

Chapter 8

Dogs, Drinks, Dads and Dante: The Life and Art of Paul Fierlinger (2000)

'Now that I was finally at home I wished I were somewhere else'
Drawn From Memory
'A family's like a gun. You point it in the wrong direction, you're gonna kill somebody'
Trust (Hal Hartley)
'... like one who unchooses his own choice and thinking again undoes what he has started, so I became: a nullifying unease ...'
The Inferno of Dante

Scene from the PBS documentary *Maggie Growls* (2004)

It might be overstating it to compare animator Paul Fierlinger to Dante. Unlike the fictional Dante, Fierlinger did not face the three beasts nor the nine circles of hell. Fierlinger is the 'privileged son' of a Czech politician and has had a healthy career as an independent animator doing primarily commercial jobs. In one person (artist Sandra Schuette), he has found both his Beatrice and his Virgil. He has two cars, two dogs (Spinaker and Gracie), and lives in a cozy cottage home studio in Wynnewood, Pennsylvania. Fierlinger's torments, like Dante, are decidedly middle class, self-induced, and at times, romanticized. He has battled his cold, uncaring father and family, gone through two marriages, produced two children, one of whom he has seen maybe twice in the last ten years, and he is a recovering alcoholic. Like Dante, Fierlinger spent a portion of his life in exile and used his work, not to create grand mythological heroes or celebrities, but to either write himself into his work as a part-fictional everyman or focus on the exploits of the average. The lame analogy of my imaginings ends there. This world isn't anywhere near Dante's poetic hell of burning flesh and three-headed dogs, it is a much more terrifying, mundane, everyday hell that all of us have encountered: the family.

During this journey, Fierlinger managed to get nominated for an Oscar (*It's So Nice to Have A Wolf Around the House*) and carve out a unique position in animation by carefully straddling that line between independent and commercial work. Whether it's a commercial for US Health Care, an autobiographical feature, (*Drawn From Memory*), a book-of-the-month club film (*Playtime*), a Nickelodeon spot, or even a *Sesame Street* short (*Teeny Little Superguy*), you are always aware of the Fierlinger presence. It's the simple James Thurber-influenced drawing style, the warm colours; but most of all it's the ongoing sense of nostalgia, memory, desire, and personal history that separates Fierlinger's work from that of his more clearly-defined colleagues.

Like the work of Norman Rockwell, one is initially tempted to reject Fierlinger's films for being commercial, folksy, sentimental, and very much a reflection of that god damn American Dream which has destroyed many lives with its hyperbolic patriotic 'just do it' justification for being. But as with Rockwell's work, or, let's say, the populist films of Frank Capra, we are attracted to this homogenous, peaceful vision because it offers the possibility domestic kindness and social accord. In these cynical times we are hesitant about Fierlinger's work because it celebrates a norm that we continually reject as a construction of corporate, political and mass media voices. And, in a sense, we are right to question Fierlinger's purified world. Normalcy at times is little more than being inarticulate, bored, violent, oppressed and generally in a state of misery and pain. The 'norm' bears little resemblance to this idealized vision of Fierlinger's films, but does that mean that we should not strive to attain this ideal? Within each of our corrupted, cynical souls we secretly long for the 'picture perfect postcard' portrait of America that Fierlinger gives us.

Appropriately, the creator of this harmonious world is a fiery, outspoken, often misanthropic man who has lived life seeking love and stability in an unstable world. From the beginning he was basically unwanted and ignored by his parents and sent from country to country, living for moments here and moments there. He is a man of in-betweens, an outsider. He is viewed by some artists with disdain because they see his work as commercial and therefore not relevant. His frankness, a compensation for insecurities and an extension of years of alcohol-induced fatigue and frustration, has pissed-off many colleagues. But beyond these surfaces lies a deeply caring, passionate, intelligent man whose portrait of the world is much more perceptive than he is given credit for.

> *At the heart of Fierlinger's work is the father.*
> *It all comes back to the bloody father.*
> *Those cursed Virgils who can't see with their clinking glasses.*
> *Between lines I sip another drink.*

Early years

Fierlinger was born in Japan but shortly thereafter moved to the USA with his parents. His father was an influential diplomat who allied himself with the direction of the random political winds. His mother is barely recalled. His Uncle was the first Communist Prime Minister of Czeckoslovakia and is loathed. From the beginning, Fierlinger never fit in. It would always be like that.

Growing up within the safe confines of Burlington, Vermont, Fierlinger remained an outsider, insecure and alone. He didn't play sports, didn't have parents (but guardians), and in general, never felt he belonged. The one thing Fierlinger did well was draw. Fierlinger's drawings won the respect of his classmates and he used the drawings as a means of escaping from a world he did not understand. He was moved to Czechslovakia at age 11 and began making films a year later. His father had a Bolex camera and Fierlinger used it to shoot a flipbook drawn on the corners of a book. In the film, a little boy jumps into a swimming pool and comes up with a fish in his mouth. Young Fierlinger was overjoyed at the sight of his moving drawings. Fierlinger went on to study and the Bechyne School of Applied Arts and spent two years in the military where he drew in his spare time and had access to a camera in the unit. 'I set up a stand made out of pieces of wood and an ancient WW1 camera that was designed to take aerial photos.' By this time, Fierlinger had decided to draw for a living. After his army career, he freelanced in Prague as an illustrator and gag cartoonist (using the name Fala). Having experience as an illustrator, Fierlinger approached a friend at an ad agency who agreed to let Fierlinger make a commercial for them.

During this time, Fierlinger set up his first independent animation studio, AKF studio. 'In the 1950s there was a law that said you couldn't own a typewriter. You had to have a permit and prove you needed it.' There was also a state monopoly on 35mm film and cameras. When TV came along, the law remained the same. Therefore 16mm, the traditional TV format, became a professional format. This enabled Fierlinger to make films at home and work for TV. 'Because I was a member of the artists' union I was allowed to work at home. I had my own camera and permission to freelance and I started making films. All the animators at the Czech studio were shocked.' Fierlinger made a logo for his new studio and produced children's shorts, theatrical films, and station breaks for both Prague TV and Kratky Film. From 1958 until his studio closed in 1967, Fierlinger made about 200 films. More importantly, television provided a valuable learning experience for Fierlinger. Not only was he practising while he worked but the horror of having virtually everyone see his work forced him to work harder at mastering his craft: 'I cringed everytime I saw the work and people looking at it. But that is the surest way to learn.' It is not known if any of Fierlinger's early films still exist, but it is known that he has no desire to show them. 'I have a friend who collected my old drawings. He had some on his walls and I had the worst

Still Life with Animated Dogs

sinking feeling. My son went to see the guy and he said, 'I saw your drawings on the wall' and he couldn't believe how bad they were. It was a very humbling experience.'

Exiled again

In 1967 Fierlinger escaped from Czechoslovakia to Holland where he worked briefly for Dutch television before moving on to Paris as a spot animator for Radio Television France and then to Munich to work as a key animator on a feature film.

In helping to ease his labour in exile, Fierlinger had developed a style in Prague where he used non-permanent magic markers. 'If you used it on a plate you could make a line and then smudge it a bit. All I needed was a ceramic tile and I would do this under the camera.' This was fine, but where can you put the camera? With so little space to work with, Fierlinger was forced to improvise: 'I'd put the camera on a tripod then put a table against the wall and put the tripod on the table. I was between the legs of the tripod with my back to the wall. I put one light to shine on the stand.' This mobile studio allowed Fierlinger to work fast and maintain some consistency between his styles.

USA and *Sesame Street*

In 1968, the now married Fierlinger returned briefly to New York where he did some documentary work for Universal Studios. In 1969, with a son in tow, the family settled in Philadelphia where Fierlinger has remained to this day. Fierlinger worked with Concept Films, a company that created political commercials for Hubert Humphrey and other candidates. He stayed with Concept for a year and half. Seeing that there was no one else in town doing animation, Fierlinger figured he had found a garden of riches. But Philadelphia, lost in the smoky shadows of the Big Apple, had little work.

Despite a new family, these years were a period of struggle and loneliness for Fierlinger. In Czechoslovakia, the art community was very close. They drank together, argued, talked and shared. There was no such community in Philadelphia. Then again, Fierlinger was not the most likable fellow and, most disturbingly, he was, horror of horrors, a commercial artist.

In 1971, Fierlinger found some much needed support in the form of Dave Connell, an executive at the Children's Television Network. Connell commissioned Fierlinger to make a variety of short films for both *Sesame Street* and the Electric Company. He also created one of the most popular series, *Teeny Little Superguy* for *Sesame Street*. '*Teeny Little Superguy* came out of insecurity. I wanted

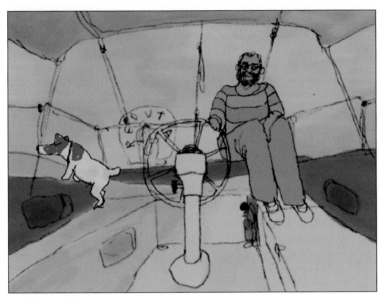

Still Life with Animated Dogs

to make a series. I needed a series. I needed a steady flow of work but Dave said that I was too small and that I couldn't produce fast enough.' Fierlinger took a plastic cup, drew on it, and surrounded the character with other household objects. 'It's like a cel and you can draw on it. You can pre-fab all the steps. Then we set up scenes with everyday household objects. Connell liked the idea and Jim Thurman (a long-time Fierlinger collaborator) wrote the first stories. Then they trusted me.' *Teeny Little Superguy* received some of the highest ratings from test groups and Fierlinger made thirteen installments. Fierlinger was surprised that he was not asked to produce more installments, but in the end the experience at *Sesame Street* turned out to be a great asset. 'It has got me work. Clients don't want *Sesame Street* but they know you are a good animator if you worked there.' Fierlinger continues to animate for *Sesame Street* to this day and has made films about the alphabet, numbers, concept films (e.g. *Up and Down*), and, most recently, the problem-solving series, *Alice Kadeezenberry*. One of the more interesting projects was an amusing *Canada Geese* spot and an Arabic version of *The Adventures of Letterman*!

While working for *Sesame Street*, Fierlinger started his own animation company, AR&T Associates (Animation Recording and Titling Services). Snuggled within his Wynnewood suburb, AR&T produced an astounding 700 films, commercials, and i.d.'s in its twenty-nine year history.

The most notable film of AR & T's early years is *It's So Nice To Have a Wolf Around The House* (1979). The film was commissioned by the Learning Corporation of America (LCA). The film was based on a book by the same name, and voice actor, Jim Thurman, ad-libbed the entire film. 'We had no script; [Thurman] just looked at the pictures on every page and said something, so we pretty much made things up as we recorded.' In the film, an old man living with his old cat, old dog, and old fish, decide to look for a 'charming companion'. The companion arrives in the face of one Cuthbert Q. Devine. Owing to the man's poor eyesight, Cuthbert, a wolf, is hired. The flamboyant wolf instantly brings life into their stagnant lives. He cooks, cleans, paints, and entertains the tired souls. Paradise falls, however, when it is revealed that Cuthbert is actually a wolf. Eventually the companions learn that appearances are not important, and in turn they learn to become more independent.

While Wolf is somewhat dated, it is clearly the first mark of the Fierlinger style. The thick black lines, the dark, warm colours, the strong, confident voice of Jim Thurman are evident. In content, *Wolf* is a tale of everyday folk; little voices Fierlinger amplifies throughout his career.

Wolf went on to receive a number of festival awards and was nominated for an Academy Award (eventually losing to *Every Child*). Again, success was not kind to Fierlinger. 'After I got the Oscar nomination, I never heard from LCA again.'

Aside from the Learning Company, Fierlinger made numerous films in the 1980s and 1990s for U.S Healthcare. Some of the more notable films are *We Sure Know How To Pick 'em*, a bizarre little film that almost seems anti-US Healthcare. The commercial outlines the care that US Healthcare takes when choosing its doctors, but what comes through in the film is a bizarre Orwellian tale about how they 'weed out those who don't fit in'. We then see doctors corralled like cattle. The commercial was shown once before being pulled.

I'll Be There (1994) is a sober piece about a father writing to his son while stranded at an airport. The father reminisces about past family trips to US landmarks (The Alamo, Grand Canyon). On one hand, *I'll Be There* is little more than a sappy reflection of the worst aspects of American marketing, yet within the context of Fierlinger's career the film is transformed into a deeply personal letter to an imagined father.

In 1988, Fierlinger made an award-winning anti-smoking film, *The Quitter*. Fierlinger got along very well with US Healthcare marketing director, Larry Alten. Alten gave Fierlinger an unusual amount of freedom when making films. With *The Quitter*, Alten gave Fierlinger and Thurman a 'really stupid brochure' for their anti-smoking program. The duo were asked to make a film out of it. This way the company could claim that they had a prevention program. Alten didn't care what the film did or said as long as it was funny. 'Jim took the booklet into my recording booth and began to ad-lib while looking at the pages. He was mostly saying put-downs and talk-backs and that's what ended up in the film.'

The Quitter is quite straightforward. A man travels to the country-side where he is confronted by a talking cloud who encourages him to become 'a quitter'. Using a Woody Allen style of self-deprecating humour, *The Quitter* is essentially a dialogue between the man and the cloud about the difficulty in quitting, the man's 'loser' charac-teristics, and the influence of movies on his smoking. While the film is at times didactic and self-righteous, there is a surprisingly human element within it that acknowledges the difficulty surround-ing this addiction.

By this time, Fierlinger was firmly established as a commercial animator and at the same time was winning awards at various 'artistically-oriented' animation festivals. Success aside, Fierlinger was also miserable, angry, and drunk most of the time.

And then I'll stop ...

> *Once it helped cure the demons, delivering the sunken soaked soul from the miseries of abandonment into a wonderful nightmare of loquacious delusions. In this drunken paradise, time froze; the hate of the outside and inside faded with each shot. Cravings, perver-sions and longings nestled restlessly within daydreams come gust-ing along with the sweet sounds of the swaggering winds. After the storm the winds calm, memories unrecalled, bruises, pain, head-aches, whispers, shits, puke, misery, slinky little bugs crawling around your floor, the voices from where? the sinking. This was gone now. There were no more deliveries. The timeless underwater oblivion soon became as miserable as the dry one above. Life became a drifting blur of insomniac inspired fragments.*

Fierlinger had known for a long time that he was an alcoholic, but stopping was not really an issue. It wasn't until the late 1980s that Fierlinger hit bottom. While at Ottawa '88, Fierlinger met NFB animators Derek Lamb and Kaj Pindal. Lamb was showing ex-cerpts from his project, *Goldtooth* and asked Fierlinger if he was interested in being the production house. 'I had never done any-thing like it, but was interested. I was insecure so it was a year's worth of work.' Pindal and Lamb visited Fierlinger's studio to discuss the project, but problems arose immediately. 'The problem was that I was drinking around the clock. Derek asked me a few times to wait until noon. I was a disagreeable person.' Lamb sent Fierlinger to Mexico to take sketches for the film. When Fierlinger returned Lamb told him that it wasn't going to work out. Ironically, Lamb left Fierlinger a case of whisky as a parting gift!

Losing the job was bad, but worse still Fierlinger had called off all projects for a year to work with Lamb and Pindal. But fate, the slithering slap in the face, pounded on Fierlinger's door. Having seen Fierlinger's work at Ottawa, Pyramid Films called Fierlinger and asked him if he would like to make a film. They had a number of topics including teen suicide and drug and alcohol abuse. 'I thought, I'm an alcoholic and if anyone can do this film, I can.' US Healthcare matched Pyramid's $20,000 fee and Fierlinger was off to the races. Fierlinger then turned to his son for some feedback. 'I told my son that I have to make a film about alcoholism and what would you want to see in school. He told me that he didn't want to see any funny stuff just real people saying real things ... so I said, OK, I'll do it that way.' Fierlinger had a friend who worked in a rehab clinic and provided him with twenty five hours of interview tapes. It was these tapes that finally convinced Fierlinger to quit drinking. ' Listening to those tapes, I knew I had to stop drinking. It's why I'm shouting at my kids and not getting along with Derek Lamb.' Fueling the fire and the bedside bottle were healthy intakes of pot, valium and nicotine.

In quitting, Fierlinger locked himself in his apartment. He told his wife and kids that he was going to work. The week was horrific: 'I had D.T.'s (delirium tremors), and saw huge cockroaches. I felt bugs crawling on me. I'd wake up naked and not remember what had happened. I didn't eat and was ready to kill myself.' Finally,

Teeny Little Superguy

from within the walls of despair, Fierlinger called his doctor. 'He held me on the line while he called my son to bring me medication. When I started feeling better he came over and gave me a shot and got me out of it and started treating me. It's a strange thing that I failed Derek because I was drunk and right then I get a call to work on an alcohol film and not only get sober but meet someone who helped me.'

Using the interviews with re-hab patients, each story takes us through the habits, downfall and subsequent acknowledgment and recovery of each addict. Fierlinger gave each voice their own drawing style. The styles range from dark, grey sketches to Steinberg-influenced geometric drawings. Accompanying the story is a haunting, minimalist track. The power of the film lies with the combination of Fierlinger's strong graphics, the soundtrack and the frank, unsentimental stories of these real people. There is not a drop of sentimentality in this film. It is very much a horror story.

The biggest twist comes at the end when we are introduced to a new character, Paul. Fierlinger's voice comes on and talks about his own downfall and recovery. It is one of the most personal and spine-tingling moments seen in animation. What's more remarkable is Fierlinger's refusal to trumpet his problem into a courageous cry for help. Instead we are given a logical, matter-of-fact admission of weakness and recovery.

And then I'll Stop met with festival success and, ironically, beat out *Goldtooth* for most of the prizes. Fierlinger stopped drinking on 7 February 1989 and has been sober to this day.

Drawn from memory

Fierlinger's masterpiece and most personal work to date is the feature film, *Drawn From Memory*. The film is an autobiographical look at Fierlinger's difficult relationship with his father, set within the background of post-World War II Czechoslovakia. The film traces Fierlinger's life, from his earliest memories of Japan (highlighted by the appropriate use of pencil test style) to his joyful youth in the USA, troubled years in Communist Czechoslovakia, and his eventual escape to the USA in the 1960s.

Fierlinger had wanted to make *Drawn From Memory* for many years but no one had trusted him to make a feature film. Producer Ron Diamond noticed Fierlinger's work and called him to see what projects he could license. He sent Diamond a treatment, and, after reading it, Diamond agreed to find money. Two years later Diamond found a producer: American Playhouse.

The production of *Drawn From Memory* was not a happy experience for Fierlinger. There were many arguments between Fierlinger and

Diamond. Much has been whispered about this relationship. Despite whatever went on, the film got made and Fierlinger again proved the doubters wrong.

Originally, *Drawn From Memory* was to be a political film, but with the guidance of American Playhouse producer, Lynn Holst, the film evolved into a depiction of a difficult, hateful father-son relationship.

Being forced to deal with his father on a daily basis, *Drawn From Memory* became an exorcism of sorts for Fierlinger. Drawing his father frame by frame and bringing him back to life liberated him to some degree from their troubled past. 'He never wanted me to be an animator. I brought him to life and did whatever I wanted with him.'

While some critics have called *Drawn From Memory* a forgiving film, it is clearly an angry film. When Paul's mother dies, he moves on, showing little remorse. 'If I were to add up all the days I ever spent in her presence, I doubt that I could put an entire year together.'

Much of the film's anger is directed towards Jan Fierlinger, Paul's father. Jan is presented as a career diplomat prepared to adapt to whichever side wins the war. The father is shown as a materialistic hypocrite and coward who cares more about his career than his family. He is also, as Fierlinger quietly suggests, an alcoholic. We see the father routinely in search of drinks. This isn't a barfly Bukowski world, instead Jan lives within a class of cognac and fine wines where drinking signifies a level of prestige. Addiction is

A Room Nearby

cloaked behind the finely-honed words: vintage, year, grapes. It is easy to see how young Paul would have found this world inviting.

When Jan dies, it merely means an opportunity for Paul to escape. Nothing more.

Drawn from Memory also details the roots of Fierlinger's love of suburban America. During the single idyllic period as a youth in Burlington where everything was a 'picture perfect postcard,' Fierlinger constructed an illusory yet very real portrait of the mass media's America. Throughout his films, he has sought to re-create this idyllic world. But the truth is that this world does not exist. It is a state of mind. It is a world that cannot be reached. Fierlinger lives in this world through his films. 'You see yourself as people in pictures on billboards because you hide from reality and conflict by dreaming. You make up stories without realizing that you are trying to transform yourself into them.' Ironically, Fierlinger's work continues to contribute to the construction and maintenance of this impossible dream.

Drawn From Memory is an emotionally complex and at times paradoxical film. At its heart is the rejection of family. Paul is unable to forgive his mother and father. At the same time, his anger and ultimate inability to escape his father's shadow led Fierlinger to alienate his own sons. At the end of the film Paul expresses hope that his sons will one day forgive him; a man who cannot forgive his own father. It is these contradictions that give this tale of abandonment and hope its power and raw humanity.

Drawn is a risky venture. Most filmmakers would have languished in self-pity, however, Fierlinger's ability to contextualize the familial relationships within the larger context of world history extends the personal into the universal and political.

Drawn From Memory was a major success on festival circuits and television. It is currently available on video. The film was also a critical success and received rave reviews from around the world. If this was live-action, Fierlinger would be living in Hollywood with five cars, five dogs and a mansion. But this is animation and unless you're an executive or a studio hack, financial security and animation are strangers. Everyone loved the film, but his wallet remained empty.

Out of work and in need of some dough, Fierlinger made two independent calling card pieces called *Marsh People* and *Rabbit Story*. Both films were made as part of a concept that Fierlinger developed called Cartoon of the Week. 'It was a well thought out and extensive proposal which described how we were capable of producing one two-minute film a week, based on stories which viewers would call in on a special line with a tape machine on the end of it. The best story would be awarded by actually making the film and showing it a week later.' *Marsh People* and *Rabbit Story* served as prototypes for the series. Although there was some interest, the response everywhere was the same: 'It's fine that you can do it in a week but we would need several weeks to approve and make changes'.

Rabbit Story is a story told by Fierlinger's composer, John Avarese. Avarese tells a tale about his grandmother's dog, a paranoid neighbour, and a dead bunny. *Marsh People*, through these twisted, patriarchally-challenged eyes, is one of Fierlinger's funniest and darkest works. Narrated and written by Fierlinger, a man takes us back to his childhood on Chesapeake Bay. The man tells us of his father's terrible temper and how he flees to the water when angry. One day the son says something the father doesn't like and the father runs for the water. A shotgun is heard. The boy finds his decapitated pop lying in the boat. The boy gently pushes his dead dad into the water and quietly returns home.

During a party to celebrate *Drawn From Memory*, Fierlinger met a variety of MTV and Nickelodeon types. He was invited to Nick Jr. to discuss developing a series for kids. Disgusted at the prospect of making television for three-year-olds; disgusted at the prospect of making television where he would have little freedom; disgusted at the prospect of dealing with a committee of twenty-somethings who were all self-appointed experts in child psychology; disgusted with an empty bank account; Fierlinger took the job.

Like *Teeny Little Superguy*, *Amby and Dexter* received a lot of positive reviews from viewers and suits, but the series was simply too tranquil for the bright, fast, loud world of Nickelodeon. There is no dialogue and the episodes are elegant, delicate odes to the imagination and creativity of young children.

In creating *Playtime* for the Book of the Month Club, fate flickered again. A Book of the Month Club producer happened to see *Amby and Dexter* at Nickelodeon and he approached Fierlinger to write stories to a series of well known songs. The Fierlingers had complete freedom in selecting the songs and writing the stories. The songs are divided by brief black and white pieces of kids at play. Of the songs, the two shorts that stand out are *Wheels On the Bus*, which interweaves the children's playtime fantasies and reality, and *Bling Bang*, a delightful geometrical interpretation of a Johnny Cash song. *Playtime* is an eloquent celebration of children's fantasies, and a portrait of rural America as a place of community and harmony.

Using the same narrative approach as *And Then I'll Stop* and *Drawn From Memory*, *Drawn from Life* is a series of two-minute shorts narrated by various women. The women in the shorts range in age and gender and class. They offer personal memories of significant moments of the past, present and future. In *Wanderlust*, a woman talks about her 'truck driving boyfriend' who sends postcards of places he has been and seen. There is a somber element to this episode and the girl's longing for escape from her often mundane job is soothed by these 'picture perfect postcard' representations of America. Like Fierlinger, the woman seems to desire to explore an America that likely exists only in postcards. The most visually innovative film is *One of Eight*. Fierlinger uses a chaotic, sketchy style to tell the story of a young athlete who relates the pressures of competition.

Throughout the series, Fierlinger manages to maintain his unique voice. The films convey an America through the eyes of six very different women and are empowering in the sense that each tale is a significant expression of personal histories. These are not tales of celebrities, politicians or Oprah, but everyday American women. Certainly these memories are slanted and misremembered, but they are folktales from the voices of the 'little' people who constructed a country that never hears them speak.

Well we've covered dads, drinks, and Dante, now life goes to the dogs. Fierlinger is currently at work on the project, *Still Life With Animated Dogs*, a series of real stories about dogs.

Dogs have provided Fierlinger with an unconditional loyalty, love and comfort that he has not found at times in humanity. 'They require absolute commitment and faithfulness – good for keeping a person from depression – not just by their company but by keeping you so busy attending to them and watching out for them that one day the dog is dead, you're still alive and have received the gift of being a survivor. They make you feel important. They sleep 16 hours a day and you can pick the hours.'

Dogs is in many ways a sequel to *Drawn From Memory*. Fierlinger traces the course of his life from Czechoslovakia through to the USA through the dogs he has owned. Each dog leads to memories of specific periods in Fierlinger's life. *Still Life With Animated Dogs* is scheduled to be finished in September 2000.

> *I find frankness and honesty.*
> *A past written with the colours of forgiveness.*
> *Where is the raging, reactionary, alcoholic*
> *I imagined?*
>
> *Where is the man who slithered through hell unguided?*
> *All I see is a hypnotic, hesitant, average voice.*
> *All I find is compassion,*
> *when I want anger.*
>
> *Then again, maybe this isn't about him.*

All images from
Drawn From Memory

So here we are in the 21st century. Fierlinger has survived, is sober, less bitter, and working. While there is no denying his talent, he is yet again an enigma within animation history. Where does Fierlinger fit in? His work is client-based, but he also has an unusual amount of freedom. We often talk about the independent Bill Plympton or the riches of the National Film Board of Canada, but are they really any more independent than Fierlinger? Plympton is not client-based, but deep down he makes films for audiences and readily admits that if an audience doesn't find a sequence funny he will remove it. The NFB, for all its success and perceived freedom, is at the mercy of a committee of bureaucrats, producers, taxpayers and social agendas. 'I certainly think it is a mistake to consider independent work to be only that work which is done with no outside money. Just because a film comes with money so you don't have to wait on tables to eat doesn't mean you lose independence. The animator-waiter is just as dependent on the tips he gets before he can finish a film as I am on my payment schedule or he's dependent on his wife's income; or she's dependent on her parent's support as she studies and makes films. Not all clients are insensitive clods, just most of them'.

Ah ... that hypnotic, warm, fuzzy, 'nullifying unease' that is the voice of Paul Fierlinger. This, for me, is the beauty of Fierlinger. He is a man who speaks truths. Sure it creates problems, but for all his anger, irrationality and contradiction, he is more authentic than most of us. Not too far within that distant shell of steel is a mild, caring man who is generous and loving. He has not reached paradise, but who the hell has. heh heh heh.

You like him. You don't. Take him. Leave Him. He Lived. He lives. I like him. His father can't say that.

Filmography of Paul Fierlinger

1979	*It's So Nice to Have a Wolf Around the House*
1987	*The Quitter*
1989	*And Then I'll Stop ...*
1995	*Drawn from Memory*
1997	*Marsh People*
1997	*A Rabbit Story*
1998	*Anna Beaumont*
1999	*Amby and Dexter*
1999	*Playtime*
2000	*Drawn From Life* (TV Series)
2001	*Still Life with Animated Dogs*
2003	*A Room Nearby*

Chapter 9

Where Memories Breathe Darkness: Underneath the Hat of Michèle Cournoyer

(2001)

'The past is never dead. It is not even past.'
William Faulkner, *Requiem for A Nun*

Addiction bottles you with the impact of thunderous silence. A force so intense you are swallowed unawares. Existence reduced to extremes. You stagger between moments accompanied by tuneless instruments. Every movement determined by invisible strings. Inevitably, you fall short. An evacuation of emotions collapses you into the hopelessness of a stained shirt. You reach an almost peaceful apathy. A mundane aftermath of despair. The echoes of memories are reduced to incomprehensible shadows. You can't see it though you know it could not but be. A life atrophied. You were. You are not. Will you be?

In Michèle Cournoyer's film, *The Hat*, an exotic dancer performs in front of shapeless figures with dark hats while remembering being abused as a child. The strings of the adultworld left this woman a child not far from the womb skulking through a lightless tunnel. Sex is without love. True love lost to the breezes of childhood. The impact of *The Hat* lies in its complexity of emotions. This is not just a film about sexual abuse. It is a film about addiction, love, seduction and emotional manipulation. For Cournoyer, *The Hat* was a personal battle. For months she struggled with technological addictions, physical demons, and creative roadblocks in order to find the voice of her film. As she tumbled farther into the pits of emotional hell, Cournoyer found her Virgil in the form of producer, Pierre Hébert. Hébert's support, encouragement and guidance lifted Cournoyer out of her circle of hell and closer to creative paradise. The result was one of the darkest, dirtiest, and complex films to emerge from the cold, scrubbed halls of the National Film Board of Canada.

Art has always been an emotional struggle for Michèle Cournoyer. Whether as a painter, independent animator or NFB filmmaker, she has fought these 'incomprehensible shadows' throughout her life. She was born. Her parents liked her. She has two brothers and a sister. While hospitalized at age 12, her father brought her an oil paint box and she started painting. She had been drawing since she was five years old. It was clear to her that painting was a refuge from a life left alone. Her formal artistic education was put on hold

Michèle Cournoyer

at age 17 when her mother became ill. She stopped to care for her ailing mother and assumed the matron role of the domestic sphere. Then her world stopped. At age 20, Cournoyer's mother died. The girl grew up fast; an ersatz mother for a heartbroken family. Still, she painted, printed, drew, sculpted and gave everything to art. After two years in Québec City, she moved to Montréal briefly before heading to London to study graphic design. 'I went to London with a $90 plane ticket and a government grant of $2000. It was "swinging" London. I was printing pillows on pillows, pearls on pillows, hands on glove. Silkscreen sequences. Here the images started to move with music and the cinema came to me one day.' Cournoyer was living in a boarding place. She became friends with a man, a photographer, and upon seeing the man with his baby, got the idea to make a simple film called *L' Homme et L'Enfant*.

A series of still photos show a man holding a baby. Eventually flowers cover up the baby. 'I did the film during lunch hour and it was quite natural for me. When I made that film it was very clear to me that I would make films.' Cournoyer lived in a surrealist world where there was always a story in motion. Cournoyer sent *L'Homme* to the Canada Council and received a grant to make another film. She went to Italy to start the next film. It was set in Venice and was about a little girl who was going to get married but her veil flies off and blows around Italy. The film was never made and Cournoyer returned to Montréal where she started working as a custom designer on feature films by Gilles Carles (*La mort d'un Búcheron*) and Mireille Dansereau (*La Vie Revée*).

Cournoyer became an active contributor to the new wave of Québec cinema. 'It was an important time for me. I did commercials, paintings for an American film series.' In 1975, Cournoyer was involved in the Atélier Graff with other artists, including Pierre Ayotte. The group made films, painted, and had group exhibitions. Cournoyer continued with her own painting. She had very few solo exhibitions because she sold her work to pay the bills. Cournoyer has none of her paintings today. All have been sold or given away to friends.

Cournoyer continued making her own films. *Spaghettata* shows a woman eaten by spaghetti to the accompaniment of the Italian national anthem. 'It was a rejection of all things Italian. After living in Italy, I had had enough of it. Cournoyer again used collage and photos for the film. The film was a collaboration with her long time friend (and NFB animator) Jacques Drouin. Drouin and Cournoyer shot *Spaghettata* in one evening while cooking the spaghetti which was used for the film. The film was presented as part of an exhibition in old Montréal. 'We had an Italian chef, an art book, a painting of a stove, and the projection of the film. It was a crazy, fantastic night.'

Her next film, *La Toccata* was based on the dream of another. A man plays Bach on a piano in a field. A woman slowly emerges from the piano. After a few flirtatious moments she runs off and cuts into the ground with a knife. Eventually she opens the ground and finds an orchestra. The woman is so moved by the new music that she jumps into a man's horn. With a definite surrealist edge, *La Toccata* is a critical view of relationships. The men are insensitive and immobile. The woman is always on the move, from one old song to another. She has no centre or stability. Throughout Cournoyer's films women are trapped, if not physically at least mentally.

Then came the lobster phase. 'I was painting a lot of lobsters. I had dreams of lobsters. I even painted myself in a bathing suit with a lobster.' Her next film, *Old Orchard Beach, PQ* (1982) dealt with, yes, lobsters. Once again, Cournoyer used a photo collage technique. The film is entirely set at Orchard Beach. The first half is akin to a Muybridge experiment. We see bodies in motion. All shapes and sizes. The film then focusses on a man glaring hungrily at a woman's ass. Suddenly the beach becomes a playground for the lecherous. The women transform into canned sardines. The lifeguard, the icon of safety, turns into a lobster as he makes love to the woman. Cournoyer creates an ugly, self-destructive environment. The woman embraces the lobster and clearly enjoys the bestial moment. Women are active participants in their own oppression. The woman is self-destructive, seemingly desperate for companionship.

Frustrated by the technical complications of *Orchard Beach*, Cournoyer turned to rotoscope animation for her next film, *Dolorosa* (The Pain and the Rose). A woman examines herself in the mirror. She sees flabby skin. She is aging. Yet inside she feels as young as ever. We see her dancing, living, and loving. She is a healthy, vibrant woman trapped within a decaying façade of mortality.

Dolorosa opened doors for Cournoyer at the NFB. The board provided Cournoyer with facilities for the film and she even had an

A Feather Tale
[©1992 The National Film Board of Canada.]

93

office in the English studio. Having received facility commitment for her next film, Cournoyer wanted to see if she was eligible for the NFB's Cinéastes Recherché competition. In her 40s and having made a number of 'amateur' films, she doubted her eligibility. However, producer Yves Leduc noted that she was indeed eligible. The aim of the competition was to allow a filmmaker to make a film in good professional conditions. This was certainly something foreign to Cournoyer. In the end she presented a scenario about an addictive relationship called, *A Feather Tale,* and won the competition.

Besides *The Hat, A Feather Tale* is Cournoyer's strongest film. The first scene opens with the shot of a cracking egg forming a face with tears. Something has been broken. A sleeping woman receives a call from her lover. He wants her to come over. She obeys and arrives in a take-out delivery box as a chicken. The man holds her, rocks her, pulls her feathers off and eats her. Initially, the woman allows herself to play this role. But she eventually takes control and realizes she must cut the head off the relationship before she completely loses herself. The final shot of the film shows the woman waking up, the man is snoring beside her. Feathers cover the ground. This addiction is over.

Following the completion of *A Feather Tale,* Cournoyer won a hiring competition at the NFB. Her first official NFB project was an entry for *The Rights from The Heart* series. She chose the topic of freedom to discover talent. Cournoyer worked on a computer for the first time using a combination of live-action, photography, and drawings. *The Artist* is about a young girl who, to the anger of her father, turns her domestic space into a creative environment. *The Artist* provides a clear example of the naiveté of *The Rights from The Heart* series. The complexity of reality is reduced to a simplistic polarization. The father goes from uninterested to supportive for no apparent reason. Cournoyer had initially proposed that the father be an alcoholic, but this was felt to be too strong. Reality had no place in *The Rights from The Heart.*

Cournoyer's next project was again for *The Rights from The Heart.* This time she selected the issue of sexual abuse. Cournoyer initially set out to make the film using photo montage and computer. She made a precise storyboard and some images on the computer. Soon, she realized this technique would not work. 'I took photos of an actor in the stairs, in a bar, and I tried to do some reproductions of the photos. But it was too precise and doing in-betweens between the photos was a nightmare. There were some beautiful parts but something was not there and I was feeling extremely sick.' Cournoyer became so sick that she was unable to work for three months. She was dizzy, emotional, and reached a point where she couldn't even go outside. The sickness proved inspiring, however. First, Cournoyer began to draw black ink on paper at home. Secondly, Pierre Hébert became the new producer of the French unit and he basically told Cournoyer to start again. 'She was going nowhere', says Hébert, 'and in my judgement it was a dead end. She showed me the very first very crude drawings that she had been doing when she was researching for the film. I thought they were very powerful and I thought she should restart from that point.' Hébert then insisted Cournoyer remove her computer and all photographic references from her office. 'He removed all my crutches and so I continued drawing with a brush. I had been working with them for two years. It was like a divorce. I had to get rid of my reality and start again.' Hébert's suggestions proved liberating, albeit addictive. 'It was like a religion. It was in my mind all the time. I was raping my brushes, staining my drawings, and taking the speed of an urgent rape. It became more and more liberating. I worked in a primitive direct communication with my devils and found the story in the execution.'

The Hat is one of the most important films to emerge from this country. It was done without compromise. Superbly edited with Fernand Bélanger, there is no cut in the film, only metamorphoses; an ambivalent endless rape. Accompanied by Jean de Rome's powerful music, memories, objects and characters mingle and merge, neglecting their temporal and spatial boundaries; past and present fuse. We are implicated in the acts of abuse. Like Dante, but guideless, we experience a hell our minds cannot imagine.

What is most disturbing about *The Hat* is not the graphics, it's the memories and imaginations that loom underneath our hats. We unwaveringly define through our eyes. What we do not see, we doubt. *The Hat,* like all of Michèle Cournoyer's films, takes us to places we do not want to see, to a darkness that lurks behind our scared small-talk smiles. In this darkness we stumble.

[This article originally appeared in *Take One Magazine*, 2001.]

Filmography of Michèle Cournoyer	
1971	*Man and Child*
1973	*Alfredo*
1978	*Spaghettata*
1978	*La Toccata*
1981	*Old Orchard Beach, PQ*
1988	*Dolorosa*
1992	*A Feather Tale*
1994	*An Artist*
1999	*The Hat*
2004	*Accordion*

Chapter 10

Ryan Larkin: Trapped in the Addictive Allure of Illusions (2000)

[Portions of this chapter originally appeared in *Animation World Magazine* and *Take One Magazine*.]

Street Music

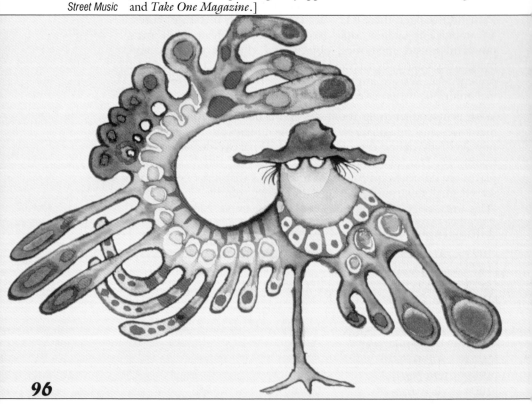

n the 1960s, Ryan Larkin was a 19-year-old protégé of Norman McLaren. With McLaren's support, Larkin was given a rare carte-blanche at the National Film Board of Canada (NFB) and subsequently made one of the most influential animation films of all time, *Walking* (1968). Today, Larkin lives on welfare in a Montreal mission house and panhandles for spending money. How the hell did this happen? Who knows? NFB personnel say one thing; Ryan says another. Truth rests somewhere in between. I'm not out to turn Larkin into a victim or a martyr. He made choices. Well, actually it was his inability to choose that caused the problem. He is living with his indecision.

Larkin's family lived in a classic 1950s suburb of Montreal, Dorval. His father was an airplane mechanic and his mom worked as a secretary. Larkin (the middle of two brothers) proved early on to be a special child. By the age of about 10, he was already doing oil paintings, and at 13 was accepted into the prestigious Montreal School of Fine Arts. The school was already old hat to Larkin. As a child, his father used to drive him there every Saturday for classes. His teacher was the Group of Seven painter, Arthur Lismer. Larkin received an extensive education in classic forms: life drawing, sculpting, and oil painting. Larkin excelled at the school and within a few years was being considered for a job at the National Film Board of Canada.

Larkin was a cokehead and is an alcoholic, but there is a much deeper and more traumatic episode behind all of these escapes. Larkin was very close with his older brother. 'I had a rock and roll teenage-hood. I played drums, was in rock bands. My older brother was very popular in the area. He drove a convertible and always had girls around him. I looked like a greaser punk and was the typical younger brother, always hanging out with him.' During the summer of 1958, Larkin, his brother and friends were playing on a boat in a lake. Something went wrong. Larkin's brother is dead. 'It was a terrible boating accident. I was unable to save him. I was on the boat and was physically unable to save his life. I felt terrible and missed him greatly.' This, more than snorts and chugs, caused his spiral.

A young Ryan Larkin

With the help of his father, Larkin got an interview at the NFB and, surprisingly, given that he had no animation experience, was offered a job at the age of 19. He initially worked as an animator on instructional films for the army and navy, including the spine-tingling epics, *Ball Resolver in Antic* (1964) and *The Canadian Forces Hydrofoil Ship: Concept and*

97

Design (1967). While the content of the films is not particularly inspiring, the overall experience was pivotal for Larkin. 'Ryan's first assignments', says former Head of English Animation, Robert Verrall, 'involved the talents of René Jodoin, Sid Goldsmith, Kaj Pindal, Ron Tunis and others – not bad company for a 19-year-old apprentice. Such programmes were part of the NFB mandate, and allowed the hiring and training of people who would otherwise not have seen the inside of the place.'

During his 2nd or 3rd year at the NFB, Larkin became friends with Norman McLaren, Guy Glover and Grant Munro. At the urging of Wolf Koenig, McLaren had recently begun holding an after-hours session in a small room at the Board. The relationship with McLaren opened Larkin up to a completely new world. 'They were sophisticated. They had huge libraries and invited me home and showed me their libraries. It was fascinating. I was just working class. In my house we had pictures of airplanes.' Larkin absorbed books, paintings and classical music. 'I was young and really impressed with all this new information.'

Within the after-hours sessions, McLaren set up a project for the eager young artists (including Pierre Hébert, Co Hoedeman and Ralph Abrams). 'He'd give us 16mm cameras and teach us the fine aspects like calibration and how to use our senses. He had a test that involved taking a cut-out of a round ball and shooting it single and double frame.' Artists were given a roll of film to shoot whatever they wanted. Animation came as naturally to Larkin as drawing. 'Norman said I had natural control over timing and pacing over any given object.' At the same time, Larkin developed a unique technique involving stop-frame action with charcoal that was easy to erase. Using a strong sheet of paper, Larkin was able to draw deeply into the paper and still erase it. Utilizing this new technique, Larkin made a one-minute test film called *Cityscape*. This dark, nightmarish view of the city is filled with animation and a mélange of strange characters coming and going. It is hesitant and sloppy at times, but also a shocking, raw and almost paranoid portrait of the cement garden.

Larkin shot *Cityscape* single frame and 'the whole thing went whizzing by in 30 seconds'. To expand the film, Larkin took it to an optical imager, reprinted the frames and cross mixed them, while developing short cross dissolves to give the film a natural-looking emotion. People at the Board noticed *Cityscape* and were taken by its originality. McLaren approached Board producers and asked that Larkin be given carte-blanche to make any film using the charcoal technique. 'They said, "Here's a budget. You've got three months to make any film.' I spent a week wondering what I was going to do. One of Norman's friends presented me with a solo

98

Syrinx

flute piece called Syrinx by Claude Debussy. A French flutist recorded it and that was my starting point.' Using the flute piece, Larkin then turned to the Greek story about Pan. In this tale of stalking, Pan is constantly hasslin' the hotty Syrinx for a little love. Tired of his come-ons, Syrinx asks Gaea for help. Gaea then turns Syrinx into a clump of reeds. Pan then takes the reeds and turns them into an instrument.

Larkin faced a number of problems before completing the film. The music was a key ingredient and had to be carefully time and paced, but Larkin lacked the necessary money to buy the music. Instead, he found a member of the Montreal Symphony Orchestra to record it for less money. The music setback was minor compared with the realization that he had to re-shoot the entire film: 'First time I got off track and the images weren't coming off as beautiful as I wanted. I was getting nervous but Wolf [Koenig] and Bob [Verrall] said, 'Go back and re-shoot the whole thing." Ah, the fortune of a court artist! Larkin re-shot the film, this time concentrating more on the images and the body of Syrinx. The final product received excellent reviews and *Syrinx* won awards all over the world including the Grand Prize at a children's festival in Iran.

Larkin was now living a princely life in downtown Montreal, continuing to paint and sculpt and surrounded by many friends. 'I was always good at sculpting and doing three-dimensional sculptures. I began to see animation as a form of sculpting.' Larkin had a few small exhibitions and many people at the NFB purchased his drawings and paintings. Larkin gleaned his inspiration in cafés and

99

bars watching and absorbing the way people walked and talked and moved. He loved to watch people and would make sketches of people walking or get friends to pose. Larkin's friends were also doing more than posing, doing what kids were supposedly supposed to do: drugs. Ironically, Larkin wasn't into drugs at the time and instead played Virgil to his LSD saturated mates. 'They would experiment and I wouldn't. I made sure they didn't fly out windows.' Things would soon change. Despite the wealth of friends and success, Larkin remained lonely. The death of his brother had quietly fractured the family. 'Because I was on the boat, nobody knew what happened, but somehow I failed to save my brother.' Something changed. 'I was always the goofy little guy and they figured I goofed up again.' Nothing was ever said to Larkin but he felt their scorching eyes. Larkin, a man who could bring beautiful images to life, could not save a life dearest to him.

After *Syrinx*, the producers told Larkin that he had to go back to applying his talents to public service films. He made, and remains proud of, a variety of educational films for St. John's Ambulance, an elaborate colour pastel clip on preventing forest fires, and a contribution to the NFB's exhibition at the Montreal Expo. 'The Board had its own pavilion, called Labyrinth, and they had multi-screens. I was asked by Roman Kroiter and Colin Low, to put in a Labyrinth, the old Greek idea, using the same style as *Syrinx*.'

Following the Expo exhibit, Larkin put in a proposal to do a film based on sketches he had drawn of people walking around. The proposal was accepted and Larkin was given a year to do the project. However, dreading the thought of repeating himself, the film took two years as Larkin spent perfecting new techniques. 'I was developing my Oriental brushwork with water colours, and the human figures and the way that anatomy works, expressions of human behaviour, how funny they look sometimes when they're trying to impress each other with certain movements. I wasn't doing any rotoscoping, I was doing a lot of self-study. I had mirrors in my little office, and I would go through certain motions with my own body and was just going with pencil, ink and paper.' In concentrating on motion and the details of the figures, Larkin abandoned background movement, instead choosing a blank white screen.

The result of this two-year project was *Walking*, one of the most celebrated films made at the NFB and one that remains a major influence on animators to this day. Using a combination of line drawing and colour wash, Larkin observes the movements of a variety of urban characters. Larkin weaves colours and sounds with an extraordinarily detailed visualization of faces, bodies, gestures and postures. A vivid imagining of the city and those within it.

Walking received an Oscar nomination and Larkin travelled to Hollywood with his girlfriend, Felicity. The Oscars provided Larkin with a chance to put his beatnik persona and wild wardrobe to practice. Larkin had hair that was about three feet long and made his own clothes. 'I would sew together my own pair of pants in special colours. It was coming out earlier I think, I was always performing, trying to look outrageous by whatever standards were established, just being a punk.' For the Oscars, Larkin selected a flashy silk, wide-sleeved shirt and tight-fitting pants with bright colours.

Death once again stepped in Larkin's path. Walt Disney, who had ceased to breathe a year before, won the Oscar for Ward Kimball's *It's Tough to be a Bird*.

Following *Walking*, Larkin once again returned to NFB public service films before being loaned out to a Vancouver art school. For eight months, Larkin ran an animation workshop. Each student worked in their own studio and Larkin would travel around visiting them, hanging out and directing them. Larkin encouraged the students to find their own voice no matter how wild their experiments turned out. Among these young voices, Larkin met a group of street musicians. 'I decided that they would make a great focal point for my abstract images. There was a whole little gang of them with their own children and stuff, hippies I guess, really good musicians.' Larkin's encounter led to his next film, *Street Musique*.

Very much a film in search of itself, *Street Musique* opens with live-action footage of two street musicians, before changing into a staggeringly animated stream-of-consciousness piece. A variety of creatures and figures float through the screen and undergo a continual metamorphosis. *Street Musique* is loosely divided into about five or six segments, all determined by the pace of the music. One of the most dazzling scenes comes in segment two with a series of extraordinary landscape impressionist paintings. As with most of Larkin's work though you can feel the hesitancy. The film ends rather awkwardly with the last image stopping to wait for the music. 'What happened was, I ran out of ideas and I didn't know how to end the film, so I just ended it on a strange little character, wiggling away in his little dance, in a way suggesting that, "This is to be continued".' Structural critiques aside, *Street Musique* is a toe tappin', knee slappin', barn burner of a film, solidifying Larkin's talent as an artist and animator.

Street Musique did the festival circuit and won a Grand Prize at an Australian film festival. Larkin is particularly fond of this award because it was a live-action festival. 'It was a ten minute film up against all kinds of complicated feature films.' Larkin received

$3000 with the prize, and because he had a regular salary he often supported other young artists with his prize money. 'I had a nine room flat in Montreal that I was renting for $100 a month, if you can believe it, and I'd give money to certain young people to experiment with their art and their music. I'd give them free room and board to hang around. In a sense I had my own school.' Larkin's generosity with people would come back to haunt him.

Following *Street Musique*, Larkin was assigned to a feature film that the Board was working on, called *Running Time*. Along with Co Hoedemen, Larkin was asked to do three short animation sequences combining the actors with animation images. However, *Running Time* soon turned into a nightmare for Larkin: 'I was trapped into it for four years because the executive producers kept putting it on the shelf, then there were endless committee meetings. I was getting pissed off because I was on hold. I had no other budgets or work to do. Frustrated, Larkin began working at home on his next project, *Ding Bat Rap*. This decision has led to one of the myths surrounding Larkin.

In the book *Cartoon Capers*, author Karen Mazurkewich claims that drugs and depression got so bad that Larkin exiled himself to his home. For two years, the NFB sent him cheques by taxi before firing him. According to Larkin, things didn't quite happen this way. 'Well, what happened was, I was seeing this feature film just flying away and in the meantime, I was developing my own idea, and I had my own setup in my apartment. I had two apartments, one that I lived in and one that I used as a studio. I was developing my own new film but I couldn't get a budget to work on it, and the executive producers of this feature film were saying, "Well, wait a couple of weeks and just stand by because we haven't got the approval from upstairs".' Rather than sit around the Board offices doing nothing, Larkin worked at home on his next film, a project he anticipated would be approved by the NFB. The situation was ideal for Larkin because if he woke at 2 am he could simply work on his film. This was something he couldn't do at the office. Larkin also notes that the producers knew that he was doing research and development for *Ding Bat Rap* at home while the feature was on hold. 'That seemed to be okay with them since I was not able to work on the project.'

About a year later, thanks to new English producer, Derek Lamb, Larkin finally received a budget for *Ding Bat Rap*, but he continued to work at home. 'I told my producers to trust me, I was working on the project, so they sent me my cheques.' Larkin paid for the cab. Larkin's producer, David Verrall was given the task of bringing Larkin back into the fold. 'I spent an exceptional amount of time and effort in trying to re-enable Ryan as a filmmaker here. I went several times to Ryan's home on Park Avenue. I liked Ryan (as most folks did), admired his work, and sincerely believed he could turn things around.' Verrall actually managed to lure Larkin back to the NFB building for a while by giving him access to one of the new animation cameras. Eventually, Larkin, either bored or stressed, would disappear for long stretches, only to be further behind when he re-appeared. In the end, Verrall reluctantly gave up.

Ding Bat Rap was to be Larkin's first 'talkie.' The film was to be set in a bar with a bunch of regulars sitting around talking nonsense with great earnest. 'A lot of people talk and talk without saying anything. They make gestures with their hands, give meaningful looks back and forth towards each other.' Larkin had experimental voice actors to re-create the 'babble.' He had originally hoped to record actual dialogue, but noticed that people froze up so he dropped that idea. He also selected swing music for the soundtrack: 'There was a beautifully organized music library at the Board, made to provide filmmakers with soundtracks for any subject. I selected that material and edited it myself. So I had edited my soundtrack but I didn't have enough animation drawing. I had drawn my characters, about five. It was a very abstract, poetic thing. I had a storyboard and filmed still images, but there was no actual animation movement.'

By this time, Larkin was a coke addict. Coke was a big attraction to Larkin. It was a magical, almost spiritual experience that took him to worlds he'd never known. 'The cocaine was giving me incredible insights into human behavior and very acute sensitivities towards what constituted human behavior.' But, contrary to Heraclitus' thoughts, the way up was not nearly the same as the way down. With the high, came the low. The neurological stimulation gave way to backlash. A flood of ideas drowns the mind. Larkin discovered a confidence he never knew, but the pace of the magic locked Larkin into a fantasy world. A magician trapped within the allure of his illusions, Larkin was no longer able to work.

Meanwhile, the programme committee was none too thrilled with Larkin's *Ding Bat Rap*. What Larkin saw as a satire on ethnic groups and nationalism was viewed with disdain as a reactionary, almost racist vision. 'I was making sound and visual jokes against all people that were too full of pride. There was an anti-Muslim thing, and anti-Christian thing. I was trying to put down the nationalistic attitude that was happening at the time.' Even McLaren backed out of Larkin's corner. 'Norman was also sort of shocked by my heavy punk material.' In Larkin's mind, he was making unsafe work for a conservative institution. But he also acknowledges that he was burning out. 'I was losing my edge because I'd been there for too

103

long. I was having a creative block that was probably the result of the coke.' In a sense, Larkin was unable to grow up or at least fit the model of maturity proscribed by the society around him. He was pushing forty, but living like a punk. He was playing in rock bands. He was still hanging out with younger people, financing their bands, writing lyrics. He was a godfather to the punks. Nevertheless, it was clear that Larkin and the Board were no longer good for each other. For Larkin, the NFB became increasingly restrictive. A coked-up, confused, talented Larkin wanted his free-dom back; whatever the hell that was.

Never one to forget an encore, in 1975 Larkin was invited to create a mural for the NFB. What he drew was likely not what they had envisioned: an adolescent with an erection who may or may not have been ejaculating. The mural was 20 x 15 feet. 'It was meant to be a satirical commentary on masculinity because at the time there was a year-long festival going on about women's rights. It was supposed to be a comical relief from all their terrible, self-con-scious seriousness.' Ryan Larkin's tenure at the NFB ended.

There was a modest effort to get Larkin back on staff, and Robert Verrall regrets not being more stern with Larkin. 'Management and friends had tried, but Ryan was determined to go his own way. [I] should have read the riot act and insisted that he work in the environment of the Board; if it was good enough for McLaren it should be good enough for Ryan'. Whatever. Larkin was free. So he thought.

However, after a brief period working at Nelvana and also working (purportedly) on *Heavy Metal*, Larkin realized that his finances were out of whack. The gal he was sharing spit with was controlling his money and apparently ripping him off. 'In the early '80s, I was getting angry with her, accusing her of stealing from me. I realized she was a thief. I tried to get rid of her, which resulted in some kitchen violence. Being a woman with a child by another man, she was able to get the upper hand with the authorities and the police. I was thrown out for being a violent man, but I wasn't.'

In addition to coke, Larkin was also an alcoholic. Unlike coke, Larkin accepts his drinking condition with the greatest of ease; in fact he claims it makes him healthier. 'I've been doing it ever since I was a child. When I was ten the doctor told my mother that I should drink 1–2 beers a day to put on weight.' Always the master of illusions, Larkin continues to conjure the spirits of illusion: 'I'm an alcoholic, not a drunkard'. The difference now is that his audience, what remains of it, sees through the tricks.

For a short time, things were okay. Larkin fell in love with a man who put him up in a studio. 'I did a lot of good paintings in the

'80s. I moved all of my work down to this beautiful home. This lasted for about 8 years, but he finally wanted to get rid of me. I'm very attractive, but evidently, I'm undesirable after awhile.' The 1990s found Larkin, now coke free, starting over again on his own. His generosity with people resulted in a variety of folks taking advantage of his home. Friends in need of a fix stole paintings, drawings and sculptures. Eventually penniless and alone, Larkin was tossed out of his home. He lived on the streets of Montreal briefly before moving into the Old Brewery Mission where he currently resides. Virtually all of his art is gone now, pawned for dope, tricks or whatever was needed to survive. He now carries only what he can: a few clothes, some books, and his little pop bottle for his daily beers. Many people have tried to help him over the years, but Larkin is either unwilling or unable to accept.

Has Ryan Larkin's life taken a downward spiral? It's really hard to say. When you watch his films, especially *Walking* and *Street Musique*, they seem to foreshadow his flâneur existence. The lack of structure, the random, carefree nature of his films seems to mirror his own refusal of order in life. Today he seems to have found some sense of freedom on the streets. He controls his time and actions. His days now consist of a regular shift outside a Montreal restaurant where he performs mime, dances and draws for change. Would life for Ryan Larkin be any better if he had remained a court artist at the NFB? Our conventional, constructed beliefs would be that his life has hit rock bottom, but I don't buy it. Everyday we see miserable souls drifting sleeplessly through life from meaningless job to lonely home. Unhappy travellers caught in a web of material constructions. Larkin may not have a home, he may not have a job, but he remains an artist. This is not to say that Larkin is content with his life. He isn't and still suffers from alcoholism, a personality disorder and other assorted demons. He routinely shifts between states of clarity and absurdity. Whatever may happen down the road, Larkin has left the world with a quartet of passionate, delicate visual poems. Beyond that, he provides some kicks, if only for a second, for those walking, weary souls on St. Laurent Street. What more is there?

[Different versions of this text appeared in *Animation World Magazine* – as Last Exit on St. Laurent St. – and in *Take One Magazine*, 2004; originally appeared in *Take One Magazine*, 2001.]

Filmography of Ryan Larkin

1965	*Syrinx*
1966	*Cityscape*
1968	*Walking*
1972	*Street Musique*

Chapter 11

Stripmalls, Hookers and Dead People: Songs of the Quickdraw Animation Society (2001)

The Wind Between My Ears by Carol Beecher

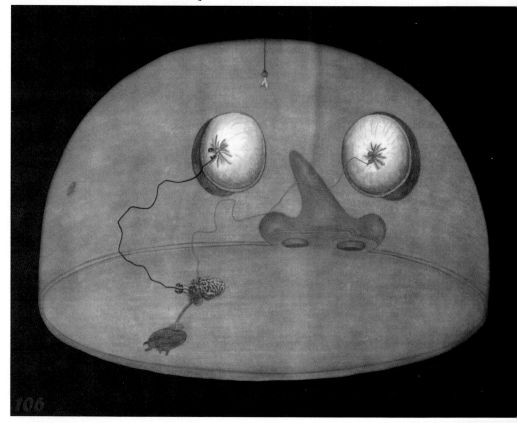

Their first home was in a strip mall. On the door was the image of a character named, Mr. Pencil Poke with a pencil stuck up his ass alongside a note that said, 'sacrifices daily'. A few years later, they shared a building with hookers. Along the way, someone died in an apartment above their office, a body was found in a car, and phone messages were written on the back of cat dissection manuals. Meanwhile, Calgary's Quickdraw Animation Society emerged as perhaps the most important producer of independent animation in Canada. Yes, Calgary, the most conservative city in Canada. The home of oil barons and raging righties like Ralph Klein. Next thing you know Ottawa will host an animation festival.

In 1980, Greg Lucier, a medical professor (that explains the dissection documents) and animation fan, moved from Toronto to Calgary. Seeing no interest there in animation, Lucier along with John Edstrom and Rita Egizii start showing 16mm NFB animations on Friday nights in an old medical building. Over time, a core group of viewers was established and the trio decided to formalize the gathering. In 1984, the Quickdraw Animation Society was born. 'At the beginning', says Lucier, 'we weren't really interested in a film co-op per se, just a group of like-minded people who enjoyed watching cartoons'. The first meeting was held 21 February 1984 Over the years, QAS expanded from a gathering animation viewers to a production and education association. In order to get charitable status, QAS began offering community lectures and classes. 'One of our milestone projects was in 1985 when we hosted Academy Award winner Jimmy Picker who came out to do a 3-day workshop on clay-mation.' NFB animator John Weldon also paid a visit to QAS, and it was during his lecture that a man upstairs breathed his final breath.

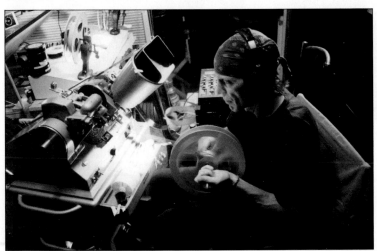

Richard Reeves at work

Linear Dreams by
Richard Reeves

In 1987, Lucier and co. left QAS and a new group of board members took over with a desire to start producing animation. The new members, who were primarily Alberta College of Art students, were a striking contrast to the founding members, who were primarily research and science people. Being visual artists, the new board expanded the animation beyond commercial work (which was dominant in the early years) towards a promotion and celebration of alternative forms of artistic creation and expression.

108

Thanks to the contribution of Operations Coordinator, Mandy Johnston, who was also a key figure in raising awareness of QAS in the national arts community, QAS used grants from the Canada Council, the Calgary Region Arts Foundation, and the Alberta Foundation for the Arts to purchase equipment and get operations happening. One of the folks spearheading the production end was Kevin Kurytnik. He became a member in 1988 so that he could take a course on animation for a patient information video he was working on for a local hospital. He took over the class in 1991 and, with the exception of two years, has been teaching it ever since.

Kurytnik became President in 1992 and one of his first initiatives was to get a real animation stand. At the time, QAS had a 'bolex camera strapped to a sewer pipe over a table with a peg bar taped to it, a professional video pencil test machine and a 16mm gang synch'. Mandy Johnston was instrumental in getting the new stand and Carol Beecher managed to secure a $20,000 grant towards the purchase. The new stand was a Mitchell Portman stand owned by Neil McInnis and used by the NFB. The new equipment paid off when Wayne Traudt's *Movements of The Body* was accepted at Cannes and short listed for an Academy Award in 1994. Since then Richard Reeves (*Linear Dreams*), Kurytnik (*Abandon Bob Hope, All Ye Who Enter Here*), Beecher (*Ask Me*) and Don Best (*Raw*) have all had international success with QAS-produced films.

At the same time, Kurytnik had a conceptual vision of QAS: 'I saw some kind of potential to do self-expressive animation after seeing work by the Brothers Quay, Jan Svankmajer, Norman McLaren, Harry Smith, and threw myself into the place as a reaction against the commercial'. Kurytnik viewed QAS as a venue for self-expression but also collaboration and the sense that you not only made work, but you encouraged work. His views were shared by Carol Beecher, who joined QAS in 1989, and became their first administrator. 'The first impression I had of the place was that it was tricked out like a daycare centre with Care Bears and Disney posters everywhere, and the only tapes in the library were Disney stuff on Beta. I figured QAS should be different and out went the Care Bears and in came the "weird" stuff.'

Mr. Reaper's Really Bad Morning (2004) by Carol Beecher and Kevin Kurytnik

109

Linear Dreams by
Richard Reeves

Kurytnik was also largely responsible, along with Beecher, Richard Reeves and, notably, Don Best, for building the Society's resource library. When I visited QAS in 2000, I was astonished at the diversity and depth of their library. It contains videos, books, and articles representing virtually every type of animation in existence. 'Kevin and I like learning and teaching', says Beecher, 'so naturally that became an important thing to share. The library is one of the big draws for QAS memberships and I think something of this scale is pretty unique for an ARC.' The library is also unique in the sense that it enables QAS to maintain a dialogue between past and present. 'We view films as living things', says Beecher, 'no matter when they were created. Works by McLaren, Fischinger and Lye, for example, are not historical documents or monuments or oddities, but models for exploration and creation of filmmaking now.'

Richard Reeves discovered QAS in 1990. 'One day during a quest for animation supplies in Calgary, someone mentioned something about a group of people who formed an artist-run co-op and they were having a meeting the very next week. I had no way of knowing that the 300km drive to QAS and back (he lived near Banff) would become a way of life for many years to come.' Reeves was instantly struck by the energy of the small group. Kurytnik mentioned that he was teaching an animation course and Reeves signed up. By 1992, Reeves had become involved with the board of directors, volunteering, presenting free film nights and instructing workshops. He was hooked.

By this time, QAS had moved to downtown Calgary and had expanded into three camera rooms, along with rooms for editing, classes, administration and screenings. Owing to incredible fundraising initiatives, unlimited coffee and many sleepless nights, more and more equipment began to arrive. 'QAS began to look more professional', says Reeves, 'and the impressive studios would attract more independents to want to make their films at QAS'.

In late 1994, Reeves became the production co-ordinator. 'The work was great, helping people, operating film equipment, building things, fundraising and seeing who can drink the most coffee.' While QAS was open to new technologies, Reeves encouraged classical methods such as pixilation, claymation and paint on glass.

Earlier that year, Reeves received a grant to produce his first film, *Linear Dreams*. QAS offered him round the clock access to the production facilities. 'You could go there at any hour and find somebody working. Without this access to special equipment, many of the films could not have been made.' The cameraless, McLaren-inspired film, which also directly manipulated the sound stripe, became an immediate success, winning prizes around the world. To this day, it remains the most successful (in terms of festival acceptance) QAS production. More importantly, Reeves' success proved that QAS was becoming a force on the international animation scene and this encouraged others to produce films there.

Quick kids

Some of the most popular activities at QAS are the children's workshops. Held every summer, *Quick Kids* (which was created by Mandy Johnston) attracts children from 9-14. There are two types of courses. One takes place on Saturdays and lasts 10 weeks. The second is a summer camp series with four week sessions in July and August. The classes include drawn and clay animation. The kids all work towards a final film. 'There's no real structure', says Beecher, 'and the kids pretty much do whatever they want as far a story content, and they get right on the pencil test machine and get to work figuring out that animation thing with guidance of the instructor'. The work is finished on video using an s-vhs system with a colour camera that the kids use. In 2000, QAS began offering a teen camp. The classes have become so popular that some kids have taken the classes every year. 'We call them "repeat offenders" ', says Beecher. 'We had one kid take the summer camp from the age of 9 to 14, and then his younger brother started taking them too.' QAS is the only media arts co-op that offers youth education at this level.

QAS doesn't just nurture home talent, they also attract international folks as well. Tanja Huber was working at the Swiss Animation Festival, Fantoche, in 1999 when she saw a retrospective of QAS. 'Carol Beecher told me more about this artist run society and seven months later I arrived in Calgary.' While in Calgary, Huber worked on a number of short projects and returned home overwhelmed by her experience: 'As far as I know there's no other place

Mr. Reaper's Really Bad Morning (2004) by Carol Beecher and Kevin Kurytnik

like Quickdraw. Quickdraw gave me a boost, I love the place and I love the people there who were always ready to help! The only bad thing I can say about QAS is ... that it is too far away from Zurich.'

Kevin Kurytnik and Carol Beecher (sort of)

Today, QAS has 172 members (20% live outside the province) and has hosted animators like Pierre Hébert, Priit Parn, John Weldon, Frederick Back, Joyce Borenstein, Helen Hill, John Korty and Bill Plympton (September 2001). QAS films have been shown at festivals in Ottawa, Annecy, Hiroshima, Switzerland, Norway, Vietnam, Singapore, and many more.

As always with an association that relies on government grants and volunteers, the future is almost eternally unclear for QAS. 'Quickdraw', notes Cyndy Ward, 'is bravely both recovering and re-defining the notion of 'alternative' that drove earlier production centres. Quickdraw is in the process of reconstructing the cultural imaginary from which it has emerged. Hopefully, it will never finish.'

Along with Carol Beecher, Richard Reeves remains the most visible member of QAS. On the back of the vhs box of Reeves' latest film, *One to One*, you see the QAS logo. I asked Reeves if QAS had financed or supported the film. He said they hadn't, but that QAS remains close to his heart: 'I am a satellite member (he now lives in BC) orbiting the earth, QAS headquarters are still mission control'.

In many ways, QAS is what the NFB once was; an enviroment with limited material resources but a wealth of creativity, dedication, passion and generosity. QAS has emerged as the true successor to the giving, innovative spirit of Norman McLaren and serves as a beacon for the future of independent animation in this country. And if this little engine that could story seems almost magical, it is: 'Even now', says Richard Reeves, 'I click my heels together three times and repeat, there is no place like Quickdraw, there is no place like Quickdraw, there is no place like Quickdraw.'

[Originally appeared in *Take One* magazine.]

Chapter 12

Fragments of Home: The Brothers Quay (2001)

'That gray, impersonal crowd is rather self-conscious of its role, eager to live up to its metropolitan aspirations. All the same, despite the bustle and sense of purpose, one has the impression of a monotonous, aimless wandering, of a sleepy procession of puppets.'
– *Bruno Schulz, 'The Street of Crocodiles'.*

The world of the Brothers Quay is one that avoids words, relying instead on sound, music, objects, movement and light to convey meaning. They give us fragments – of poetry, sounds, music, mise-en-scène, dialogue and characters. What we inhale depends on our temporal and spatial positions. Each of us enters through a different door, at a different time, in a different setting. We leave with fragments – of thoughts, memories and emotions unraveling uniquely into our compartments of conspicuous memory and understanding.

In a medium where studios tend to overshadow individual creators, twin brothers Stephen and Timothy Quay are a rarity. Like Jan Svankmajer and Norman McLaren, the Quays have worked within the 'art' world, which has given their work credibility. At the same time, along with Walt Disney, Bill Plympton, McLaren, Svankmajer and a handful of other animators, the Quays have achieved recognition outside the animation community. This is unusual, given that their work is decidedly cerebral and seemingly far removed from the mindset of a public that generally defines animation as a gag-oriented fartfest for kids.

The Quays were born in Philadelphia, which seems a long way from the worlds of Kafka and the angst gang. Yet witness *The Street of Crocodiles* (1988), based on the book by Bruno Schulz, in which we enter a Polish city that has become artificial and sterile in the face of industrial decay. The alienated individual wandering through the dark streets of boredom is rooted in the existential literature of Kafka and Beckett, yet is also something very close to us. When we look at our globalized world, we see the same thing: Callous, cold-hearted bureaucracy; a society lost in a simulacrum. Consider that the Quays grew up in fifties America – where the citizen became the consumer, where materialism and kitsch grew out of false, war-torn dreams – and South Philly doesn't seem that far from Communist Poland.

The Brothers Quay

The twins studied illustration at art school, but 'always felt a strong pull towards cinema and because of our graphic formation it became quite a natural step to head towards animation'. In the seventies, they headed to London's Royal College of Art. They made their first puppet film, *Nocturna*

115

Artificialia, in 1979. 'Puppets always held a strange mystique for us – the power of the mask, its "otherness", the fact that you had to "read" them. And in this sense, we saw them instinctively allied to dance and music. But most of this was simply vague intuitions and hunches. We were never formally trained as animators or in puppetry. We picked up by watching and by making a lot of mistakes (mostly the latter).'

Their next film, *The Cabinet of Jan Svankmajer* (1984), 'was an open homage to a 'maestro'', – the Czech animator Svankmajer, whose work the brothers watched closely – in which a young pupil visits a professor and receives 'life' lessons. Following *Cabinet*, the Quays made a series of personal films based on the writings of lesser-known authors (*The Epic of Gilgamesh [or This Unnameable Little Broom]* (1985), *The Street of Crocodiles* (1986), for example). Other films were inspired by images (*Rehearsals for Extinct Anatomies* (1987)), or dreams (*The Comb (From the Museums of Sleep)* (1990)).

Along with their independent work, the Quays have made more commercial work, including interstitials, music videos and commercials. *De Artificiali Perspectiva or Anamorphosis* (1991) is an 'educational' film for a series on art that explains the concept of perspective and how we see things. In 1995, the brothers completed their first feature film, *Institute Benjamenta*. Based on the writings of Robert Walser, the film follows a Keatonesque figure who enrols in a servant school filled with repressed desires and imaginings.

In 2000, the Quays completed their first short film in almost a decade. The appropriately-titled *In Absentia* was made for a BBC series that pairs filmmakers with composers; the brothers worked with Karl Heinz Stockhausen. Intrigued by an exhibition of letters from an insane woman to her husband, they developed a scenario based upon her writings. *In Absentia* offers a flurry of conflicting images and startling sounds and screams, in which time and space dissolve as we stumble through a world of the insane.

The Quay world is akin to that of science fiction. Within their strange universes reside quiet metaphors that reflect our own time and space and the fears within them. Each Quay film gives a glimpse of a world of the dead, alive. Inside, we encounter all sorts of crippled, dirty, grotesque objects. Time and space splinter. Dream and reality merge. Character and décor blur. Everything is possible, nothing is certain. We step on the bridge to a past that is no longer. The Quay world is like a museum at night. Strange sounds emanate through decaying, dirty walls. We catch a flicker of movement out of the corner of the eye. Headless, broken figures move here and there. The camera moves with the grace of Max Ophuls and the intensity of Carl Dreyer. Watching a Quay film is like entering a fairytale gone wrong. Lurking beneath this surreal surface is a world of decay and illusion and emptiness – a world very much like our own.

[Originally written for the 2001 Toronto Worldwide Short Film Festival]

Filmography of The Brothers Quay

1979	*Nocturna Artificialia*
1980	*Punch & Judy* (*Tragical Comedy or Comical Tragedy*)
1981	*Ein Brudermord*
1981	*The Eternal Day of Michel de Ghelderode*
1982	*Igor – Chez Pleyel – The Paris Years*
1983	*Leos Janacek: Intimate Excursions*
1984	*The Cabinet of Jan Svankmajer*
1985	*The Epic of Gilgamesh* [aka *This Unnameable Little Broom*]
1986	*Street of Crocodiles*
1987	*Rehearsals for Extinct Anatomies*
1988	*Dramolet* (*Stille Nacht I*)
1989	*Ex-Voto/The Pond*
1990	*The Comb* (*From The Museums of Sleep*)
1990	*De Artificiali Perspectiva or Anamorphosis*
1991	*The Calligrapher Parts I, II, III*
1991	*Are We Still Married?* (*Stille Nacht II*)
1992	*Long Way Down* (*Look What The Cat Drug In*)
1992	*Tales From The Vienna Woods* (*Stille Nacht III*)
1993	*Can't Go Wrong Without You* (*Stille Nacht IV*)
1994	*Institute Benjamenta*
1999	*Duet – Variations for the Convalescence of 'A'*
2000	*The Sandman*
2000	*In Absentia*
2000	*Dog Door* (*Stille Nacht V*)
2003	*Poor Roger/Oranges and Lemons/Green Gravel/Jenny Jones*
2003	*The Phantom Museum*

Chapter 13

If I Forget Thee, Lenica
(2002)

To have toiled and moiled through a lifesworth of delusions, for an approximate-minimum full-life's duration, and have it add in a flash to undifferentiated molecules on the slag heap of undifferentiated nothing – now THAT is a frightening outcome to grapple with.
From *Geezer* (2001), by Richard Meltzer

Labyrinthe

He was. He ain't. It's that simple. Time that once stood between him and a dreamless sleep collapsed into a rubble of ashes. It's not all bad; with the threat of mass extinction once again rearing its head, at least Jan Lenica had the benefit of ceasing in his own individual way. He got out before we were all obliterated en masse anyway so at least there are a few of us left to go through his luggage. Aside from daughters, wives, family and friends, he also left behind some cartoons, posters, and ideas that will enrich, provoke and amuse a few of the few of those with time on their metre.

When writing of those who have laid fresh tracks within the gates of Hades, we construct complimentary sentimental gushes to honour our 'old friend' and remember what a great person they were. I can't do that. I didn't know Jan Lenica. The fragment of Lenica I encountered sporadically through letter and sight over a three-month period, in the summer of 2000 (we were honouring him at the Ottawa 2000 International Animation Festival), was one of a grumpy old man who appeared unappreciative and uncooperative.

But you know what? That's what makes him so important to me. He was in his early 70s and suffering from diabetes and heart disease. I encountered a man who was tired and scared. I felt his pain, frustration, weakness, and fear. He didn't hide it. He couldn't hide it. I saw his humanity in all its humility. He could hear the songs of the angels in the breezes behind him getting stronger and louder with each difficult breath. Each step was selective. Each response contained.

Now it isn't.

Jan Lenica

119

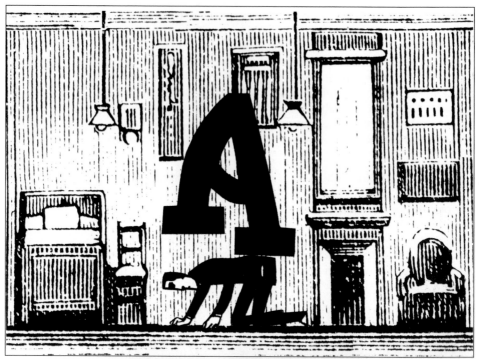

A

If Lenica had shown up with a rose in his lapel and played the role *Adam* of grateful, polite diplomat, I would have appreciated it, but soon forgotten it. It would mean little. The darkness within Jan Lenica left an impression on me. His sourness led me to try and grasp why he was the way he was. He was a son, father, husband and friend, and worst of all, just a man. Jan Lenica's naked humility shattered my fears for a moment and inadvertently led me to reach farther inside to scour through my own blood and guts.

My STUFF aside, there is a danger in freely throwing roses on the dead and living. One of the most dangerous systems we've created is the myth of the hero. A bar has been set and more often than not it's bogus and unreachable even by those supposedly in possession of these ideals. The heroic system celebrates sameness. Sameness removes what is unique, diverse and contradictory from each of us.

Heroism captures a fragment of a life and the tendency in our society is to simply re-write that life without the naughty bits. As such we grow up aspiring to become someone who never existed. We learn more from the shadows and shit holes than from the plastic palaces we often make believe within.

'Know Thyself', said a wise Greek.

To know thyself, one must find oneself.

To find oneself one must search.

To search is to live.

To live is to know thyself.

We are always in the process of becoming. Life is a process. To stop is to die. The search for self is at the core of every Lenica film. His protagonists (think Jan Lenica as performed by Buster Keaton through Beckett and Ionesco and Gilliam) travel through a world of violence, paranoia, anxiety, and absurdity. They do not know how to, nor are sure they want to, fit into an increasingly dehumanized society. Lenica's characters encounter various forms of oppression in the face of paranoia (*Rhinoceros*), language (*A*), exile (*Labyrinth*), humans, and even themselves. Each character is simply trying to define and establish a unique blip on life's map.

The characters mirror Lenica. Their search was his. He denied politics, but he was affected by it throughout his life. He was born in Poznan, Poland in 1928. Poland was an economically unstable country, but the Lenica family (father, Alfred, was a musician) enjoyed a relatively cozy existence, until 1939, when the Nazis forced the family into exile in Southern Poland. It was in exile that Jan Lenica began his career as an artist.

After the war, Poland was in a shambles, literally, spiritually, and economically. The new generation of artists that emerged was characterized by black irony and sarcasm. By late 1948 (a year after the Russians took control of Poland), Lenica was firmly established in the Polish graphic art scene. Then, as later, his drawings were rooted in black comedy, violence and paranoia.

Animation emerged in Poland in 1956. Not surprisingly, animation was viewed as a serious graphic art form, as opposed to kiddie cartoons. Lenica, along with Walerian Borowcyzk were among the first to make animation films, in 1957, when they made the film, *Once Upon A Time*. After two more collaborations, Lenica found work in Paris, Poland and Germany and made his most famous films, *Monsieur Téte*, *Labyrinth*, *Rhinoceros*, *A* and the short feature, *Adam II*.

Existential themes and an ironic tone aside, Lenica's films were intentionally primitive. The cut-out animation was awkward giving the characters a thoroughly dehumanized manner. His characters, modeled after Buster Keaton, had plain, deadpan faces as they moved about a world that was designed with more complexity, often using cut-out figures and photo collages.

By the 1980s, Lenica had received the flowers, heard the trumpets, and stored the prizes. He moved to Berlin in 1984 where he taught poster design at a local arts school. He retired in 1994 and remained in Berlin until his death. In 2000, he was at work on a new short film – the making of which was documented in the documentary film, *The Island of Jan Lenica* (Marcin Gyzinski, 2000) – but it's not clear whether he completed it.

At the end of William Faulkner's *The Wild Palms*, his protagonist, after being convicted of manslaughter for a failed abortion attempt, momentarily considers swallowing a cyanide capsule. Facing a life of grief in prison and without his lover, he chooses grief:

because if memory exists outside of the flesh it wont be memory because it wont know what it remembers so when she became not then half of memory became not and if I become not then all of remembering will cease to be- Yes, he thought Between grief and nothing I will take grief.

Jan Lenica gave me grief. That was it. That was all. To forget that is to forget Jan Lenica. To forget Jan Lenica is to forget life. To forget life is to be nothing. I will take grief.

[Originally appeared in the January 2002 edition of *Animation World Magazine* (www.mag.awn.com). Reprinted with permission of Animation World Network.]

Filmography of Jan Lenica

1957	*Once upon*
1957	*Rewarded feeling*
1958	*House*
1959	*Monsieur Tete*
1960	*The New Janko Musician*
1962	*Labyrinth*
1963	*Rhinoceroses*
1964	*A*
1965	*Flowerwoman*
1968	*Adam 2*
1969	*Still life*
1972	*Fantorro*
1974	*Landscape*
1979	*King Ubu*

Chapter 14

Beyond Good and Evil: Piotr Dumala's Crime and Punishment (2001)

'... [C]an it be that I will really take an axe and hit her on the head and smash her skull ... slip in the sticky, warm blood ... Lord, can it be?'

Turning books into cartoonies is nothin' new. Virtually all of Disney's early features were adapted from books. The Russians were also especially apt at adapting – but without getting the rights first (e.g. Fedor Khitruk's *Winnie the Pooh* and Alexei Karaev's Dr. Seuss takes, *Welcome* and *The Cat in The Hat*.) More ambitious adaptations include Jan Lenica's bizarre take on Ionesco's absurdist classic, *Rhinoceros*, Svankmajer's *Faust*, and Alexander Petrov's recent *The Old Man and The Sea*. Some, like Lenica's work well, others, like Petrov's tepid Hemingway film, do not.

Now it's one thing to adapt fairytales, plays and novellas, but it's an entirely different task when you're dealing with a mammoth work like Dostoevsky's *Crime and Punishment*. Cinema has already attempted a number of adaptations, most notably by Josef Von Sternberg and Aki Kaurismaki. Most recently, Polish animator Piotr Dumala, already well known for existential films *Kafka* and *The Gentle One* (based on a Dostoevsky short story) tried his hand, literally, at Dostoevsky's novel. While it's not the first animation attempt at *Crime and Punishment* (In 1999, student Zack Margolis made a short but inspiring take on it called *A Trip to the Building*), it is the most ambitious.

The cinematic temptation is obvious. For all its multi-layered philosophical, social and economic critiques of Russian society and humanity in general, *Crime and Punishment* contains all the tension and suspense of a Hitchcock film. As with *Shadow of A Doubt, Rope, Frenzy*, or even *North By Northwest*, we know almost immediately who committed, or in the case of *North by Northwest*, who didn't commit, the foul deed. Like Dostoevsky, Hitchcock implicates the viewer in the crimes (e.g. the voyeurism in *Rear Window*, the shower scene in *Psycho* or the murder in *Rope*). Throughout the course of the works, the viewer/reader must live with what it

knows. The tensions evolve out of this self-awareness. With our implication comes a variety of mixed messages that shuffle and confuse our own moral values and sense of right and wrong. Despite his monstrous actions, we (well, at least I) do not want Raskolnikov to get caught. Not only are we witness to the crime, but also to the motivations behind it. And despite its intimidating reputation, *Crime and Pun-*

Piotr Dumala

125

Franz Kafka   *ishment* reads like a mystery novel. Indeed, the book was originally a serialization for newspaper readers.

'Man gets accustomed to everything, the scoundrel!'

Dumala, it seems, also picked up the Hitchcock theme. *Crime and Punishment* opens with a marvelous Saul Bass-inspired credit sequence. Thumping, repetitive piano notes accompany the reddish-brown visuals that appear in and out of shadows. In between, we see what is almost an overture of images (including the murder) revealing, in an almost Brechtian style, what exactly we can expect to see in this film. The fusion of red and brown throughout the film captures 'the intolerable stench' of this sick world, while the elliptical, paranoid, dimly-lit images perfectly capture the increasingly blurred line between dream and reality in Raskolnikov's disturbed mind. As with the novel, the crime is very much a before and afterthought. What interests Dumala is less the crime and more the emotional and mental state of this troubled soul before and after the murder. The search for love and good through Sonia also functions as a major thematic element along with the murder. This is not Dostoevsky's *Crime and Punishment*, nor should it be.

Adaptations, like essays, should strive to be personal re-creations of the feelings and ideas inspired by the adapted work.

Unfortunately, Dumala has been criticized for his apparently un-faithful translation. 'People wanted a standard adaptation. People expect to see what they read in the book. This is something else so they feel cheated. It was not my aim to copy the book. I was really close to the book. I took one level of the book. It's not possible to show everything from this book. I got what I wanted.'

Dumala's film takes only the main plots: the killings, and meeting Sonia. This is not a tale of evil or like in St. Petersburg. This is about love and how obsession can destroy love. Dumala limited the film to five characters: Sonia, Raskolnikov, the old lady, and the old man who is always peering from the shadows. He also created a new character based on the dream that Raskolnikov has of himself as a young boy, trying to save a horse from a severe beating. 'I felt that I could make another hero who can exist like an angel repre-senting his innocence.'

'Occasionally he would stop in front of a summer house decked out in greenery, look through the fence, and see dressed-up women far away, on balconies and terraces, and children running in the garden. He took special interest in the flowers; he looked longer at them than at anything else.'

Dumala worked for 3½ years on *Crime and Punishment*, but he was introduced to the book in secondary school. 'I was very moved when I read this story about a 20-year-old good guy who wanted to kill someone without any reason.' The idea of a young man struggling to find his limitations appealed to Dumala, who, in

Dumala's *Kafka* inspired spot for MTV

127

typical teenage fashion, was drinking too much, causing trouble, and fighting with his parents. Beyond the juvenile attraction, there was something much deeper in the book that embraced the young Pole. The atmosphere in *Crime and Punishment* is one of dirt and scum. Everyone is dirty. They live in dirty houses with dirty children and have dirty thoughts. We see criminals, prostitutes, low-lifes; the dark side of society. This was a world very familiar to Dumala. He grew up in a poor district of Warsaw with 'lots of criminals living in the court'. The court was built in 1938 but was destroyed during WW II. 'Many people were killed in this area. My childhood was among these surroundings. It was dark poetry. People were living in ruins. A single mother with two kids lived in the basement, while another family occupied the top part. Criminals were fighting everyday. There was blood everywhere. Prostitutes lay in the stairway shitting on the stairs.' At the same time, Dumala, in love with a schoolgirl, had his Sonia within this landscape of darkness. In *Crime and Punishment*, Dumala 'found a book about my life'.

At 15, Dumala was not mature enough to make a film of Crime and Punishment. Ten years later, Dumala had started making comics consisting of about 300 drawings. 'It was the best drawings I'd ever made in my life, so after I thought about a film. My professor said you should do Crime and Punishment, but it was too early for me.' It would take Dumala another 17 years, making hundreds of films before he was ready to make the film of his life.

Dumala is, of course, already a well-known artist on the international animation circuit and his work is acclaimed for its philosophical themes, but especially for his innovative plaster technique. The technique involves the use of slabs of plaster covered with normal glue (with hot water to make the surface stronger and smooth). Once dry, Dumala scratches on the plaster with sandpaper and paints it with oil paint. 'It goes very fast. I put the paint on the surface and it's absorbed very quickly. I scratch on it with a sharp tool and can achieve very nice effects from dark tones to white plaster. The animation goes onto one piece so I make one drawing and change it on the same plaster and re-paint it.'

Dumala invented the technique in 1983. 'I had a piece of wood covered with a special preparation – I kept it as a lesson of technology from art school – and I covered the wood with brown oil paint as background – I always liked Dutch painting and I knew they covered their paintings with black – I really liked this and scratched it with a needle. It was an illumination. It was possible to scratch and make a drawing. I could continue this and make a film.' After one year at the academy of fine arts, Dumala made two films (*Little Black Riding Hood* and *Lycantrophy*) in traditional drawing style, before using the new technique on his next film, *Flying Hair*. 'It was a fantastic technique. Everything was influenced by this technique. It was smooth and poetic and black.' While the first two films were done on a white background, *Flying Hair* was made on a black background. 'This started my series of black films. So all films take place at night or between night and day. It's not possible to explain time of the day (timeless). Is it real light or dark sun?'

The process is time-consuming and Dumala never quite achieves the most desired effect. 'There are no line tests. Everything is done the first and last time.' With the life of a new image, comes the death of the old one. 'It's really destroying my mind. It's like killing your own children. Only what I get is the effect on the screen. The movement. I'm very much linked to my drawings. Sometimes you still have some of the past drawing and parts of the next one. It's something really interesting, but you can't keep it. I work slowly to keep it as long as possible. So I'll got to the bar and eat something and then it's time to destroy it. It's a punishment.'

If there is a crime to go with this punishment, it comes courtesy of the film's sountrack. Faced with deadlines, Dumala had only days to complete the soundtrack. 'There were technical problems and I couldn't start earlier. When I finally went to the studio I had two nights. I couldn't see the result until Ottawa (where the film premiered in September 2000).'

Fortunately, the completion of *Crime and Punishment* was mildly therapeutic for Dumala. 'When I was finished I felt like after the crime. I knew that something was passed. I am free of an idea that I was keeping for twenty years. It is done. It's over. I felt free to make something else.' Old women the world over are rejoicing.

[Originally appeared in the January 2001 edition of *Animation World Magazine* (www.mag.awn.com). Reprinted with permission of Animation World Network.]

Filmography of Piotr Dumala

1981	*Lycantrophy*
1982	*Little Black Riding Hood*
1984	*Flying Hair*
1985	*Gentle*
1986	*Jittery Life in Space*
1987	*Walls*
1988	*Freedom of the Leg*
1991	*Franz Kafka*
2000	*Crime and Punishment*

Chapter 15

The Spectacular Sounds and Images of Studio Filmtecknarna (2001)

Body Parts

Formed in 1981 by Jonas Odell, Stig Berqvist, and Lars Ollson, the Swedish animation studio, Filmtecknarna has developed into one of the most respected and innovative animation companies in the world. Filmtecknarna have merged a low and high end mixed-media aesthetic to produce a visually exciting body of work that includes award-winning commercials for a variety of clients (Madonna's *Music* video, Boddington's Cream Ale, MTV, Cartoon Network) along with a unique body of personal films (*Revolver*, *Exit*) that have received wide acclaim from international film festivals.

While Filmtecknarna has no consistent graphic style, there is a distinctive humour and rhythm to their work. 'The studio', says Odell, 'is made up of individuals with distinctly different approaches, but I do think there are things you recognize from film to film'. Diverse films such as *The Man Who Thought with His Hat*, *Dawning*, *Exit*, *Revolver*, and *Otto*, all feature a unique combination of surrealism, social commentary and black comedy. Many of the films are situated in suburban working class environments. Within these seemingly average spaces we find a darker and often humorous world.

The studio's first film, *The Man Who Thought with His Hat*, was, like most Swedish animated films, adapted from a children's story. 'We thought that was what you had to make', says Odell. 'We found a children's book that we liked and bought the rights (the author didn't want any money, but insisted that we draw characters with five fingers on each hand). The producer at the film institute was actually looking for someone to adapt this author's work to film. I still like the story, but the film definitely isn't "us".'

Exit

Although *The Man Who Thought With His Hat* certainly contains a number of elements usually found in a children's story, the film is a decidedly adult tale that examines class and power while suggesting that social attitudes are inherited, not natural. The film follows an oppressive President who does his decision making with a hat. The society he has created is one of conformity and repression. One day, the wind blows the hat away and the President loses his ability to think. After a rather bizarre interlude between the hat and some animals, a small boy returns the hat to the President, but teaches him how to think without it.

Their second film, *Dawning,* was closer to the studio's tastes. The protagonist is a 'cute' teddy bear who awakens early one day and wanders through the city streets. Along the way, he encounters a variety of people going about their daily routine. The unassuming narrative then takes a dramatic twist as it turns out that boy was wandering through a film set.

One of the studios' first films to receive international acclaim, and arguably their best work to date, is *Exit*. This was the first film written by the studio and it had two starting points. One was a nightmare that Berqvist had about a bizarre amusement park/department store. The second was a story told by *Dawning* writer, Joakim Pirinen. 'Joakim told us about the trip he made to Berlin.' says Odell 'When you enter East Berlin you had to exchange a certain sum of money into East German marks but you weren't

Otto allowed to bring them out of the country.' Law abiding as he was,

132

he desperately tried to spend the money on what there was to buy (i.e. Cheap souvenirs and nylon socks). This developed into a satire on the entertainment industry and the desperate race to have a 'good time'.

Exit opens with Ike and his three friends riding the train to town to visit a mammoth amusement park/shopping mall facility that bears a striking resemblance to the White House. Once inside, the quartet is greeted with a visual assault of neon signs (including a fabulous and ominous opening shot of a 'Get Happy' sign directly above a 'No Exit' sign) offering the allure of sex, violence and immediate pleasures. But what begins as a paradise turns into a nightmarish Orwellian consumer hell of violence and excess.

One of the subtle achievements of *Exit* is its deceptively simple design, which is more aligned with classical animation (like *Dawning and The Man Who Thought with his Hat*) than with the more expressionist design of *Revolver*, *Otto*, and *Body Parts*. Initially, one laments the lack of stylish graphic design until you understand the consciously alluring effect of the 'cartoony' nature of *Exit*.

Following *Pesce Pesce*, a bizarre stop motion piece about fish, Filmtecknarna made *Alice In Plasmaland*, a series of 21 short, clay-animated segments that fuse surrealism, Lewis Carroll and cut and paste hip hop with well known 20th century dialogue. The segments include an old white redneck rapping Martin Luther King's famous words, 'I have a Dream' before turning into a 'sexy' black woman; King Kong pulling his female victim apart to the words, 'loves me, loves me not'; a sexual relocation of George Bush's famous line, 'read my lips'; and a disturbing piece with Santa Claus masturbating to a peep show booth within which two young children open presents. While many of the segments border on the

2000 MTV European Music Awards

133

Dawning

absurd, *Alice* re-contextualizes well-known dialogue with images that subvert the original meanings by re-locating them in an ugly, but perhaps more honest, environment.

Alice was commissioned for SVT broadcasting company in Sweden and marked the first time Filmtecknarna worked with clay animation, but also the first time Odell worked with fellow Swedish animator, Magnus Carlsson (director of Radiohead's *Paranoid Android* video): 'Neither of us had done any claymation so we decided that would be a fun thing to try. We made a couple of episodes as a pilot and showed it to the head of the youth department at the SVT broadcasting company in Sweden who liked it and commissioned 26 episodes. During this period we spent a lot of time in bars in Stockholm, and most of the ideas were written down on napkins. We shared a common interest in music and decided to use sampled lines of dialogue in the same way it was used in music at that time.'

Filmtecknarna's most famous production is *Revolver*, a dazzling black and white film with a bold graphic style and a striking minimalist score. The film won awards around the world and to this day continues to be included in best of animation programmes. Says Odell: 'We had long wanted to do something in black and white but somehow one or two colours always sneaked in and before we knew it were always back to full colour. We had long wanted to do something using loops, this is usually done to save time and money in animation, but we noticed that looping a movement always added new qualities to it, either it suddenly turned out very comical or annoying or even frightening, and this was something we wanted to use. Animation from the silent era, especially the Fleischers and Victor Bergdahl were a major inspiration, with their extensive use of cycles. We wanted to structure the film in the same way as a piece of music; to start with a couple of themes and let them develop and merge into new themes. Of course, this way of working made it impossible to obtain any funding for the film, so we had to finance it mostly from our commercial productions, and strangely enough it turned out to be the film that got us the most new commercial jobs, so I guess it was well spent money, even from a strictly commercial point of view.'

Revolver

Revolver is comprised of a series of disparate repeated images that flow to the rhythm of a nightmare. The theme of domesticity, however fragmented and vague, seems to be the defining thread of *Revolver*. A housewife kneads a fish; a *literally* two-faced father fishes with his son. While the son's gaze is elsewhere, the father's face turns inside out, before quickly reverting back to 'normal' when the son looks back at him. In this one clever image, the film conveys the complexity of parent/child relationships. To the children, parents are a sign of order, normalcy, maturity, but this scene conveys the fragility of such notions, instead presenting the parent as a deceptive, multi-faceted being. Later, we see a wedding in a revolving church that cynically links marriage to that of the temporary nature of a revolving restaurant. This image is followed by a bickering couple who exchange lips (notably the revolving church is in the background) so they can yell at each other. In the end, *Revolver*, like a dream, can be read in a variety of ways, or merely savoured for its formal aural and graphic beauty

Following *Revolver*, Filmtecknarna made another compilation film, this time exploring, in their usual absurdist way, fifteen parts of the body. Similar in pace and tone to *Alice*, *Body Parts* was made 'in a kind of 2½-D technique', says Odell, 'with flat cut-out, animated-like puppets, improvised and held together by the soundtrack'. While there is a prevailing sense of alienation and loneliness, it's hard to take a film that shows a man playing *Ode to Joy* with his armpits too seriously. Other surreal highlights include a man who uncovers a lover and child when he pulls out his nose hair; a man pulls out his brain while cleaning his ears, and a couple who find love in their common gastrointestinal disorders.

Filmtecknarna returned to the Swedish suburbs for *Otto*, the story of a young boy who, lying in bed, imagines what exciting adventures his siblings might be having. Filled with bold, bright, UPA-influenced colours and design, *Otto* is a striking contrast to the stark black and white imagery of *Revolver*. 'The script for *Otto* was written even before we had started work on *Revolver*', says Odell, 'but we didn't quite now what to do with it, design-wise, to begin with. The experience of working within a very limited style on *Revolver* made it possible for us to approach design and the use of colours in a new and freer way.' While Otto was never picked up as a series (it was intended as a pilot), much of the design has found its way onto the Filmtecknarna animated series for Oxygen, *Mom's Online*.

One of the distinguishing marks of Filmtecknarna, and especially Jonas Odell's work, is the soundtrack. Using a clever amalgam of cut and paste dialogue, electronica, hip-hop and reggae, music plays a pivotal role in establishing and maintaining the mood of the work and in orchestrating the direction of many of their improvised films.

Commercial for
Boddington's Ale

Odell has created most of the soundtracks, most notably *Alice in Plasmaland*, *Body Parts*, *Revolver* and *Otto*. 'I used to play in bands and I enjoy doing the music myself, it might not be the world's greatest music but making it yourself does make it a part of the overall vision. Besides, I am the cheapest composer we ever worked with.'

Although Filmtecknarna was created to make 'personal' films, commercial projects have been a necessary part of their survival. Owing to the festival success of their short films (especially *Revolver*) Filmtecknarna has been hired to make a wide array of commercials in Sweden and abroad. 'The situation in Sweden has been kind of special. When we started out, there was no commercial television in Sweden. When it arrived in the 1980s, there was a big boom in commercials production, but not a lot of people with specialized skills in fields like SFX and motion graphics. We soon got a reputation as problem solvers and were called in to work on all kinds of things. We suddenly were model makers, we did on-location effects, television graphics, visual effects, puppeteering etc. I have even done sound editing on other projects. So the directors at the studio today have a basic knowledge of the possibilities of most conceivable animation techniques, and are able to choose from them when they design a new project.' The success of their recent commercial exploits owes a lot to the studio's remarkable diversity and innovation.

137

In the past couple of years alone, Filmtecknarna has produced a number of spots, including some real gems for *Music is my anti-drug*, MTV (a very clean/minimalist design), the MTV European Music Awards, Boddingtons Cream Ale (one of the funniest and lewdest commercials of recent memory), retro shorts for the Cartoon Network's *Cartoon Shorties*, and a nifty animated segment for Madonna's *Music* video.

Filmtecknarna landed the Madonna segment largely because of their previous collaborations with the video's director, Jonas Akerlund. 'The basic brief', says Odell, 'was to make something that looked like an animated *Madonna* TV series circa 1970s so we tried to keep CG effects and 3D stuff at a minimum and only do things that could have been done on an animation stand'.

Created for the Cartoon Network's 'shorties' series, *Atom Ant* is one of a series of reinterpretations of old Hanna Barbera characters. Using a cold war/atomic 'look', Odell works with, similar to *Body Parts*, a cut-out style, using samples from the original soundtrack. Aside from *Atom Ant*, Filmtecknarna also created re-interpretations of *Wally Gator*, *Jabberjaw* and *Josie and The Pussycats*. The *Josie* spot is particularly interesting because it uses a variety of techniques (cel, cut-out, CGI with live-action explosions!) as we follow the theme song and the girl's style through a series of metamorphoses based on music stylings over the last thirty years (disco, punk, country, electronica, heavy metal). When discussing Filmtecknarna, Cartoon Network director, Mike Ouweleen, gushes with enthusiasm: 'We stumbled upon their reel three years ago and they began doing a piece called *Things to do*. They just "got it" from the beginning. Their design and textures are absolutely brilliant.'

Music is my Anti-Drug was part of a series done by various animators, all featuring a young person and their particular anti-drug. Wanting to give the spot a dance music style, the studio looked a rave posters and flyers and out of that developed two styles: 'a stylized flat drawing for the main character and the mettallic shiny basic 3D style for the characters surrounding him'. Rendering the 3D city several times in different techniques and then compositing it together created the imposing backgrounds.

The spot for the 2000 MTV European Music Awards mixes rotoscope with a retro-futuristic style as it plays with the idea of the year 2000 as a symbol of the future. The opening sequence opens with a line of text saying 'Stockholm in the year 2000' and follows a 'hip' young couple through their futuristic leisurely life (that oddly enough looks nothing like Stockholm in the year 2000!). 'We did several ideas when we pitched to get the project, one featured a herring called Sven sporting porn star style sideburns. They liked the ideas but added another element to the brief: the stage was to be designed in the style of Ken Adam (the art director for several 1960s' Bond movies as well as for Kubricks' *2001*). The characters were shot as live-action and then hand rotoscoped. The backgrounds were built as 3D models in the computer and rendered as line images to fit the style.'

A new challenge facing the suddenly in-demand studio is balance. The success of their commercial work has meant that there is little time for personal projects. In fact, the studio has not made an independent film since *Revolver* (*Otto*, while technically an independent film, was targeted as a TV series). 'We were used to being able to use the time in between commercials to work on our own films', says Odell, 'but that time doesn't exist anymore. It took us a while to understand that and to devise new ways of planning the studios work so we actually will be able to do both. We have now stated as a policy to create independent films regularly.' In fact, Odell is currently half way through a new 'slightly autobiographical' short called *Family and Friends*. Jonas Dahlbeck (who became a studio partner in 1994 along with Magnus Carlsson) and Boris Nawratil have also started on a couple of projects.

While the animation industry heads into a drought, Filmtecknarna seems flexible enough to withstand it. 'We have been lucky', says Odell, 'to get almost all of our films theatrically distributed in Sweden and that's not really a normal thing when it comes to short films'. At the same time, any studio that can create inventive and exceptional animation using either the latest digital technology or a simple fax machine is probably going to turn out just fine.

[Originally appeared in the October 2001 edition of *Animation World Magazine*. Reprinted with permission of Animation World Network.]

Filmography of Studio Filmtecknarna

1984	*The Man Who Thought With His Hat*
1985	*Dawning*
1988	*Pesce, Pesce*
1989	*Exit*
1993	*Alice in Plasmaland*
1993	*Revolver*
1995	*Body Parts*
1997	*Otto*
2000	Madonna *Music* video sequence
2000	*Atom Ant*
2001	*My Anti Drug: Music*
2002	*Family and Friends*
2004	*Take Me Out* (music video)

139

Chapter 16

Pierre Hébert and Animation in The Age of Digital Reproduction (2001)

La Plante Humaine

Walter Benjamin wrote his seminal article, *The Work of Art in the Age of Mechanical Reproduction* as a response to the technological innovations such as a cinema and photography that permitted, through reproduction, mass access to previous sacred or unique works of art. One of the interesting questions Benjamin asked was just how this reproduction will change the process of creating and reacting to art. Owing to digital technology, we are at a stage where we must perhaps return to Benjamin, if only to consider the effect of this new technology on art.

In a 2000 article for the Holland Animation Film Festival, Canadian animator, Pierre Hébert argued that animation, in its fervent desire to protect and promote itself, has instead become an inward-looking practice: 'It has let itself drift into an embittered, corporatist and willful isolation, valuing good craftsmanship and good animation and slightly losing sight of the philosophical position that underlies the act of animating'. Similarly, where animation once had a meaningful, but undefined relationship with cinema, and especially experimental film, this is no longer the case today despite the obvious, but unspoken, influence of animation on almost every fiber of cinema. In the rush to protect and promote itself, Hébert suggests that 'auteur' animation has isolated itself from other plastic arts.

Animation, and specifically independent or 'auteur' animation, which is often the feeding ground for any and all new trends in commercial animation, is at a dead end. Stylistic and narrative innovations certainly continue, but all within the same abiding walls; walls that have been pushed as far as they will bend.

In recent years, Hébert has put is words into action. While his interest in alternative methods of creating and presenting animation goes back to the early 1980s, his recent performance piece, *Between Science and Garbage,* is suggesting radical new possibilities for viewing, creating and defining animation. As it stands at the moment, Pierre Hébert appears to be the most visible voice capable of leading animation out of its almost forty year period of isolationism.

Pierre Hébert

Much to the chagrin of me, myself and I, outside of the animation festival crowd, very few people even know who Pierre Hébert (let alone, Svankmajer, Pärn and The Quays) is; so let's go back to Hébert's beginnings as an artist.

141

The abstract years

As a child growing up in Quebec, Hébert was always interested in drawing and painting. For years he wondered where the desire came from. Neither of his parents were artistically-oriented. His father worked in the steel industry as an office worker, accountant and later as dossier builder to help land contracts. It was only recently that Hébert found the seeds of his creativity. While courting his grandmother, Hébert's grandfather used to send her a painted postcard every week. 'I saw the about 50 postcards. It showed that he had talent. So I have this small seed.'

Not surprisingly, when Hébert wanted to attend the Fine Arts school, his parents frowned upon it and insisted he was better off enrolling in university. Hébert studied anthropology and archeology, but visual arts remained foremost in his mind. Then came Norman McLaren, who indirectly planted the next artistic seed in Hébert's mind. 'I had friends at school who had started to wash out 8mm films and draw on it and the idea of that came from McLaren. I saw it and thought it was cool.' Hébert began making his own cameraless films and was excited by both the process and result. Meantime, a producer at the National Film Board was putting on screenings of experimental films at museums and other venues. Increasingly, Hébert began to see the connection with animation.

Meantime, Hébert was calling up McLaren and asking for advice about creating scratched soundtracks. McLaren would give Hébert film leader to practice with. Hébert later brought the results for McLaren's feedback. Obviously impressed with this new talent, McLaren referred Hébert to producers Wolf Koenig and Bob Verrall who had just started a student program and were looking for students to hire.

Hébert was hired. Consequently, Hébert and the NFB began what would be a thirty-five year relationship.

Initially, Hébert did not find the NFB very compelling. While he was given encouragement to do his own thing, he also worked on sequences for documentaries and other service-oriented work for various government ministries. One of the most interesting projects he directed was a film called *Population Explosion*. This warning against overpopulation was not much, but it did feature an original soundtrack by jazz legend, Ornette Coleman. Hébert spent most of his evenings and weekends at the NFB, working on his own films. Two of these 'spare time' films were *Op Hop* (1966) and *Opus 3* (1966). These almost violent abstract films use geometrical shapes – which randomly flicker and float across the screen – to explore theories of optics and perception. Hébert's first 'official'

NFB film, *Around Perception* (1968), was a continuation of the theories explored in the first two films.

From the start, Hébert's work was, oddly enough, given that he is deeply rooted in the work of McLaren and René Jodoin, an anomaly. While McLaren undoubtedly influenced many of the young animators of this period (e.g. Ryan Larkin, Francine Desbiens), he had virtually no influence on the direction of the Board. During the 1960s, the NFB concentrated on 'cel' animation and assembly line structures. Fortunately, the creation of a French animation department led to the hiring of former McLaren colleague, René Jodoin, who, from the beginning, insisted on reawakening the McLaren heritage. It was within this new environment that Hébert began making his own films.

Personal politics

In the 1970s, clearly influenced by the increasing political climate of his era, Hébert began to combine his artistic innovation with political commentary. Following a cinematic attack on the commercialization of Christmas called *Père Noël, Père Noël,* Hébert made *Between Dog and Wolf* (1978). Hébert mixed a variety of techniques (including cut-out and scratch animation) into a multi-level narrative that merged Brechtian dialogue with sombre images of people waiting at a bus station. Alas, the animator's output began to appear reductive and didactic during this phase – not to mention that its formal complexity distanced the work from those whom Hébert claimed it was speaking to and for.

After taking a sabbatical from the Film Board in 1979, Hébert returned to the NFB rejuvenated and with a clearer sense of his artistic direction. *Souvenirs du Guerre* (1982) marks a turning point in Hebert's early career as he moves away from both abstract formal and political concerns to a more personalized, tangible politics.

Motivated by the birth of his son, Etienne, and the war in Afghanistan, Hébert wonders how his child will survive in a harsh violent world where children are little more than 'leaves on a tree'. Hébert uses scratch, cut-out animation and live-action images to create an unstable and ominous world, always on the brink of violence and destruction. While the rigidity of Hébert's earlier films rear their ugly heads occasionally (the link between family-labour-war is a little too simple), in general, Hébert's vision is more flexible and constructive. Hébert understands that war and politics are a complex infrastructure involving labour, the family and the individual. As he shows us, we are participants in our own destruction, but do we have the power or ability to participate in our salvation?

As early as 1984, Hébert was involved in multimedia performances. Usually they involved a projected film accompanied by improvised sounds. The challenge for Hébert was how to create a way of improvising the images. Eventually he started experimenting with film loops in the projector. In 1985, Hébert began to extend this improvisational style to his films. *Le Métro* (1985), for example, was collaboration between Hébert and musicians Robert Lepage and René Lussier. Each artist improvised his impressions of the dehumanizing effects of the underground world of the urban subway.

Increasingly encouraged by his improvised results, Hébert made a film version of his collaborative performances called *Lettre D'Amour*. *Lettre D'Amour* evolved out of a series of small workshops that Hébert and his wife and writer, Sylvie Massicotte were involved in. Subjects were chosen out of a hat. One subject that seemed to offer infinite possibilities was a love letter and the variety of emotions and thoughts confronting a person as they await its arrival. Hébert and Massicotte expanded the performances to include dance (Louise Bedard) and music (Robert Marcel Lepage). *Lettre D'Amour* is a film of one of those performances.

Akin to a jazz performance, each performer has his/her turn to riff on the subject. The result however is interesting but flawed. *Lettre D'Amour* fails to capture the spontaneity, tension and freedom of the performance setting. The dance, in particular, is reduced to a poorly flickering image on a TV screen, adding nothing to the piece. Let's just say that *Lettre* is an interesting experiment and a step in Hébert's progression towards performance animation.

In 1996, Hébert completed his first feature film, *La Plante Humaine* (The Human Plant). The film, which combines scratch

Souvenirs de Guerre

animation and live-action, follows the rather uneventful life of a retired librarian named Michel. His days are spent walking his dog, reading about Leonardo Da Vinci, reading a book of traditional African stories, and watching television (and specifically news-casts). He acquires a variety of knowledge about the world but he does not do anything with it (he's essentially a couch potato).

Interestingly, Hébert plays off his old activist days as we expect a critique of the Gulf War, television, or this inactive protagonist. However, Hébert does not succumb to these easy targets of attack. Michel and his life are merely observed and we, like Michel, are left to figure out our own solutions.

What hope is there if we can no longer actively participate in, let alone change, the direction of our vast world? The answer, for Hébert, is modest. In the final scene, Michel leaves his house and goes to the library where he shares his stories with a group of children. Talking to each other, Hébert seems to suggest, and sharing our knowledge and experiences, offers hope for the present and future. However, Hébert again throws a loop into what we're seeing because Michel has now become a well-dressed professorial live-action character. The live-action character, it seems, is merely a projection of Michel's imagination. If this is a part of his imagi-nation, has he even left the house or does he remain planted in the seeds of his imagination?

In having Michel dream in live-action, Hébert reverses our ten-dency to see live-action images as genuine or authentic. In doing so he reminds us (à la Walter Benjamin) that all images are constructed from a particular point of view.

Le Métro

Time for a change

After thirty-five years, Hébert left the National Film Board of Canada in 1999 to concentrate on his independent artistic career and specifically performance art. During 1999 and 2000, Hébert traveled to a variety of International Festivals (Switzerland, Canada, Holland) to present a series of scratch animation performances (usually accompanied by a musician). Over the past year, he began working with noted musician, Bob Ostertag, on a new type of performance that would be created and performed using digital technology. The result is *Between Garbage and Science*, an hour-long multimedia performance about the disposability of culture.

What Hébert and Ostertag are creating is, within the context of independent animation, radical. Ostertag has collected a variety of music samples on a Mac Power Book. Using a program called Max, Ostertag is able to virtually do anything he wants to the sounds. Meantime, Hébert has a digital video camera hooked up to a small homemade animation stand. The camera is connected to Hébert's Power book. Hébert also has about fifty images stored, along with a handful of QuickTime movies (taken primarily from news footage). He can alter the sequence, pace, texture and color of these images. Hébert's performance consists of a combination of these archived images with about 80% improvised live animation (ranging from cut-out, object, paint on glass, chalk on board, and basic drawn animation). The title of the performance refers at once to the disposability of the technology (the computer could crash during the screenings) and the content (which changes with each performance).

In artistic terms, this is by no means revolutionary. Hollywood has made digital features, and music has long collaborated with film in a performance context. Yet within the world of independent animation, Hébert's work is radical. The process of creation is no longer hidden from the viewer in a different time and space. The animator performs, not for a 'mechanical contrivance', but an audience. While you could suggest a return to sacred art because of the uniqueness of each performance, we should remember that each performance is also disposable. There is nothing to prevent Hébert from having his computer crash and losing all his images. So while each work is unique, there's this sort of casual attitude that shrugs if it's lost.

The collaborative aspect of the performance enhances the ability to create something new. Music is no longer subservient to the animation.

One of the more interesting aspects of Hébert's work is the liberation of time. 24 frames per second has for the most part remained the defining slice of time for many animators. Now 24 frames is merely an option among many: 'When I first encountered the parameter controls in the first versions of the Max software, for example, the control button of the speed of the loop in buffer-1, it was like a mental landslide because all my animator skill had been up to that point locked to a fixed value, that is 24 frames per second.' Suddenly Hébert discovered that the program (which was designed for music) could measure in 1000th of a second. 'I could set the different parallel flows of events happening in the computer at independent values in 1000th of seconds, also independent of the frame rate it would be sliced into by the video projector. The elimination of 24 frames as a measure of time provides an opportunity for animators to fundamentally change the way they construct their work. The digital technology means that the work is mobile and compact. After the initial cost of the computer and essential gadgets, there is no need to strike prints, no shipping dynamics to negotiate, and no projectionist to shout at.

This is not to say that animators should all rush out and pick up laptops. This is not an either/or situation or a criticism of existing animations. Instead, Hébert's work is merely opening a door to new possibilities of animation. 'I just feel like trying to assess in a radical and experimental way what is already widely happening in the audiovisual media as a whole. And also trying to understand that historically and find a ground to help define new conditions of artistic creation when dealing with technology.' At the very least, it means that those animators who've often cringed while watching their films, often wishing they could go back and change this or that, will perhaps soon be in a position where they can do just that.

[Originally appeared in the October 2001 edition of *Animation World Magazine*. Reprinted with permission of Animation World Network.]

Filmography of Pierre Hébert

1966	*Op Hop – Hop Op*
1966	*Opus 3*
1968	*Around Perception*
1968	*Population Explosion*
1974	*A Piece of Cake*
1974	*Santa Claus Is Coming Tonight/Père Noël, père Noël*
1978	*Entre Chiens et Loup*
1983	*Memories of War*
1984	*Étienne et Sara*
1984	*Songs and Dances of the Inanimate World: The Subway*
1989	*La Lettre d'amour*
1997	*La Plante humaine*
2004	*Between Science and Garbage*

Chapter 17

Masculinity in Crisis: The Animated Films of Andreas Hykade (2001)

We Lived in Grass

ndreas Hykade learned to draw in a Bavarian pub. His father dragged him along so Mother could have time to herself. The men wanted to plays cards. To keep the boy quiet they gave him some pencils and paper. He stayed quiet. The men played. The men drank. The men talked. Andreas kept drawing but between strokes he heard their words and their laughter. Life was good.

The bar days long in the past, the 33-year-old Hykade has emerged as one of the bright spots on the animation film festival scene. His most recent films *We Lived in Grass* (1995) and *Ring of Fire* (2000) are startling, uncompromising personal insights into the deep contradictions lurking beneath the flesh of masculinity. Hykade's young protagonists enter what they perceive to be a man's world – a trough of sex, booze, violence and, ultimately, power. But as his characters' journeys continue, they encounter other possibilities and emotions, coming to realize that their learned masculine ideals actually conflict with the world's true nature. In other words, Dad was full of shit.

Prior to making *We Lived in Grass* and *Ring of Fire*, Hykade made *The King Is Dead* (1991) about his first hero, Elvis Presley. With choppy animation, *The King Is Dead* is technically unpolished and hesitant. But beyond that there exists a surprisingly wise explora-tion of the thwarted myths of heroism. Hykade opens with a nostalgic Elvis quote: 'When I was a boy I saw myself as a hero in comic books and movies'. To the accompaniment of Presley's fat-ass Vegas standard, *My Way*, the film shatters Presley's boyhood dreams. The 'boy' we see now is an old, tired, hideous fat man. He leads a mundane life popping pills, eating and watching television; he has to be strapped down and into his costume to conceal his gut and prepare him for the ol' Vegas birds. Using few images and a simple narrative, Hykade considers the price of fame and the death of this once innocent, hopeful child.

Brought up in the Bavarian country-side, Hykade had no formal contact with art until he studied animation at the Filmakademie Baden-Württem-berg in Stuttgart, Germany. 'It was the only thing to do', Hykade recalls. 'I couldn't stay in the village because I would have become a freak. I had this artist myth in my mind that you go to art school and smoke, drink and have discussions about deep things, but it was just bored kids hanging around.' Any hope Hykade had that art would save his life drifted away in the smoke

Andreas Hykade

149

Andreas Hykade:
self-portrait

he lazily blew from his stale cigarette. Between puffs, Hykade made little drawings based on his village life. 'We had this neighbour who was a complete alcoholic. He had six or seven children and he had testicular cancer. He died in 1974, when I was six years old. Our doors were always open and you could see their life.' Soon Hykade found a thread connecting the images, a vocabulary with which he could create a portrait of his childhood village. This became the basis for *We Lived in Grass*.

Superbly animated, *We Lived in Grass* is drawn in an almost child-like style, reflecting the frenzied, fragmentary nature of an unnamed young boy's mind growing up in a small village. His father is a massive, grotesque man who does nothing but drink and fuck; his mother is little more than a sperm receptacle. Children are scattered around the chaotic house. The crux of the film again rests with its opening words, spoken by the father to the boy: 'All woman is whore and all man is soldier'. The seeming simplicity of the father's words is initially confirmed as the boy travels between nightmare and reality through an often violent, imposing and dark world.

The boy's impressions change when, out hunting for a tiger, he comes across a young woman. She is a happy, flirtatious, and generous soul (all beautifully conveyed with just a few gestures) who offers the boy a lock of her 'dandelion' hair. Her gentle, loving nature stirs strange emotions in him. 'Papa didn't tell me about this', he says, referring to the warm feelings of love and tranquility that lie nestled inside his soul. As the boy bathes in the warmth of his new discovery, his father dies; with Papa go the whore and soldier. The nightmares stop. When the boy next sees the 'dandelion' girl she is standing, almost meditating, her eyes closed. The boy tries to get her attention, but she does not notice him. In frustration he yanks and twists her hair. Unmoved, she straightens her hair and continues her meditation. 'All woman is whore', the boy says. The nightmares return. This time he burns down the dandelion girl. The father is dead, but his words find new life. With an economy of impressions that would not be possible in live-action, Hykade manages to capture just how deep the roots of heredity and environment are planted.

Using prize money earned from *We Lived in Grass* (notably for Best Student film at the Stuttgart International Animation Festival in 1996), Hykade started work on his next film, a Felliniesque, neo-noir Western. A striking departure in terms of graphics alone, *Ring of Fire* catches a few moments in the life of two cowboys as they arrive at a sex bazaar – two ignorant boys who see the world as a playground for their dicks. However, after the protagonist violently beats and rapes one of the women, his sidekick aids her, soon discovering a vibrant soul beneath the flesh he once so desired. The story is complemented, at times overshadowed, by a wide-screen format with loud black-and-white graphics featuring a series of strange, sexually absorbed characters and a twanging, tremolo-tinged guitar score.

Ring of Fire

151

Such a disturbed piece of work has many interesting stories behind it. The root of the film is a real-life love triangle. 'I had a very good friend and we went out to get pissed every night. And then I fell in love with his wife.' The love was lost. The friendship was redeemed. A film was found. Hykade spent a year-and-a-half on the script and knew that the setting would be a bazaar with all sorts of sexual figures. He placed ads asking people to draw figures representing their sexual desires and sent them to prisons, art magazines, schools and friends. Together with his colleague, Sabine Huber, Hykade sorted through the 350 drawings they received and created 30 figures for *Ring of Fire*. These erotic peripheral figures dance in and out of the film adding a layer of dementia to the sex-crazed protagonists while providing a palette of metaphorical accompaniment to Hykade's vision of sexuality.

Facing page: Top is from the music video *Ten Little Deerhunters*; bottom is the music video for *Just A Gigolo*

Like almost all independent animators, Hykade cannot exist solely on his personal films. He has done animation for commercials, kids' films and a multimedia show for Expo 2000. His music videos, *Zehn kleine Jägermeister* for the band, Toten Hosen, and *Blablabla* for Gigi D'agostino resemble Hykade's personal work only in terms of graphics. He is also fortunate to have the support of the young German film production company, Gambit. The company, led by Michael Jungfleisch – who became friends with Hykade when both were studying at the Filmakademie – has been involved with Hykade since *We Lived in Grass*. Their arrangement is simple: Hykade presents ideas to Jungfleisch and if he likes them, he'll find money. Considering that many independent animators must find their own backing, Hykade has it a little better than most.

Hykade recently presented Jungfleisch with an idea for a feature film called *Jesus*. 'The film is my interpretation of Christ', says Hykade. 'The bible has the four gospels, but there are better ones, like the gospel of Thomas. The Jesus described there is more down to earth. He offers a series of wise statements on how to live your life. The Catholic Church will butcher me.' Controversy is likely to follow Hykade for his whole career – a few voices have whispered 'sexism' in relation to his work, especially *Ring of Fire*. Far from discriminating or oppressing the female gender, *Ring of Fire* constructs sexuality from a male point of view, through the eyes of a couple of morons. 'They are kids', says Hykade, 'who have a desire for flesh and learn that there is a soul behind the flesh. That's it. It's nothing more.' *Ring of Fire*, like *We Lived in Grass*, explores the nature of machismo in order to expose its ugly roots. When people are given the choice between beauty and honesty, most will take beauty. Beauty is simple. Honesty is complex, frustrating and often ugly. In the end, people see what they want to see.

Filmography of Andreas Hykade

1990	*King is Dead*
1995	*We Lived in Grass*
1996	*Zehn kleine Jägermeister* (music video)
1999	*Blablabla* (music video)
2000	*Ring of Fire*
2003	*Tom* (TV Series)
2004	*Walkampf* (music video)

(originally appeared in *Cinemascope Magazine*, 2002)

Chapter 18

Thou Shalt Covet Phil Mulloy (2002)

The Chain

If Disney is animation's heart, then British animator, Phil Mulloy is it bowels. (Or wait – maybe that's the other way around.) Very, very far from the colourful cartoony world of bunny rabbits, cuddly ogres, and assorted sexless wide-eyed moral crusaders who make the world safer and linear for us, are Phil Mulloy's deceptively crude and intentionally primitive animation films.

Mulloy made an animation as an entrance film requirement for the Royal College of Art in London (he graduated in 1971), but subsequently spent almost 20 years working in television and documentary film. It wasn't until the late 1980s, when Mulloy moved to Wales and turned a cowshed into a studio, that he returned to animation; he's made 24 films since. His films are drawn with bold, black lines and feature skeletal figures with black skulls, white eyes and noses resembling flaccid penises. Mulloy's black comedies drip with cynicism and sarcasm as he explores the repressive effects of the world's social, political and religious systems. The *Laughing Moon* spots (1993–94), made as part of a campaign about social injustice for MTV Europe, summarize Mulloy's view that these systems have forcibly polarized the world into black/white, good/bad, up/down –- and in doing so, they oversimplify our life experiences. A man runs back and forth on a train track between two brick walls. It's not clear where he wants to go or what he's seeking, but occasionally he bangs his head against the wall until he stumbles and falls off the tracks. As he gets up, he sees a forest with many paths, panics, and jumps back on the track to resume running at the wall. Here, Mulloy uncovers what he perceives to be the root of humanity's problems: we've created an either/or system that fails to meet our multifaceted needs and desires.

In Mulloy's short series, *The Ten Commandments*, he applies each commandment to contemporary life. In *Thou Shall Not Bear False Witness*, a man and woman who failed to please their parents as children marry each other, solely to appease them. As a result, the couple lives a loveless life. They pretend that everything is peachy keen, but have erotic homosexual dreams at night, forgetting their fantasies come morning. When they die, they're considered a model couple in the eyes of others. In *Thou Shall Not Covet Thy Neighbour's Wife*, a man is so determined to win the love of his neighbour's wife that he switches

Phil Mulloy

155

Thou Shalt Not Bear False Witness

places with her beloved dog, who he trains the dog to walk and talk, in order to win her adoration. In both instances, Mulloy presents characters forced to live in a world of stifling polarity. Having chosen to step outside this accepted framework, these transgressors go to extreme lengths to fulfill themselves while maintaining an illusion of normalcy. Under Mulloy's analytical eyes, *The Ten Commandments* becomes a system of absurd rules that leads people to live under an uncracked shell, never having found the courage to crack open their lives to find greater possibilities.

In *The Chain* (1997), Mulloy shows us that the systems we've inherited stem from a history of ignorance, miscommunication, and greed. An uncaring parent discards a child's drawing. A street

Sabbath Day

drunk subsequently picks up the drawing and mistakes it for a treasure map. Soon everyone wants his map and world leaders are rallying their troops to find the treasure. A 200-year world war erupts until a king believes he's finally found the treasure. He digs his way down a hole but his people, fed up, revolt and bury him. There is celebration, peace, and joy until a hungover man stumbles across a piece of paper that looks like a treasure map. *The Chain* is at once a ferocious denunciation of religious and political greed, and the mass killing it begets in the name of peace and love. What elevates Mulloy's work from mere rant is his awareness of the complexity behind these systems. With strong Hegelian echoes, the final scene suggests that humanity will never learn from history and will keep making the same costly mistakes.

At the same time, Mulloy's cynical, punk view is almost textbook raw-raw anarchist generalization. His films offer such sweeping denunciations of humanity that they can become repetitious and downright hopeless. Also, he occasionally succumbs to cliché. For example, *Cowboys* (1991) attacks US consumerism, and *Thou Shall Keep Holy The Sabbath Day (1996)*, fundamentalism; in both, Americans are presented as little more than hicks, and Mulloy succumbs to the very stereotypical tendencies he ridicules. That said, Mulloy's work is almost always provocative, nasty, and quite funny (as in the Monty Python inspired *Sex Life of A Chair*). More important, it shows that animation is not just a medium for kids and teenagers and can instead serve as an important intellectual and artistic tool to excavate the subtleties of existence.

[Originally appeared in *Cinemascope Magazine*.]

Filmography of Phil Mulloy	
1991	*Cowboys; Possession*
1992	*The Cowboy Collection; Ding Dong*
1993	*Laughing Moon Films; The Sound Of Music*
1994	*Laughing Moon; The History of the World* (Episodes 10, 16, 65)
1994	*Destruction*
1995	*Great Moments in Film*
1995/96	*The Ten Commandments*
1996	*The Wind of Changes*
1997	*The Chain*
1998	*The Sex Life of a Chair*
1999	*Season's Greetings*
2000	*Intolerance*
2001	*The Henries; Intolerance II – The Invasion; Flik Flak*
2002	*Love Is Strange*
2004	*Intolerance III – The Final Solution*

Chapter 19

David Ehrlich: Excavation of a Flawed Soul (2003)

'It's all error … There's only error. There's the heart of the world. Nobody finds his life. That is life.'
Philip Roth *I Married A Communist*

Dryads

158

American animator David Ehrlich lives in the woods, but he's not lost like Dante, for he knows his way as well as any of us can. These Vermont woods offer Ehrlich a modicum of harmony through their indispensable songs of nature. Films like *Vermont Etude* (1977) and *Dance of Nature* (1991) evoke these natural melodies and their mysterious cyclical routes. Ehrlich's life and all its borrowed breaths are rooted in the same uncertainty, ugliness and beauty. His images are restless and at times it's as if they, like Ehrlich, are in search of their life; a life that fits; a life that unleashes the soul from confusion, anger and frustration.

This year, at least, life appears to fit David Ehrlich just fine. In May, Dreamland Publishing in France released *David Ehrlich: Citizen of the World,* by scholar, Olivier Cotte. In June, Ehrlich received the prestigious ASIFA Achievement Award at the Zagreb Animation Festival. And in October he served as Honorary President for the Ottawa International Animation Festival alongside a retrospective of his work which included not one, but two new films: *Taking Color For a Walk* (2002) and *Current Events* (2002). Not a bad year for ANY independent animator let alone an experimental one.

So Okay fair enough, this guy got some nice accolades, but who, you ask, is David Ehrlich? First and foremost, Ehrlich is an independent experimental animator. He's been making almost one film per year since 1975. His most acclaimed works include *Precious Metal* (1980), *Dissipative Dialogues* (1982), *Dryads* (1988) and *A Child's Dream* (1990). Since 1992, he's been teaching animation at the ol' Animal House stomping grounds at Dartmouth College, and since the mid-1970s, he has taught numerous children's workshops around the world. From 1988-2000, Ehrlich was Executive Board member of ASIFA International.

Ehrlich was born in Elizabeth, New Jersey in 1941. His pops, Max, was an eye surgeon and his Mom, Jeannette raised David and his

David Ehrlich

younger brother, Jeff, and wrote poems in between. As a youth Ehrlich did the things boys were supposed to do (boxing, football) and not supposed to do (draw, paint, sing, and tap-dance). He began pre-medical study at Cornell but soon realized that he was taking this road for his parents, not for himself, and switched to pre-law where he also breathed in courses in international relations and a boatload of Eastern languages and philosophy. His interest in all things Eastern led him, like many after him, to visit India, where he ap-

159

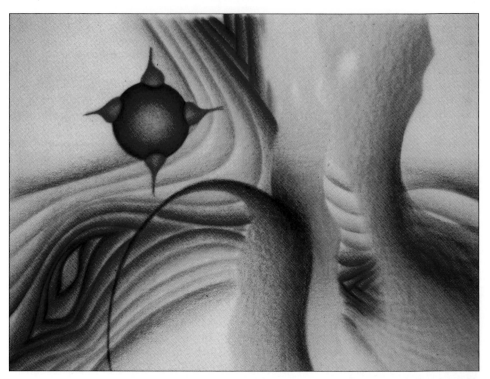

A Child's Dream prenticed as a sculptor and studied a sitar-like instrument called the veena. Perhaps afraid to get on with life, Ehrlich continued to study after he returned to the USA in 1964. By the 1970s, he became increasingly interested in the process of creativity and even taught courses on the subject at the State University of New York from 1971–75. All the while Ehrlich continued to paint, sculpt, compose and dance. Animation emerged out of a desire to integrate these different arts, and around 1974, he began toying around with an 8mm camera. By 1975, he made his first animation film, the aptly titled, *Metamorphosis*. He was hooked.

In 1977, Ehrlich began sending his films (*Vermont Etude,* 1977 and *Robot*, 1977) to ASIFA festivals (Annecy and Zagreb). Incredibly, given the amount of activities and initiatives Ehrlich undertook, he was, in essence, a shy guy. Fortunately, animation has always been dominated by open, modest, faulty, and caring human beings. Ehrlich was quickly welcomed into this new world and specifically the International Animators' Association, ASIFA.

Ehrlich had joined ASIFA-East (New York chapter) in 1975, but didn't become formally involved on an international level until 1982 when he became part of the ASIFA Workshop Committee. (By the way, during this time, Ehrlich, motivated by his father's

160

struggle with colon cancer, researched and wrote a book about bowel health called *The Bowel Book*). Beginning in 1985, he co-chaired an ASIFA committee on International Cooperation (remember this was Cold War days) and two of his great initiatives were the collaborative films *Academy Leader Variations* (1987) *and Animated Self-Portraits* (1989). The first film featured a series of film leaders interpretations by artists from Poland, USA, Switzerland, and China, while the second featured a series of self-portraits from US, Czech, Estonian, Japanese and Yugoslav animators. Both films went on to win a variety of awards including a Jury Prize at the Cannes Film Festival for *Academy Leader Variations*.

In 1988, Ehrlich was elected to the Executive Board of ASIFA and served as Vice-President from 1991–1997. In 2000, he retired from ASIFA. During his tenure, Ehrlich was the conscience, voice, and legs of ASIFA. While he was never elected President, he was always ASIFA's leader, serving as an active bridge between Eastern and Western artists, and as an often-vocal defender of the rights of animation artists.

Ehrlich's support of 'less fortunate' animators was not limited to words. In 1982, he started the Vermont Visiting Animators Program to bring international animators to do children's workshops in Vermont. Ehrlich then arranged additional screening tours in places like Montréal, New York and New England. The list of animators is astounding: Yuri Norstein, Priit Pärn, A Da, Piotr Dumala, Jerzy Kucia, Michel Ocelot, Borivoj Dovnikovic, and on and on. Even more amazing is the fact that from 1984 onwards, Ehrlich funded the visits himself. His motivations were manifold. It gave him a chance to hang out with some friends and was a way of, in his words, 'opening up naïve, unexposed Americans to different cultures and socio-political systems'. The program, which he stopped in 2001, was a success and eventually expanded to California via ASIFA-San-Francisco and ASIFA-Hollywood.

As an artist, Ehrlich is like a Pre-Socratic philosopher, convinced that the essence of life is to be found in the materials of nature (fire, water, and air). Throughout his work, Ehrlich sorts through the wreckage of the collision between the individual and society, space, and self. Even in his most 'scientific' films like *Precious Metal, Precious Metal Variations* (1983), *Point* (1984), *Pixel* (1987), *Interstitial Wavescapes* (1995), and all those other dots, lines and circle type films, there remains a strong connection to the material world of Ehrlich's existence. This is what, for me anyway, elevates him above the cold world of formalism or structuralism or whatever friggin' 'ism' 'you' want to use.

Echoing another fine experimental artist, René Jodoin, Ehrlich sees

161

the sights unseen by most of us. He recognizes the subtle effects that time and space have on our (and his) daily lives, and the routines we create within them (e.g. *Robot Rerun, Dissipative Fantasies*). Whether it's trees (*Dance of Nature*), bees (*Point*), women (*Dryads, Dissipative Dialogues*), or himself, life is always flowing, expanding, contracting, evolving, and, most importantly, interconnecting. Potential is the only certainty.

Facing page:
Top: *Dance of Nature*;
Bottom: *Radiant Flux*

In films like *Dissipative Fantasies* (1986), Ehrlich shatters the gap between him and us. 'We' are implicated in everything that contacts us. Ehrlich not only shows us the world he sees, but also the eyes with which he sees, the ears with which he hears, and the hand with which he feels. For Ehrlich, the separation of individual and world is simply not possible. All is personal and political.

Until 1991 (when he suffered temporarily from a blepherospasm, which diminished his sight, and he began working tactilely with clay painting animation), Ehrlich's films were entirely drawn by hand using prismacolour pencils and, later, ink markers (*Pixel* and *Point*). Visually, colours dominate the films. They're an integral part of any understanding of his films. Using a 12-tone system (or for you laymen like me – sorta like a single colour colourbar.) Ehrlich's expressive, powerful, and varied colours not only capture the external flavour of the world around him, but also an internal and deeply personal sense of joy, hope, and harmony that is at the core of Ehrlich's humanistic being.

If you look through the back of the *Citizen of the World* book, there are a variety of tributes to Ehrlich from many animators. Most of

Robot

163

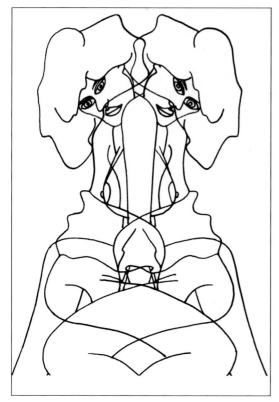

Dryads

these tributes speak of Ehrlich's character and seem to avoid dealing with his films. For a variety of reasons, some people (especially fellow animators) are very shortsighted when it comes to Ehrlich's work. Perhaps there are those who cannot get beyond the visual style which often seems like a leftover ode to the psychedelic blots of hippie culture (but in fact is more rooted in Chinese art). Certainly, the 12 tone colour scheme (picked up from serial and Indian music) that Ehrlich uses often looks like a remnant from an acid trip circa Jefferson Airplane. Furthermore, the animation, especially in early films like Robot and Precious Metal appears hesitant, awkward, and downright slow (we post-*Sesame Street* kids expect animation to be fast and seamless). Ehrlich also happens to make non-narrative works in a narrative world. But perhaps the biggest obstacle is rooted in economics. These are big films made with small material means. These are one man films made using pencils on paper and as such they (especially the early 16mm films) have a very raw, primitive appearance (i.e. cheap). All these criticisms are understandable but superficial. And fortunately, it appears, given the long overdue recognition that Ehrlich is receiving this year (his films are also available on video), that the shortsighted are in the minority.

Ehrlich's films are beautiful, complex, and passionate excavations of a flawed soul who seeks, like we all do, a harmony or rhythm. Ol' Chuck Olson once said, 'he who controls rhythm, controls'. Ehrlich's work is a means of articulating the tuneless tensions in order to find that groove that we all need to ride through life comfortably … man. Ehrlich's films, like his life, sometimes fail, they succumb to redundancy, and occasionally the GRAND softie in him creeps too strongly into his work and pushes aside the calm quiet of wisdom. But failure, error, it's all life. Yet defeat is momentary. Ehrlich doesn't pitch a tent stake in the ground. He gathers his strength, mends his aches, soothes his ego's sorrow, and gets right back into the game. Led by the same stubborn determination, he resumes his struggle all over again. The sun is new again, each day.

[Originally appeared in the October 2002 edition of *Animation World Magazine*. Reprinted with permission of Animation World Network.]

Filmography of David Ehrlich

1976	*Metamorphosis*
1976	*Album Leaf*
1977	*Robot*
1977	*Vermont Etude*
1978	*Oedipus at Colonus* (45 Second Animated Hologram)
1979	*Robot Two*
1979	*Vermont Etude, No. 2*
1980	*Precious Metal*
1981	*Fantasies*: Animation of Vermont Schoolchildren (Producer and Co-Director)
1982	*Dissipative Dialogues*
1983	*Precious Metal Variations*
1983	*Ranko's Fantasy* (45 Second Animated Hologram)
1984	*Albert Bridge Presents Olympics* (Producer)
1984	*Phallacy* (45 Second Animated Hologram)
1984	*Point*
1985	*Kunin Inauguration Psa*
1985	*Perpetual Revival* (Co-Director with A. Petringenaru, Romania)
1986	*Dissipative Fantasies*
1987	*Pixel*
1987	*Oedipus at Colonus, No. 2* (45 Second Animated Hologram)
1987	*Academy Leader Variations* (Producer And Co-Director)
1987	*Animation '87* (Producer)
1988	*Dryads*
1989	*Animated Self-Portraits* (Producer and Co-Director)
1990	*A Child's Dream*
1991	*Dance of Nature* (Co-Director with K.Sletten, Norway)
1993	*Genghiz Khan* (Producer)
1994	*Etude*
1995	*Interstitial Wavescapes*
1996	*Robot Rerun*
1997	*ASIFA Variations*
1999	*Radiant Flux*
2001	*Color Run*
2002	*Taking Color for a Walk*
2002	*Current Events*
2005	*Three Songs*

Chapter 20

Steven Woloshen's Fun With Science (2002)

Didre Novo

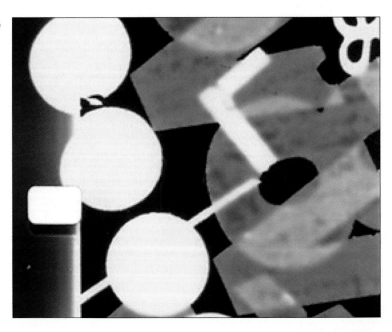

Experimental animation implies experimentation, experimentation implies science. A scientist enters the lab with a question and when he leaves, he hopes to have an answer. And it's certainly an apt analogy of the scratch films of Montreal animator, Steven Woloshen. Since he was a child, Woloshen has been using film as his lab. On it, he has simply wanted to see what he could get away with, to find that point when film is no longer film anymore. But don't be fooled, Woloshen's work is not cold and analytical; each scrape, slash and stroke is fuelled by a deep passion, love and even mischievousness.

If his method doesn't convince you, then check out his means. Woloshen receives no bursaries or grants to make his films. They are self-financed from his day job as a driver in the feature film industry. Between pedal pushing, he works on film concepts and at night gives them light. Woloshen is about as close as you can get to the essence of independent animation. Woloshen's reasoning about not applying for funding grants is twofold. On one hand, he simply doesn't have the patience to sit around waiting for decisions. 'I am in awe of people who can make an application for a grant and wait six months before they even lift a pencil to do it. I've got these ideas in my head and I've got the let them out. The only way to do that is to do them.' Secondly, there is a puritan component; 'Independent to me means all the raw materials are sitting around me. If I have an idea I can wake up tomorrow and do it. I've got five or six pieces on sound transferred onto magnetic. I've got thousands of feet of clear and black leader and if I want to start right now on something I can just do it. That's really liberating.' Of course, the independence has had its setbacks; despite making animation for almost twenty years, Woloshen is virtually unknown in the animation world. So let's end the obscurity here and now.

'I found animation by accident', says Woloshen, 'I was kind of bored. I was interested in what film would look like if I just played around on my own and I had no other means to make a film. What could I do with film and scraps lying about the house?' Well, Woloshen didn't hold back. He smashed open super 8 cartridges, took a pair of scissors and scraped along the film. He filled his parent's bathroom sink with bleach and dumped film cans in it. And he even attached film to the wheels of his bicycle and then rode the bike through their Laval suburb

Steven Woloshen

Ditty Dot Comma just to see what would happen. Throughout his scientific experiments, his parents never blinked an eye. 'They never stopped me at all. They never looked at me and said, "don't waste our precious bleach". If I wanted to spend the entire day in the basement projecting films, they let me.'

Film was an ideal release for a pent-up boy. 'When I was growing up, I was really into destruction. I thought it was a great thing. It wasn't vandalism. Not against anyone else. Once my dad gave us a project to dismantle our shed. Most people would do it plank by plank, but I really got off on the idea of literally destroying. I like the chaos in that. In the first super 8 films there was a lot of rage, the scraping, emulsion shards flying everywhere. It was nice to let loose.'

Woloshen continued to hammer, bang, saw, and grind on his own until 1972, when, at the age of 12, he joined a casual YMCA film club. 'All they had a budget to do was show NFB movies and when we did stuff all they did was give us some clear leader and a sharpie marker. They told us to draw pictures between each sprocket. We'd edit them together and projected them. I was surprised that if you had no money, you could still make a film.'

In 1980, Woloshen enrolled at Montreal's Concordia University. He took film production. The course was divided into production and studio. Woloshen opted for the latter, which meant that students did individual projects with minimal crew and money. Woloshen focussed on producing small documentaries, but on the side, he started making scratch animations. 'I had all this footage and art material, so I laid film across a big table and started scratching here and there. After about a year, I liked the scratch films better.' When the year-end screenings approached, Woloshen found that his documentary, *You're No Fun*, (1983), collage film, Hey Papa Dey (1983) and animation, *Didre Novo* (1983) were all accepted. 'I thought that if these scratch films were being received in equal proportion to these documentaries that I was working way too hard on and spending way too much money on, I might as well keep doing them.'

During his studies, Woloshen was exposed to more experimental films. 'I saw Len Lye and *So Is This* by Michael Snow, and of course McLaren's films. I had watched McLaren's films in high school. We had no choice. You always saw a McLaren film. He was a big influence. You see the materials he's using, the marker, clear leader etc. ... and it's nice to watch.'

Thanks to McLaren, Woloshen also began to understand exactly what he wanted and didn't want. 'McLaren had such good ideas and I felt that the NFB reduced it to a small idea. His films were always 1:33, the prints were awful, and they never seemed to be re-done. So I said ... if I'm gonna do this ... I'm gonna take a small idea and make it look big.' Woloshen then and there decided only to work in 35mm cinemascope. 'I'm not gonna show it on video. I want to show it on film to people sitting in cinemas.'

Ironically, given the McLaren influence, Woloshen's attempt to land a job at the NFB met with a negative result. 'After Concordia, in 1984, I knocked on Douglas McDonald's door [McDonald, the head of the English Animation Department, was generally pooed upon for his mediocre bureaucrat-inspired 'vision'] and showed him what I was doing. He saw my three Concordia films and his response was basically, "thank you" and "goodbye". That was discouraging.'

Aside from a few commissioned pieces including the loop *Love Stinks* for Bachar Chabib's film, *Memoirs* (1984) and *Los Endos* (1996), a homage to Stan Brakhage, Woloshen stopped producing films. Throw in his inability to get a job, and you've got one frustrated young man. In 1993, Woloshen bought a one-way ticket to Vancouver. He floated around doing odd jobs in the feature industry (where he had worked since graduating) and then got work at the Vancouver film lab, Alpha Cine. 'What really got me back into doing my own things was working at Alpha Cine. I had access to everything: clear leader, editing equipment (which I worked on because I was a negative cutter). I could play around with the film without destroying it. I learned a lot at the lab. Everything I wanted to make film with surrounded me on a bench.'

Despite the access to equipment, he quickly became frustrated with the film scene in Vancouver and returned to Montreal in 1999. 'I started *Get Happy* in Vancouver, but otherwise, Vancouver offered me nothing. I went to Cineworks a few times, but everyone was into narrative fiction films. I got no inspiration there, so I came home and suddenly it all started coming out.' Since returning to Montreal, Woloshen has made six films in just over three years.

And how does one manage to make films as a hobby of sorts? There are innumerable stories told about young dreamers working high paying studio gigs by day and turning to their own projects at night. In most cases, the scenario fails. They either become too enticed by the nice salary or are simply too burnt out at night. How does Woloshen succeed while others fail? 'I've been working in the feature industry since 1984. I've done all sorts of jobs: boom operator, cut rushes, driver, whatever … They pay good money, the film is over, and I'm free to be me. I'm walking a thin line right now.' Still, Woloshen has managed to find a system. As a driver, he spends a lot of time not driving so he often uses that time to work out the concept for his films. When the feature work ends, he can go home and toss his brains on the film. Woloshen sees nothing strange about this process and points out that many artists have had to juggle their work with 'real' jobs. 'I remember that artists used to wear suits and ties, have real jobs, like Brakhage. If they can do it, why can't I? Why do I have to sign up for a grant of $40,000, sit in a café, get disillusioned (ok, that's an extreme example)? Why go that way when others have done it the other way?'

Of course, Woloshen's method requires a lot of self-discipline, but on the other hand, it certainly brings up the issue of WHY one creates. In a time when kids are spending thousands of dollars to, if they're lucky, come away with a short film from their school, one has to wonder what the motivations are behind, not the schools (we know their angle), but the students. 'I can't imagine anything more sad then spending $15,000 to make a 30 second pure animation and that being in your hand as the only thing you've got to show people until you get a job. These technologies really suck people's money dry.' Ideally, one makes art out of an urgent need to unleash whatever the hell it is that swallowing their head. This means you absolutely MUST find a way to get rid of that fog, ache, or itch; whether it means maxing credit cards, pumping gas, flipping burgers; whatever. When Woloshen gets that itch, he doesn't wait for someone to tell him when he can start, he simply opens his closet door, rips off some feet of leader and let's loose.

Woloshen is a rarity. He's a man well aware of the power of origin. 'The more we go to the future, the more I want to go back. I keep on going back. What are the roots of light, vision, and motion? What about the projector's role in beaming light? How is film made anyway?' Like an 18th century British empiricist, Woloshen is a tinkerer, hobbyist, and a philosopher of experience. Knowledge for Woloshen comes from getting your hands dirty, from doing, from being. The toe-tapping, body-shaking sensations that you get while watching *Get Happy* and *Ditty Dot Comma,* or the more slithering sensual vibration unearthed during *Babble on Palms,* are the message. There's no secret society code. Every scrape, chisel, colour, shape and mark IS the meaning.

By creating a fairly strict series of codes for himself, Woloshen is liberated from the pressures that face many other contemporary artists. He doesn't make films to get jobs. He doesn't make films to make money or even to break even. He makes them simply because he thinks people might be interested in seeing what he has to say and because he needs to relieve that relentless ache. Harmony comes from finding a rhythm in life. Once you've got your tune, you're set, you're in control. Woloshen, it seems, has found his pace. 'There is nothing that's going to stop me from making more films. There is no reason for me to stop because there was no reason for me to start.'

Filmography of Stephen Woloshen

1977	*Brushstrokes*
1978	*Line and Dot*
1982	*Son of Dada*
1982	*Cat's Cradle*
1983	*Didre Novo*
1983	*You're No Fun ...*
1983	*Hey Papa Dey*
1984	*Pepper Steak*
1984	*Love Stinks*
1996	*Los Endos*
1999	*Get Happy*
2000	*MeMeMaMa*
2001	*Ditty Dot Comma*
2001	*The Cave*
2002	*The Babble on Palms*
2002	*Bru Ha Ha!*
2003	*Cameras Take Five*
2003	*Minuet*
2004	*Two Eastern Hair Lines*
2004	*Shaving Shania*
2004	*SNIP*

Chapter 21

The Odysseys of Mati Kütt (2002)

Little Lilly

Mati Kütt was born in Tallinn in 1947. His father worked for a transportation company in Viljandi and his mother was a housewife. As a boy Kütt studied art for a year in Viljandi: 'Mother supported the idea and I remember a smock was sewn for me and paints were bought, but as other boys did more realistic things, I quit after a year. Kütt finished secondary school in Viljandi and then went to the Technical University where he stayed for four years, until 1968. 'Young children are asked what they want to be', says Kütt, 'and I always wanted to be an artist. But, as my grandfather and father had real jobs, I followed their wishes and instead went to university to become an engineer. But I didn't like it and left university.'

In 1974, Kütt learned that a man named Rein Raamat was having a competition to find animators for Joonisfilm, a new drawn animation division of the state studio, Tallinnfilm. 'Rein Radme, whom I knew from the university and was a book illustrator, and I, discussed the competition and applied even though we didn't think we would be accepted. But we were picked. I still don't understand why because my drawing ability was quite weak', says Kütt.

With new directors needed and extra money available, Joonisfilm assigned three directors to make episodes for the short film *1+1+1* (1981). Kütt's contribution was *Monument*, about a man who has the overwhelming task of carrying gigantic monuments to their places of display. He becomes so overburdened by the monument's weight and his surroundings that he stumbles and falls; the monument he carries lands on him and he in turn becomes a monument.

Mati Kütt

Monument is a fairly lightweight and unremarkable piece about the pressures that we place upon ourselves, but it certainly shows signs of Kütt's later black humour.

Kütt would not make another film for eight years. He spent the rest of the 1980s working primarily as an animator and artist on Avo Paistik's (one of two directors in the studio) films. His next film was *Labyrinth* (1989). With its frantic and dirty atmosphere – created with a scratch-on-film technique, and populated with feckless characters who run about feverishly, *Labyrinth* (as the title suggests) explores the theme of entrapment and aimlessness in contemporary society.

In 1992, Kütt produced, in Estonia's puppet studio division, Nukufilm, what remains his masterwork: *Smoked Sprat Baked in The Sun*. *Sprat* is a comically surreal opera about a man who lives unhappily under the sea. In this inverted fairy tale, the man under the sea catches a fish from the dry land above. When he releases the fish, he is granted three wishes. When he releases a fish he has caught from dry land, the fish grants him three wishes. After a night of contemplation, the man asks for a woman, a big tool (penis),

Button's Odyssey

and a minister's portfolio (a cushy government job). *Sprat* is an incredibly unique and beautiful anti-fairytale. The happiness that the man finds through his wishes is clearly sarcastic, especially when one considers that Kütt has created an inverted world where people live in the water and fish on land. In our world, it takes more than a big dick and a career to find happiness.

Sprat wasn't all that fantastical, as the film also reflected the challenges facing the newly independent nation of Estonia. For the

175

first time in over fifty years, the Estonian people had their own political representatives. There was now an opportunity to express and act upon one's desires and wishes. But these desires appeared to be as crass and selfish as they were under the other ideological system.

With his next film, *Little Lilly*, (1995), Kütt again creates a tale both comical and philosophical. This time it concerns a little girl, Lilly, who is angered by her father's contradictory nature. He yearns to fly, yet continually kills flies. In protest, she decides to starve herself until she is as small as a fly. The magic of Kütt's films is found in the way they seamlessly weave between dream and reality. The viewer is never certain about what is true or false. And this is precisely the point in *Little Lilly*. Too often adults reduce the world to binary opposites instead of allowing their rich, but now dormant, imaginations to evolve and create new and varied possibilities.

Kütt had the idea for *Lilly* as early as 1981, but because of his strained relationship with Raamat, he wasn't able to make the film for about fifteen years. While making *Sprat*, Kütt realized that his daughter was growing up fast. 'People started asking me', says Kütt, 'why don't you ever make films for children?' and I thought they were right and I should do something like that'.

But *Little Lilly* is not a typical children's film. A common theme in Estonian children's literature, theatre and film is the conflict between the rich imaginations of the young and the increasingly stagnant, matter-of-factly nature of adults. In *Lilly*, for example, the father wants to fly but is unable to see the hypocrisy of his on-going killing of flies.

Little Lilly actually led to some lucrative commercial work. Some Japanese advertisers saw *Lilly*, liked Kütt's style and commissioned four short commercials from him. With one exception, the pieces are conceptually weak, although they remain stylistically interesting.

With *Underground* (1998), Kütt headed into different technical territory combining his oil paint style and pixillation. In the pixillated scenes, we see a young dancer making a series of ordered, carefully structured movements. But under the three dimensional world inhabited by the dancing girl, perhaps orchestrating her movements, is a two-dimensional world (painted and traditionally animated) of randomness and chaos. 'It was an absurd enough approach', says Kütt, 'but something that was necessary to bring out the desired effect'.

Heraclitus's words immediately come to mind: 'The cosmos works of harmony and tensions … From the strain of binding opposites

comes harmony'. The idea that life is a continuous flow is but one of the themes in *Underground*. There is also the issue of perception. The two dimensions and their two viewpoints suggest that reality is subjective. One person hears harmony while another hears noise. There is no single eye from which to see, but many, from different perspectives, with different minds, at different times. Nothing is fixed, all is changing. As Aristotle noted in *Poetics*, if I see a blanket,

Little Lilly (both images)

maybe I miss the bed, but if I see the bed, I miss the room. Conversely, if I see a room, perhaps I miss the details within. Everything moves; nothing remains the same.

'It's the tendency', says Kütt, 'that as one becomes more experienced and sees more and grows, that one should be able to make more sweeping generalizations, be able to bring aspects of one's life and experience together and mix them, come to some conclusions'.

Kütt's most recent film, *Button's Odyssey*, (2002) follows the journey of a button as it travels in search of its place in life. Along the way, Button meets a variety of strange characters, becomes separated from his brain and, finally, comes to rest on a scarecrow's coat. The matter of free will and determinism is central to this bizarre tale. Do we determine the course of our lives or are we simply unwitting participants led by outside forces? The unpredictable nature of the journey itself that leads up to this moment seems to answer that question. This is an age-old philosophical question, which certainly Kütt poses from the unique position of Estonia. Estonia is now free, but did Estonians really cause their own freedom or was it just the result of a series of outside factors? Is Estonia even really free now? Kütt seems to suggest that Estonia, like Button, remains in search of its function or purpose.

Kütt brings this strange tale to life though a dazzling array of visual images created with oil paint, stop-motion metal figures, cut-out, bits of drawn animation, live-action, what looks like sand or even coffee animation. Kütt clearly remains at the top of his game, continually producing strikingly original imagery with content that is paradoxically complex and yet fundamentally simple. And like his colleagues, Kütt never lets his work delve too far into heavy-handed pretentiousness. Almost every scene is laced with moments of comic absurdity (e.g. cows performing a pyramid, mundane opera lyrics like 'the cow is out of breath') that keep audiences guessing and laughing – once they realize they are actually allowed to laugh!

Kütt had to wait four years to get funding for *Button's Odyssey*. Even then, he was forced, for the first time, to look beyond Nukufilm and Joonisfilm for support. It's not clear what the problem was, but Joonisfilm's explanation was that they only had money left in the budget to make a small film. So Kütt was presented with the opportunity and accepted, but proposed a more ambitious and expensive project. He was asked to create something more in line with the budget, but apparently refused. Kütt's feeling is that the film could easily have been made by Joonisfilm, 'but as they are dealing more with real drawn animation and computer graphics, they somehow decided that my mixed technique wouldn't suit them very well. Although a work place was available and no one was using it, evidently there wasn't enough good will on their part.' Who knows where the truth lies, but Kütt certainly possesses an often hard-line and uncompromising artistic nature. But why should he compromise? Stubbornness aside, Kütt is easily one of the most interesting and innovative animation artists in the world. His investigations into the nature of humanity are tinged with a soulful mix of classical philosophy and absurdist humour and are enhanced by a consistently interesting, modern stylistic and technical approach that combines classical painting with pixillation, cut-out and 3D technologies.

Unfortunately, Kütt has not received the same international acclaim as that bestowed upon fellow countryman, Priit Pärn. But there are those who'd argue that Kütt is a more interesting artist than Pärn. Whereas Pärn has settled into a comfortable graphic style and has influenced a swarm of followers, Kütt's work, while recognizable, is always changing, always in search of itself. 'Of course, I continue my way. It's normal for an artist to try to find his aesthetic. When I look at these young animators at Joonisfilm I see that their work looks so much like Priit Pärn's. This is very sad because they should be going their own way. It's better. That's just my opinion though', says Kütt.

'I still don't feel that I know what my personal style is. My opinion is that an artist should be changing all the time. Otherwise it becomes boring for you and the audience if you deal with the same topics all the time. Jüri Arrak, for example, claims he's found his style or god and closed the door. For me', says Kütt, 'this means stagnation'.

For Kütt, making films is 'simply' about living life. 'What's the purpose of making films? What's the meaning of life, I ask? It's to live. It's how people choose to express themselves. I paint and make films. Another drives a taxi.'

[Excerpted from the book, *Between Genius and Utter Illiteracy: A Story of Estonian Animation*, Varrak Press, 2003.]

Filmography of Mati Kütt	
1981	*Monument* (from 1+1+1)
1988	*Animated Self-Portraits*
1989	*Labyrinth*
1992	*Smoked Sprat Baking in the Sun*
1994	*Little Lilly*
1997	*Underground*
2002	*Button's Odyssey*

179

Chapter 22

A Moment, Please: Koji Yamamura (2003)

Your Choice

A moment. I was 13. Hog's Back Falls. Ottawa. Summer. Doing a tongue dance with Traci Ridgewell. First girl I shared spit with. She had braces. Cut my lip. By summer's end she ditched me like a weighted leaf in fall. Heartbreak.

A moment. 13-year-old Koji Yamamura wants to see his drawings move. He reads a short column about animation, gets a Super 8 camera, and makes his first animation film. It was a silly film, a collection of gags. Who cares? He felt exhilarated.

I've been thinking a lot about childhood lately and re-visiting many moments from those times. It's nothing new. Everyone does it. Memory is a dialogue. We re-visit the past (a fictional past at that) and uncover the roots of various ailments of the present. Memory gets us off our island and helps us negotiate the present.

Within memory, moments flourish. Memory uncovers the small moments we usually overlook in everyday life. In each case, the process of working through a moment, with its fever of scattered senses, mattered more than the actual kiss or film. And it's in these small moments that we find the essence of our lives. It's a choice between living in the moment or for the moment. To live for the moment is to reduce life to an illimitable blur, to ignore those moments that ultimately comprise your core. To live in the moment is to savour each morsel. No matter how seemingly insignificant, the crumbs make the man.

Japanese animator, Koji Yamamura's films seek the essence of life within these small, and too often overlooked, moments. In this world, life is sacred. Every ounce is consumed and enjoyed. Life is

Koji Yamamura

Above: *Mt. Head*

Facing page:
Top: *Sandwiches*
Bottom: *Mt. Head*

pleasure. Pleasure comes from those individual moments. Yama-mura's early characters, Karo and Pyrobupt are the anti-Vladimir and Estragon. They await no one. They embrace the moment. In *A House* (1993), they build a house together before winter approaches. In *Imagination* (1993), they use their imagination to forget about a rainy day. Friendship. Collaboration. Communication. Imagination. Satisfaction. That's it. That's all. Life shared. Life loved.

In *Bavel's Book* (1996, inspired by Jorge Luis Borges) and *Kid's Castle* (1995), the excitement, power and realism of the objects only exist because of the tenacity of imagination within each child. Without the children's ability to let go and share themselves with their book or toy, they remain objects, fragments of a dead tree littered with indecipherable ink stains.

In *Your Choice* (1999), moments are defined by choices we make. Will it rain or shine? Do I need an umbrella? Shall I visit the barber or dentist? Choices involve the untangling of emotions and reason. Choices involve communication with experience, the experience of our past or the wisdom of those who've gone before us.

182

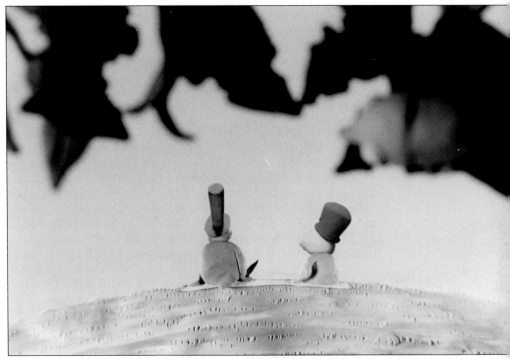

183

To choose does not necessarily mean to be free. Raoul has choices forced upon him. If he had chosen to take care of his hair and teeth, he would not be making these painful choices. In the end, Raoul avoids making a decision. His pain becomes so bad he runs to the dentist. The waiting room is full. The only choice is the barber. What Raoul doesn't yet understand is that if we avoid choices, they will be made regardless.

Sometimes, as Yamamura's 2003 Oscar nominated, *Mt. Head* (2002) suggests, we make bad choices. Sometimes we can go too far and turn a moment into a womb, a shelter from those around us. In the cave, the stingy man lives not as an echo, but as a shadow. He is surrounded by garbage, a rubbishy ramification that staves off the threshold of despair. He wastes nothing. He shares nothing. He enjoys nothing. Cherries are shoved into his mouth untasted. When he chooses to let a tree grow on his head, it becomes an attraction for Tokyo workers. They take and take. He can't handle it and pulls the tree out. All that remains is a hole. People come to fish instead. The man flees in horror and finally kills himself by jumping into the hole in his head. Ecological warning aside, a man who embraces only himself, lives and dies alone.

You're born. You die. In between you try and do a bit of this and a bit of that while mingled together with a bunch of other people *Bavel's Book* who were born at the same time and who are also trying to do a

Bavel's Book

bit of this and a bit of that. We're all strung together in a single book trying to create our own verse before the page turns. To leave a unique ineradicable stain of memories and moments that bleed through the pages is not the best we can hope for, to try is.

Those who deny the past, deny memory. Without memory they are nothing. Those too who seek escape in the past live in dreams and nightmares not in the moments of memory. For Yamamura, the past is a bridge to the present. He fuses the adult's memories with the child's moments. Unframed memories breathed as the irrevocable instant of a child.

It is this innate ability to speak as both child and adult that ensures the permanence of Yamamura's stain. He has unearthed the forgotten spaces, the cracks, gaps, and out-of-frame moments that embody the essence of adult and child. Without them, like the stingy man in *Mt. Head*, we remain as alone as islands.

[Originally appeared in the 2003 Tough Eye Animation Festival catalogue.]

Filmography of Koji Yamamura

1985	*Nature History*
1985	*One Night Serenade*
1987	*Aquatic*
1989	*Japanese-English Pictionary*
1990	*Perspektivenbox*
1991	*The Elevator*
1993	*A House*
1993	*The Sandwiches*
1993	*Imagination*
1995	*Pacusi*
1995	*Kipling Jr.*
1995	*Kid's Castle*
1996	*Bavel's Book*
1999	*Your Choice*
1999	*Jubilee* (music video)
2002	*Mt. Head*

Chapter 23

Ode To Martha Colburn
(2003)

Background: This is definitely the oddest piece of the bunch. Martha Colburn is a Baltimore born filmmaker. Most of her work is super 8 – a fusion of scratch, collage, drawing and cut-out. She currently resides in The Netherlands. Go to google.com and type in her name to find out more, and do your self a big favour and find her work. It's funny, provocative, sexy and nifty. I found it difficult to sit down and write a straightforward piece on her work, so I sat down, watched all of her films and jotted down my reactions. Here is the result. It's confusing, but I think it really captures the essence of Colburn's manic work.

XXX Amsterdam

186

Oh heavens above thank you thank you thank you. Ya see I've been at a crossroads with ol' animation of late. All they seem to offer me are all these tender precious oh-so-fucking sensitive carefully crafted take forever to make HIGH ART 'works' or these bland ha ha goofy fart vomit gags fooling themselves and the shits who watch them into thinking theyre real original unique rebellious punk rock like avril lavigne (shes from round here ya know) give me a break but oh baby thank you for Martha first off Martha is real sexy I'd like to suck her toes or even naw on her bones any ol day we met in Utrecht I was rude She was rude She won Took the damn chair we said we were saving Bitch Didn't know who she was then I saw her films sort like umm albert ayler hangin with betty page roger corman and William castle crazy out of control in your face constant zoom pop art collage painted over with occasional photo-cut out figures trash culture at its finest a THANK YOU in the faces of all those craft/technique perfections who dominate the animation world martha's having a good time and so am i No high falutin deas here just groovy bug attacks cat loving dogs a world gone zombie dogs getting off on cats hey loser xray vision doesn't mean youre gonna see titties and skin just ba ba ba ba bone buddy you wanna see what's underneath them panties Really underneath tis all bone that's it all if there's a punk rock animator tis Martha images like boxers they shift duck dance and jab manic zooms like non-stop jabs teasing you tappin your chin before the right comes smash smash smashin into your jaw knockout don't look for no safety net no hand to grab onto there aint no core no fixed no nothing to protect you sex sex sex so much sex it aint sexy no more even Martha strips ala betty page choppy blurry those damn zooms

Evil of Dracula

I Can't Keep Up (left)
Lift Off (right)

cant focus not getting turned on her antitease spread eagled women all over the place but they aint doing so well getting their toes flossed eyes are all zombied out with fangs Martha likes poets and musicians jad fair does a lot of crazy non sequitor accomp. and check out this 99 Hooker dude especially his manic apeshit world gone mad I cant keep up guys lost pace with a world what's on tv in marthas world I never had a pervert in my pool but is Clinton really a perv He got his wang chunged big deal what guy doesn't are all guys perverts aren't there any woman perverts is Martha a perv hey maybe fatty did put the bottle up her stream but shit man she went with it whose the perv the perv or the one who follows the perv? Are animals into kink like us are we animals for being kink what's kink Lola? Ever seen an 8 legged cock swallowing spider or web shooting titties do spiders smoke after sex everyone else seems to smoke why do people smoke they smoke everywhere what the fuck its gonna kill you no ifs and butts (heh heh) course life is killing you too what's the diff between eating bigmacchocolateeggsfriesoilgreaseanimalfat and smoking fuck a duck is this trash culture one mans jewel another gals trash? Trash is used lived loved absorbed dumped eaten shitted trash has gone through the system it's been taken to the ropes jewels just touched admired behind glass protected precious what kinda life is that Life unlived

188

is a liveless life toe-tar-tar we neglect the obvious like toes toes toes toes pedgsicles ha ha why not toes probably tastier and better than fudgsicles but I like fudgesicles so fuck you marta what's with toe sucking anyway never tried it either way lots o folks seem to dig it toe jam do farmers get their toes pecked by chicks my not real pops had this little fuck of a dog who likes to bite toes that freaks me out leaves my fucking toes alone doggie go watch some cat porn freak did napoleon have a foot underneath that coat he was capital nut. Man oh man I could go on and on but I need to get some lunch Like being in a world with a personality disorder thats what so real bout Martha cause this world that seems so weird is really pretty damn accurate s'like shes making uncensored documentaries unhindered by narrative free for all guttural automatic concrete poetry maybe ill have some fat but hey dey giggly day lets just say that I dig Martha whos living and loving it all and not fussing about polish just seeing the world as it is not as we delusion makes me feel fucking free free free possibilities. life IS beautiful.

Martha Colburn and friend in disguise

Filmography of Martha Colburn

1994   *Asthma*
1996   *What's on?*
1997   *I Can't Keep Up*
1997   *Persecution in Paradise*
1997   *Evil of Dracula*
1998   *Lift Off*
1998   *A Toetally Soleful Feeture Pedsination*
1998   *There's A Pervert In Our Pool!*
1999   *Spiders In Love: An Arachnogasmic Musical*
2002   *Skelehellavision*
2002   *Cats Amore*
2002   *Big Bug Attack*
2003   *Secrets of Mexuality*
2004   *Amsterdam XXX*

Chapter 24

Top left:
Somewhere;
Top right:
Time Streams;
Bottom left:
Passe-Partout;
Bottom right:
Reflecting Pool

Fragments of Stephanie Maxwell (2004)

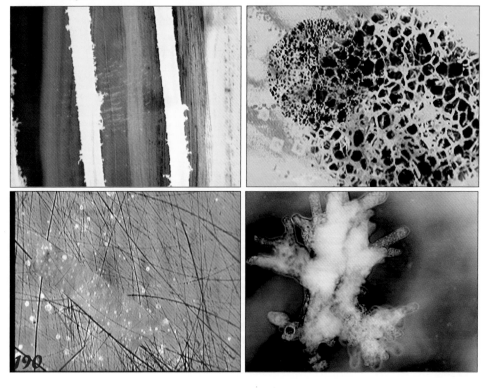

ackground: *Another odd piece. Stephanie Maxwell is a Rochester-based experimental animator. Stephanie visited me in Ottawa during the summer of 2004. I interviewed her about for about three hours. As I went through the tapes, I just loved so much of what she said. There were all these little fragments that captured that I thought captured the spirit of her work better than anything I might write. Stephanie's films try to take us beyond the surface to see the many minute little worlds and realities that our eyes don't often show us. It seemed appropriate that a piece about her work should also be experimental and philosophical. I don't think Stephanie liked the piece.*

Ramble Bamble Preamble

Stephanie Maxwell's work gets me. Her work is fuelled by a breathless, giddy energy and passion that seeps through every whore of a pore. Like a child, she is excited by a seemingly minute discovery – like an anthill, river or a rock. Maxwell's work is an extension of that explorative part of our childhood. She has a tenacious fascination with the natural world; a world that too many of us (myself included) have left behind in favour of simulated realities.

Fragments

Family worked in Hollywood in the movie industry. Didn't want to do it. It wasn't interesting to me. Spent a lot of time on movie sets.

A vacation without tourist markers, just the peripheral sights, sounds and sensations experienced whether it's trolls in Norway (*Nocturne*), night driving (*Driving Abstractions*), water, or time itself (*Time streams*)

During the summer we camped a lot because it was cheaper to camp than pay rent. We'd catch fish for dinner. Brother and I would split a wetsuit and we'd spear trout. We'd snorkel and catch dinner. My mom would buy peaches and potatoes.

Stephanie Maxwell

Time Streams = my time is not your time but it is THE time.

Was interested in science and math. Went in and out of college. Spent time overseas, under the pretext of going to school, but then quit and travelled. Painting and collaging and trying to make myself an artist at the same time studying science because it was an aesthetic experience.

I'd been diving since I was 12. It was so incredible underwater. Studied marine

191

biology. All the crud I'd see underwater ... all this stuff under the water that I didn't understand as a teenager I learned were colonies of incredible organisms.

The whole physical sensation of being in this other place. After a while I felt completely at home. It was very second nature to me. That also gave me an experience to create these other experiences... you really feel it. I know what it is to be in other places. Cinematically, you go for a ride, create other places. It was so visually beautiful as well. It was escape into beauty and colour and difference.

Connecting with disconnectedness.

We went on a lot of car trips ... as a town was approaching ... they'd say ... it's coming ... and I'd drop down in the car and look up ... and I'd see the lights of the town flashing above me ... and then they'd be gone. That was entertainment for me. Sometimes I'd only concentrate on my peripheral stuff.

I lived in an abstract world because it was fun.

They called me the 'philosopher' in class. Sewed my own clothes. Do I become a scientist or do art? Artists were more fun.

Used to find film in the streets and would chew on it.

Biology, geology, science, diving, ...real hands on-ness ... working small, crafts, sewing ... I loved watching ants. I'd stalk ants to find out what they do. I was always looking small.

Patterns and colours of minerals. Gems. Patterns of rocks. I still love it. Looking at what's out there. I love to beachcomb.

It was always play for me.

I was just going on the ride. I felt that I'd find something, but I needed to enjoy myself. I was always moving onwards ... it was always self-improvement.

One day the shit-luck thing happened ... I was driving in Berkeley and hadn't remember that there was a Len Lye show at the Pacific Film Archive. I wanted to see it and forgotten ... but I was driving and drove by the archive and saw the sign. I was like, 'Oh yeah ...', and ordinarily there is no parking on the busy streets but I found a spot right out front, went inside, and my whole life changed.

After seeing Len Lye's work, I went home and started doing drawing on 16mm film ... but I knew he did his work on 35mm ... so the next day I went to this 35mm lab that did a lot of porn films. I asked them if they had some spare footage and they pointed to a bin of film. So I worked on 35mm.

I had a little antique movieola ... and it had a magnifying lens and I could do a strip and immediately watch it and study the results of my experiments. I noticed that I could make things appear in front or behind objects and define a three dimensional space.

Portability. Didn't need lights, cameras, crew.

Worked on Twice Upon a Time *and* Ewok's Adventures ... *assistant animator doing these pixie things ... I felt that my own work was more important.*

Sounds, especially those by regular composer, Allan Schindler work with and often against the music. Often the sounds seem to be taking us to a different space.

I don't see myself so much as an animator because of what that connotes ... I feel myself more as a filmmaker ... but I'm using digital ... maybe it's moving imagery ... visual motionist.

Even within the indie/art side there's this strange realm of experimental/abstract

... 'absolute animation' because there's nothing to follow ... how to communicate through this different way ... you can't rely on trendy or traditional drawing styles or processes ... you're on your own.

And yet you're all continually accused of looking the same ... you're all apparently derivative of McLaren or Lye.

Yes, people sometimes say, 'oh you mean like Norman McLaren'.

People are disappointing.

In experimental circles, Maxwell is criticized for not being experimental enough ... almost narrative ... and in animation it's not accepted by most animation Festivals.

The works are open ... they go into these worlds ... and its not ending ... it keeps going ... you're getting a moment with it and then it says okay ... this is the end of your ride.

Filmography of Stephanie Maxwell

1984	*GA*
1989	*Please Don't Stop*
1997	*Driving Abstractions*
1998	*Outermost*
1999	*Nocturne*
1999	*Somewhere*
2000	*Fragments*
2001	*Terra Incognita*
2002	*Passe-Partout*
2003	*Time Streams*
2004	*Reflecting Pool*
2003	*Time Streams*

193

Chapter 25

Top left:
Son of Satan;
Top right: *Chestnuts,
Icelolly*;
Bottom left:
Son of Satan;
Bottom right:
*9 in a Chimney, 10 in
a bed or Hates a
Strong Word*

JJ Villard: An Angel Betrayed (2005)

194

I see 1000 new animation shorts a year, and I'd be hard-pressed to find 100 worth viewing more than once. Every so often, however, I encounter a film that rattles, shakes, and wakes the soul; a work that shows you that at its best, animation can you take you further and deeper through the senses and intellect than any of the other arts. Over the last decade, Priit Pärn and Janno Põldma's *1895* (1995), Andreas Hykade's *Ring of Fire* (2000), and Chris Landreth's *Ryan* (2004) have been those soul-shakers. Recently, an adaptation of a Charles Bukowski story by a young Cal Arts student shook me out of my festival pre-selection numbness.

Son of Satan is told from the perspective of the informal leader of a trio of mischievous boys. To alleviate their summer boredom, the 'leader' suggests that they beat up a freckle-face kid because 'he fucked a girl under my house'. After they pummel the innocent kid, the trio forms a mock court and vote to hang him. The leader begins to have misgivings, but he feels he's gone too far to turn back. They gag and hang the boy, leaving him barely conscious. The film ends with the leader returning home to his menacing father, who mercilessly beats the boy. It's a tense, powerful, and ugly story that provokes and challenges the viewer. By revealing the doubts of this troubled kid and the obvious history of violence in his home, we are asked to sympathize with a character who initially sickened us.

Visually, *Son of Satan* looks like the remnants of an unfinished student's sketchbook. The drawings are rough and disorderly. Barely legible scribblings litter many of the frames. The voiceover is distorted and, at times, poorly acted. The soundtrack (featuring excerpts from The Stooges' Raw Power) appears suddenly like a cut-and-paste afterthought. However, when you string all the rusty bits together, *Son of Satan* transforms from apparent chaos into something special: a raw, urgent punk scream at the pain of abuse, bullying, and the cyclical nature of violence. It stands firmly against those who believe that animation must be clean, precise, and polished.

What makes *Son of Satan* all the more exceptional is that its director, JJ Villard, has already made a handful of impressive films (most students are lucky if they can make one complete film, let alone an impressive one), including two (*9 Chimneys, 10 in a Bed or Hates is a Strong Word* and *Chestnuts, Icelolly*) that stand alongside *Son of Satan* as unique, provocative explorations of scorned, abused, and lonely individuals.

Villard, who was born in England and grew up in California, was fixated on drawing at a young age. Before his senior year of high school in 1997, Villard met John Teton, an animation instructor. Teton had recently started the Earthlight Pictures Animation Train-

Son of Satan

ing Program. The program was unique in that they invited students of any age to study there. Villard was the first student.

Two years later Villard followed Teton to the Otis College of Art and Design in Los Angeles. At Otis, Villard made *Me*, a great example of a student taking a test film to its full potential. What is clearly an exercise in character animation becomes a swirling mini-tale about a raving, neurotic man suffering from self-doubt and anxiety.

In 2000, Villard decided to leave Otis for the character animation department at the renowned California Institute of the Arts. 'I knew the reputation Cal Arts had, and I wanted it', Villard says. 'My parents, along with a few loans, and a small scholarship, paid $25,000 a year for me to be fucking crazy and it was worth every penny. I did drugs, met very few girls, drank far too much and drew.' During his four years at Cal Arts, Villard produced five animation films along with a bizarre live action piece about the spiritual journey of a soccer player. Perhaps it's a symptom of his age, but all of Villard's animation films are about troubled young individuals. They are loners haunted by parents, teachers, classmates, and life in general. In *Tummy Beast* (2001), taken from a Roald Dahl poem, a little boy tries to convince his mother that there is someone living inside his stomach. In *God is So Close Now* (2002), a child flees from his parents, doctors, and teachers, fights the Pope – loses – takes the Pope's hat, and then runs, swims, and walks until he comes to a quiet forest where he decides to stay.

Villard first landed on the international festival scene with *9 in the Chimney 10 on the bed or Hates A Strong Word* (2002). Accompanied by a haunting gothic interpretation of 'Que Sera Sera' (by the band Pink Martini) that drags along like a body being drained of life, a young girl uses her sketchbook to imagine what the future holds for her. Anticipating *Son of Satan*, Villard's drawings – like those of an angry child ferociously scrawling away – are rough, almost violent, as though you're looking through a notebook of a madman.

Villard's latest film (his graduation project) is called *Chestnuts, Icelolly* (2004). A cross between Tim Burton, Diane Arbus, and Gary Panter, it's the story of a chestnut vendor who traps a boy named Rye inside a box. The vendor hopes that this will force Rye's friends to come to the stand and buy chestnuts. What the man doesn't know is that Rye has no friends. Rye is chased by a cop, booted out of school, and finally chased through the fields by the bully, Sassy, and her wild boyfriends. Accompanied by fragments of the songs 'Crimson and Clover' and 'Waiting for the Man', Villard's often jarring, off-kilter framing gives *Chestnuts* a freakish and claustrophobic intensity that aptly reflects the precarious nature of its troubled protagonist.

Given the eternally fragile state of independent animation (especially in the USA), Villard's graduation from Cal Arts in 2004 is bittersweet. Many fine student animators have teased us with brilliant works only to graduate and never be heard from again, swallowed into anonymity by animation studios. With bills and loans to pay, Villard is currently working in the story department of *Shrek 3* for Dreamworks.

What elevates Villard's work from mere adolescent angst is its soul. His characters are lost and sometimes angry, but they have a spark of faith in themselves. They see that life can be shit, that it can sometimes pummel them into the dirt, but they don't give up. They fight back. In the end, it's that acknowledgment of the darkness, the conflict, and the willingness to fight against the demons that makes his worldview life-affirming. Sure, the boy in *Son of Satan* is sitting under the bed with his menacing father within reach. He's probably going to get another beating. But he forgets for a moment and instead listens to the birds and cars, the sounds of life going on around him. The angels.

Villard's films are raw, sloppy, intense, and honest reflections of the cycle of good and bad that lives within us all. Where there is light, there is darkness, and darkness, light. We are neither one thing nor the other. With uncertain hands, Villard shows us that we're flawed and that ... you know ... THAT'S life.

[Originally appeared in *Cinemascope Magazine*, 2005.]

Filmography of JJ Villard

2000	*Me*
2001	*Tummy Trouble*
2001	*God Is So Close Now*
2002	*9 In the Chimney 10 on the Bed or Hates a Strong Word*
2003	*Son of Satan*
2004	*Chestnuts, Icelolly*

Chapter 26

Signe Baumane: Woman Mountain Horndog World

(2005)

The Witch and the Cow

I'm generalizing, but when many people think of women's films, they think of goddesses, nature, cats, flowers and pastels. Women are offered as gentle, almost virginal beings that face the daily task of fending off evil lecherous men. If they have been corrupted, it is usually the fault of a man.

Latvian/American animator and illustrator Signe Baumane makes honest women's films. In her films, women are stupid, mean, greedy, lusty, dangerous, sexy, and smart. Women are not pure, innocent creations soiled by lascivious men. They are just as faulty, contradictory, evil, and horny as any man. And what makes Baumane's work all the more potent is that she doesn't just talk the talk. Throughout her life she has challenged society's myopic gender roles.

Baumane was born in 1964 in Auce, Latvia. Her mother was a teacher and her father was an engineer. Most animators will tell you that they were drawing as soon as they could hold a pencil. Not Baumane. At age six, she wanted to be a writer. At eight, she'd written an adventure novel. At fourteen, her writing was published in a local newspaper. Baumane credits her mother for nurturing her love of storytelling. 'I think my Mom felt frustrated that she married and had to have children. I think she felt unfulfilled and put her hopes for fulfilment on her daughters. She thought that imagination was something to be developed in her children so she encouraged any seed of that.'

Baumane's parents were supportive of her writing, but felt that she needed more experience and education. 'The best education you could get in Soviet Union was in Moscow University so I went there to study philosophy.' It was a difficult process for Baumane because she had to learn to read and speak about complex philosophical concepts in a foreign language.

Frustrated by the limitations of language, she took a strong interest in drawing and dancing. 'Neither of them required a language that I didn't have and both of them expressed my eternal soul just wonderfully. After a few years of dancing and drawing I committed to drawing only when I saw that I could tell some longer stories via series of drawings.'

During a philosophy lecture in her final school year, a friend pulled out a newspaper clipping that said that Pilot Studio in Moscow was looking for animators. During the process of preparing for the interview, Baumane had an epiphany: 'I had three days to make up a portfolio. I forgot about lectures and started to draw. For three full days I was immersed into the logic of my imagination. There was no food, no sex, no outside interests. At the end of the three days, I knew that this was what I really wanted to do.'

199

Baumane didn't get the job. She was told that her drawing was okay; her imagination was great, but that she'd be better off finding work as a director. Pilot Studio needed animators, not directors.

In 1989, Baumane returned to Latvia and approached the Riga Animation Film Studio with her portfolio. They hired her on the spot after telling her that her portfolio was a work of genius. Baumane was so excited that she accepted a position without even asking what the job would be. It turned out to be cel painting, one of the most tedious jobs in the animation process. 'I was bored to tears. I sabotaged the work. I was late or didn't show up.' To keep Baumane from fleeing, the studio producer, Ansis Berzins, let her direct a commercial for a product of her choice. She chose socks.

In 1991, with the Soviet Union on the verge of collapse, the government gave the Riga studio more money than they knew how

The subtle side of Baumane

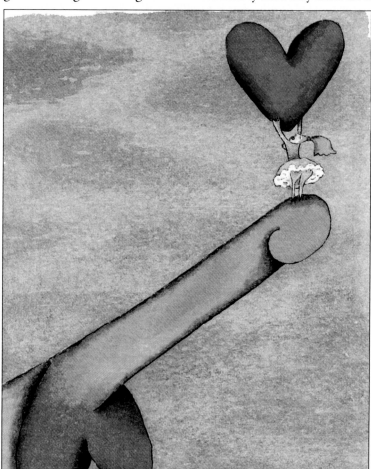

to use. They decided to find eight aspiring animators to make their own films. Baumane was chosen and she produced her first film, *The Witch and The Cow* (1991).

In *The Witch and The Cow*, Baumane uses simple drawings to tell the story of a witch who goes to the cattle barn each day to collect huge piles of cow shit. One day the witch flies into the barn and gets swept away by a stream of cow's milk. Fed up, the witch takes an axe and cuts the cow's head off. To her surprise, many smaller cows appear and charge towards her. She manages to save herself by turning into a wolf.

On one level, *The Witch and The Cow* (which was inspired by Baumane's 3-year-old son, Haralds) deals with our hypocritical relationship with animals. It also presents an overwhelmed individual who chooses to close the door on a problem rather than try to solve or confront it. 'It is all about me', says Baumane, 'My instinct when I was young was to end any situation that didn't make me happy. But the situation then becomes worse than it was.'

Following *The Witch and the Cow*, Baumane married a Russian man named Yuriy Gavrilenko, resigned from the studio and moved to Moscow. 'We got very poor and had nothing to eat and if we ever got money, Yuriy drunk them off. I decided to take things in my own hands and make some money.' Baumane took a short-lived job illustrating children's books. Baumane was offered a lot of illustrating work but the economic uncertainty due to the collapse of the Soviet Union was causing publishing companies to declare bankruptcy.

With her marriage also on the verge of collapse, Baumane learned of a competition for animated film projects in Latvia. 'I had only three days so I feverishly looked through piles and piles of storyboards and written stories to find one that may be good enough for this competition.' She found an old story called 'Tiny Shoes', submitted it, and won the grant.

Faced with financial and personal pressures in Moscow, Baumane embraced the opportunity to run home and make *Tiny Shoes* (1993). The film is about a girl who, against her father's dying wishes, goes to a castle to marry the prince of her dreams. During her journey she blinds a dragon. The dragon then eats the prince and forces the girl to marry him. After killing the dragon, the girl returns to the prince who she frees from the dragon's stomach.

Despite its fairytale overtones, *Tiny Shoes* is about as anti-fairytale as you can get. This is not your typical fairytale heroine: a weak, innocent virgin sitting around waiting for the prince to come by and swoop her up. This is a woman on a mission. She knows what she wants and will stop at nothing to get it even if this involves

201

betrayal and murder. 'Women can get that way', says Baumane. 'They want something that doesn't exist and they go like tanks after it, crushing everything on their way. If you say human race is violent and aggressive it includes women too. Where does this idea come from that women are as dainty as flowers and as sensitive as a blade of grass? Women are tanks and men are rockets.'

Visually, *Tiny Shoes* is more colourful and inventive than *The Witch and The Cow*. The backgrounds are more detailed and there is even a dash of early *Simpsons'* influence in the colour and jagged design of the characters. The fresh style came from two very different sources. Baumane's work as a children's illustrator gave her a new appreciation for backgrounds. 'Something I liked in picture books for children were the little countless details and hidden treasures in the backgrounds.' The second influence, oddly enough, was *The Simpsons*. 'The Soviet monetary system collapsed so fast that my Dad had only few days to put money of his life earnings into something. He decided on satellite antenna for the Television. I will never understand completely why he went for it but there it was and me and my son spent at least three to four hours a day watching Western civilization via small window of our comprehension. *The Simpsons* was on. I didn't understand English at that time at all but those *Simpsons* shook my world. I have never seen anything like that so stylized and alive at the same time.'

Tiny Shoes was well received internationally and remains a favourite today. The film won a Grand Prix at the Minsk International Women's film festival. Ironically, all the judges at the festival were men.

Following the completion of *Tiny Shoes*, Baumane began work on a book called *The Book of Tigers*. It was written in Russian and published in Moscow. During this time Baumane found a new prince in Swedish animator, Lasse Person. 'We met in August 1993 right after I finished *Tiny Shoes*. We met in Denmark at the Nordic Lights festival.' Within weeks the two were married in Sweden and on their way to live in Toronto. The Prince, though, was not to be. The marriage lasted four months and by January 1994, Baumane was back in Latvia.

Once again there was a call for animation film proposals and Baumane quickly turned *The Gold of the Tigers* into a film synopsis. She received a grant and began work. *The Gold of the Tigers* is undoubtedly Baumane's strangest and most mystical film – although thematically it is not so far removed from her other work. The story is about the Tigers who rule the land. The King tiger has a nightmare of a man murdering him and taking his power. *Gold of the Tigers* is a meditation on the nature of power and the violence and paranoia that it triggers. Unfortunately the film is diminished by weak drawings and, in the English version, poor narration.

During this time Baumane made a life-changing decision. 'I set a date in September to leave Latvia for New York. I was pissed off at the Studio and at the whole grant system. I guess I was also pissed off at myself for living at my parent's house at age 30. I was pissed off that my relationships with men were not more successful. I was pissed that Latvia was so small and there was a very little room for roaming and breathing.

'I wanted challenge. I wanted space. I wanted a bigger pool of bigger money and possible mates.'

Five Fucking Fables

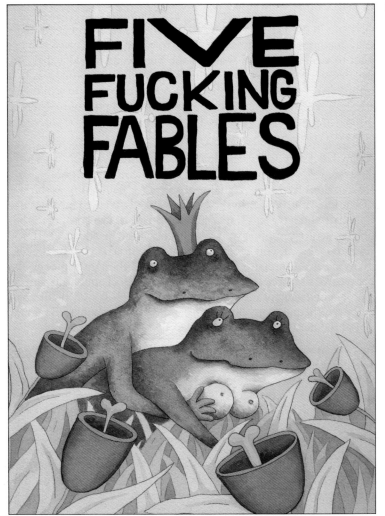

This was not, in itself, an unusual decision, except Baumane had decided to leave her eight-year-old son behind. Most people are appalled that a woman could move away from her child. However, I know of many male animators who have done the same thing and their decision is rarely questioned. 'You know how some animals when they are trapped or cornered to free themselves chew off the limb that is caught?' asks Baumane. 'I felt like the trapped animal and my son was that limb. It was a question of life and death. I had to go otherwise I wouldn't live. I didn't leave my son on a street or in a bad situation. He lives in a good house with people that brought me up and they know what they are doing. He is loved and cared for. I love him very much too. I just can't be in that house in that country right now.'

Arriving in New York with $300 in her pocket, Baumane initially sold drawings on the streets of Soho to eat and pay rent. When her plan to find illustration work in the publishing world failed, she decided to try and meet some animators. 'Bill [Plympton] was first on my list. I gave him a call and brought over my portfolio. He spent an hour with me looking at my films and portfolio. Then he offered me a project. I started work on his feature, *I Married a Strange Person*.'

Baumane didn't make another film for three years. 'I was very frustrated. My creative juices were overflowing. I was going crazy. Like an unmilked cow.' A major problem for Baumane was the lack of a studio or producer in the USA. Unlike Latvia or countries like Canada (who have the National Film Board of Canada), the US is not particularly supportive of independent art production. If you want to make art, you have to use your own dollars. 'I didn't believe in myself as an animator nor as a producer. I thought someone else has to give me money and a studio and hordes of animators and cel painters in order for me to make it happen.' However, thanks to a hefty paycheque from illustrating children's textbooks, Baumane found the nerve to try and make her next film, *Love Story*.

In *Love Story* (1998), a man and a woman's attraction for one another is interrupted by the presence of a dog and a crocodile. The woman's sexuality, represented by the dog, scares the man whose own desires are represented by the crocodile. At the film's conclusion, the man and woman unite, as do the dog and crocodile and the final image is of the dog licking the crocodile's cock. Love and sex become one.

Love Story not only marks a turning point in Baumane's geography, but also the tone of her films. The animal symbolism remains, but the tone is now more explicit. A simple white background replaced the rich settings of *Gold of the Tiger* and *Tiny Shoes*. Because of budget and time restrictions, Baumane had to do without detailed backgrounds and make do with as few drawings as possible. In the end, this three-minute film was composed of only 200 drawings. As a comparison, Baumane worked on a short commercial production the same year that used 2000 drawings. Whatever the reasoning, the minimalism is effective. The images are less cluttered which enables the viewer to engage with the characters and action more directly.

A year later, Baumane was invited to work on a project that involved fifty-two filmmakers each creating a short film based on a poem of their choice. The participants were free to choose any poem and use any technique. Influenced by the work of Jorge Luis Borges, Baumane completed *The Threatened One* in just four months.

The Threatened One opens with a hungry fox chasing, catching and killing a rabbit. Again, the animals are human stand-ins. The rabbit represents the man's fear of the sweeping effect that love has on him. The woman's love, the fox, scares him because he doesn't care about anything anymore. All rational thought has left the building. Everything that once mattered is gone. He thinks only of this

Dentist

DENTIST

an animated short by Signe Baumane

woman. This love is a threat to his identity and to his life. To be consumed by love is to lose yourself, to become one with your lover. For Borges and Baumane, love triggers the death of the individual.

In 2000, working with animator Josh Rechnitz, Baumane came up with a storyboard for a film called *Natasha* (2001). Tired of her sterile marriage to a man obsessed with watching the television, Natasha discovers the sexual potential of her vacuum cleaner. After she fucks herself a little too deeply with the vacuum hose, her eggs get sucked up and two vacu-children are born. Baumane pokes fun at the absurdity of contemporary relationships and again, the power and drive of female desire. As absurd as the vacuum scenario seems, is not her husband doing the same? He has betrayed his wife with a Television; a mechanical device that clearly gives him the pleasure and satisfaction he feels he doesn't get or need from his wife.

The production of *Natasha* was not among Baumane's favourite experiences. 'Working on *Natasha* was fun till very soon it turned to hell. We had a fun time creating the storyboard but then it went to hell. We had totally different visions. I thought it is an independent animated film and Josh thought it was a cartoon, so we fought like two raging bulls. In the end Josh's vision won.' That vision included a flaccid final scene – a fight between the husband and the vacuum – that undermines and betrays the rest of the film by turning a relatively cerebral and funny work into a vacuous cop-out.

Five Fucking Fables (2002) is Baumane's most explicit and popular film to date. It was also her most enjoyable to make. '*Five Fucking Fables* is probably my only film that I really truly enjoyed the process of making it. It was after *Natasha*. After that controlled storyboard and the fights and compromises, I was so happy to get up in the morning and not know what I was going to draw. Not having to share the vision made me so free and so happy.'

The film's synopsis pretty much says it all: 'The ones who fuck live better'. In a sense, *Five Fucking Fables* is Baumane's answer to Plympton and to the notion that women cannot make dirty films. Almost all of the fables feature explicit sexual imagery: a man sucks a woman's cunt with a straw; the decapitated head of a woman gives a guy head; a group of female flowers grope a guy; two dwarves perform oral sex on a couple while they have dinner. However, Baumane uses these images with purpose. Behind each image is a theory about sexual relations. In one fable, for example, a woman flirts with a man just before getting her head cut off. The decapitated head flies off the body and lands on the man's cock. 'A lot of people get turned off by this scene', says Baumane. 'I was surprised that something like that came out of me then I realized it was a symbolic representation of me losing my head during sex; of losing control.'

To confront the problem of low budgets and to give her drawings a more animated look, Baumane has used colour pencils on all of her New York films. However, along with the more explicit images of sex and violence, this has triggered comparisons to the work of Bill Plympton. Baumane does not deny Plympton's influence. 'I learned from Bill how an independent studio works', says Baumane. 'I learned about festivals, about keeping good relationships with people, keeping low overhead and making films cheaper. Everything else that they say that I got from Bill – sex and violence and comedy – was in me before I met Bill.' While Plympton's work simply tries to shock and amuse, Baumane's explicit imagery is used as much for introspection as it is for laughs. 'I like shock value', says Baumane. 'But I can't quite understand why sex is a taboo to talk about or piss and crap is a taboo – they are just normal ordinary important things like eating, walking and breathing.'

Baumane also has more freedom with the tone of her films than she did in Latvia. 'I like to be direct with my images and a lot of Latvians were put off by blood in *Witch and The Cow* and *Gold of the Tigers*. When I did *Tiny Shoes* I was asked not to use blood. My first draft of the storyboard was so violent and bloody that the head of the studio sent me home to rework it.'

Baumane notes that there are vast differences in film production between Latvia and the States. 'In Latvia, people do get grants for their projects, but you can't get a government grant for project where pure fun of sex and violence. I like the feeling of team and support we give each other. I like the protection of a studio and the promise it gives you. But I don't like making films in Latvia because I have to sell my idea before I have it. I can't be spontaneous because I have to stick to a storyboard. Mainly I don't like politics of getting a grant. I like making films in NY because I am on my own. I can get up in the morning and start working without knowing yet what the main idea is. I love that. I hate making films in NY because I have no money and I have to make them fast and cheap. I can't make a complicated film like my new project "Veterinarian" in NY because it would take four years.'

In fact, in 2002, Baumane returned to Latvia to make a film she could never have made in New York. 'In late 2001, Vilnis Kalnaellis, a producer from Rija Films, called me and asked if I had a storyboard to submit to a grant committee. I pulled out a few story boards I had in my drawer and picked, *Woman*, a story that I had written in 1994.' Baumane received funding and spent the summer of 2002 in Latvia.

207

Like *The Gold of the Tigers*, *Woman* is ripe with symbols and has a dream-like quality. You know what you see, but you're not sure what it means. A woman is made from drops of the moon and is then carried on the back of a running bull. A wall, which turns out to be a large goblet, suddenly stops the bull. A boy with an animal for a dick sits nearby. Inside the goblet is water, out of which emerges an alluring woman. She lures the boy-animal into the water and when he returns to the surface, the man and animal have reversed positions. Now the man and woman are able to love. As with all of her work, female sexuality is presented as a threat, potentially fatal to men because it can destroy their essence with the wave of a tit. But once men and women work their way through the confusing signals of lust and desire, they can begin the process of love.

Baumane has just finished a film called *Dentist* (2005). There are no animals, no men and women trying to figure out how to fuck each other; instead Baumane looks at the relationship between dentist and patient and specifically our fear of dentists, who represent power and the unknown.

It's a bit extreme to call Baumane the female Charles Bukowski, but her work is certainly closer to his than it is to the work of most female animators. In much of Bukowski's work, it is an aggressive, primitive, often beastly male sexuality that drives many of the

Split Personality

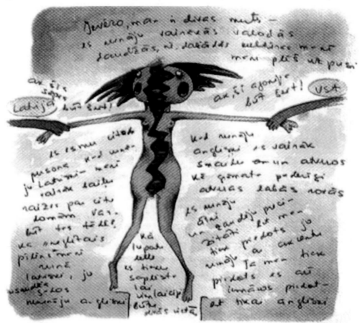

stories. In Baumane's work it is the reverse. From *Witch and Cow* through to *Woman*, the woman is the aggressor. These are women with powerful desires and, as Baumane stated earlier, like tanks they will let nothing stand in the way of fulfilling that urge. Men, who have been nurtured and conditioned to think of themselves as the hunter, are often scared of this power. It's a threat to the so-called rules of masculinity. Baumane does not buy into the myth that women are somehow more pure and innocent than men, that they are magically connected with nature, that men are the evil and violent ones. 'Men and women in essence are the same', says Baumane. 'Why is such a big deal made out of the gender? Gender sometimes is exciting when it comes to sex but it's not so important when it comes to doing dishes or feeling lonely.'

For a person who isn't all that enamoured with drawing, Baumane has put together a decent body of work.

'All I want is to tell a story. I don't concern myself with a quality of drawing (well, I am concerned about it, because most of the times I can't draw what I intend, and I get frustrated because of that.) I may not have a temperament of an animator – I have one of a dancer – I want immediate satisfaction of live performing and delayed effect of my performance and audience reaction sometime drives me crazy. Even writing – you can write a short story in a weekend and show it to a friend on Monday.

So what is it that holds Baumane to animation? 'Well ... I don't know ... have to think ... there is something ... something really deep ... a challenge? A mystery of moving drawings? A way of living? A way to torture myself? I don't know.'

Filmography of Signe Baumane

1991	*The Witch and The Cow*
1993	*Tiny Shoes*
1995	*The Gold of the Tigers*
1998	*Love Story*
1999	*The Threatened One*
2001	*Natasha*
2002	*Five Fucking Fables*
2002	*Woman*
2005	*Dentist*

Chapter 27

Roughing it in the Bush
(2005)

Dr. Jeckyll and Mr. Hyde

It's hard to pin down the work of British animator, Paul Bush; and that's precisely what makes his work so intriguing. He's experimented in scratch animation, stop motion, time-lapse, engraving, and even video collage, never satisfied to stick with one technique. What doesn't change is Bush's on-going commitment (obsession?) to exploring how we perceive the world around us, examining how time and space affect our interpretation of everyday objects, environments and people. Don't be afraid though. Bush's work may be philosophical, but it's often funny, created with a sly wink that reminds us that in the end it's all just a big game.

Born in London in 1956, Bush's father was a composer and his mother worked part-time as a physiotherapist. 'I think my father was quite successful in his earlier years', says Bush. 'But he wasn't a modernist and by the time I was a teenager his work was being passed over particularly by BBC radio which was the main source of commissions in the UK. He was a little embittered by this but not discouraged and he worked at home all morning composing at his piano, he rested in the afternoon and taught history of music for London University in the evening. He never earned much money from his work but thanks to his evening job we were never short of money.'

Both parents were liberal intellectuals with a strong interest in the arts. The family was very social and when they weren't entertaining friends, they were taking their sons to concerts and the opera. 'In retrospect', says Bush, 'it was strange to be brought up in this bohemian atmosphere but in what appeared to be a very middle class domestic nuclear family. I sometimes think I was taken to [art events] at too young an age and my interest was engaged by elements of the performances not usually noticed by people. This led me later to ignore some of the larger themes of art and instead become involved with working on the minor details. Hence my offbeat films.'

As a teenager, Bush, to no one's surprise, had a strong interest in art and literature. 'I wrote as well as drew and painted. I only remember once expressing a desire to do anything else and that was when I was about ten; I wanted to be a priest. I remember my Dad saying, 'but priests don't earn any money' as a way of putting me off which I later used to tease him about as he was a christian and a socialist.I never expected that to be an artist was going to be easy but I was encouraged to believe that I had a vocation – and that people should pursue their vocations. When I went to art school and met people whose parents were trying to discourage them from becoming artists, I realised how important my family's support was.'

211

After studying fine art at Central School in London, Bush attended Goldsmith's College. Goldsmith, in particular, had an important influence on Bush. 'Conceptualism and minimalism were very strong influences and both of these ideas have informed the processes of all my work; for instance with the scratched films I am recycling and re-presenting old engravings precisely by using the engraver's technique – but on film.'

Having completed his studies in 1978, Bush began teaching and running a film workshop in South London. During this time Bush taught himself filmmaking and, between 1984–1991, made three live-action films. 'They all had modest success', says Bush, 'The second [*So Many, So Magnificent*] was bought by Channel 4. It looked like they might fund my next film so by the late 80s I thought things were taking off.' Unfortunately Bush didn't get another dime to make films during the 1980s. 'When I look at that period now with so little happening and then being in my thirties with a small baby and having achieved nothing, I'm surprised I wasn't more down about it.'

Bush's career began to turn a corner in the 1990s. He received funding to make a short film called *Lake of Dreams* and a short experimental film, *Lost Images,* for TV. Then he became aware that the Arts Council of England and Channel 4 were funding experimental animation films. 'It was going to people who were known as filmmakers but who weren't necessarily animators'. Phil Mulloy, who started in live-action before becoming an animator, was one of those filmmakers who got funding to make an animation film.

'While I was teaching I used to give students some clear 16mm film at the end of the first day and tell them to draw, paint or stick stuff on it. I always liked the painted and scratched films of Len Lye, McLaren and Harry Smith, particularly the extraordinary depth and complex spatial dimensions to the images.' Bush had an old book of Gustav Doré's engravings of The Divine Comedy. 'These engravings', says Bush, 'have a huge depth and each one is a narrative in itself'. After a year of making tests, Bush received funding to make the film, *His Comedy.*

His Comedy (1994) is based on Doré's engravings of Dante's Inferno. Bush scratches on footage of both Doré's etchings and live-action images; some of them archival footage of war and explosions. Bush's innovative approach brings Doré's images to life with a haunting, mystical dimension. The use of modern imagery adds a modern touch to Dante's timeless romp through hell. By scratching himself into the story just as Dante wrote himself into The Divine Comedy, Bush becomes at once Doré's craftsman and

Furniture Poetry

also a Virgil to the viewer, guiding us through the images and sounds of hell.

His Comedy was a success on the animation festival circuit and Bush found himself a home. 'I became known in the animation

His Comedy

community and it became much more easy to get animation projects off the ground.'

After *His Comedy*, Bush decided to look for different stories illustrated by different engravers. He settled on an etching called Still Life with Small Cup by Italian artist Giorgio Morandi. For *Still Life with Small Cup* (1995), Bush uses Morandi's etching to take the viewer back into the artist's world. The film starts with a series of seemingly abstract lines. It is unclear what these lines are or where they are going. Only at the end of the film does Bush pull the camera back to reveal that these lines form the cup in Morandi's etching. In taking us from the micro to macro, Bush simultaneously celebrates Morandi's work; explores the beauty and abstract quality of everyday objects (something Bush will return to); and takes us through Morandi's own creative process. As with *His Comedy, Still Life* is a bridge of time and space that unites two artists and two worlds. 'Doré is a fine illustrator', says Bush, 'but his work was old-fashioned in his time and frequently veers towards sentimentality and kitsch so it feels safe to use it and try and update. It's a little scarier working with something you really admire and knowing you are going to change it a lot. How can a film compare with these tiny intense engravings that Morandi made? It can't of course so I attempted to make a story out of the engraving, one that describes the process of making an engraving.'

After a decade of uncertainty, Bush became firmly planted in the animation world. Then in 1995, he risked his stable career by making a twenty-six minute experimental film called *The Rumour of True Things* (from a Walter Benjamin text) comprised entirely of excerpts from various industrial films. 'It seemed a huge risk to make it just as I'd seemed to established myself as an animation director', says Bush. 'I had tried to get the money for the project since 1990 and I think when I finally got funding in 1995, it was a reward from the Arts Council for making *His Comedy*. Trouble is you're only given one chance so I was risking another plunge into obscurity by making this film.'

Bush spent two years collecting films and originally intended to build an archive. When he couldn't find funding for the archive, he decided to continue to collect films for *The Rumour of True Things*. 'None of the stuff I collected came from an archive, it was all original research and as I only had a small budget I couldn't offer any royalty payments, but had a couple of thousand to make Ex Gratia payments, usually to medical research departments. So I got all the rights to everything and as the film has sold very well that has been extremely useful.'

214

Industrial films are made for a single instructive purpose. But

Paul Bush by Finnish photographer Timo Viljakainen

anyone who has ever watched an old social and sexual education film from the fifties or sixties knows that these films take on additional, often comical, new meanings when watched by later generations. They often tell us much more about the values and ideals of the earlier generation than they intended. Technically speaking, many of these films are quite accomplished, filled with striking photography and sweeping camera movements. However, because they are made for a specific context, their existence is usually brief, and their creators anonymous.

In *Rumour of True Things*, Bush removes the films from their

Still Life with a Cup

original context. The result is a fascinating collage of industrial film and video game images that together create an ominous portrait of a society obsessed with technology, violence, and images. Watching the often people-less images, you feel like something terrible is about to, or has already happened.

Rather than collect moving images from different eras, Bush chose only footage from the mid-nineties in the UK so that the audience would be able to view a specific place at a specific time. 'I grouped images according to their subject matter', says Bush. 'At the same time I wanted to make the film short enough for the audience to make a connection between every single image in the film – to be able to see the whole world of images together and weigh up what they mean. I felt 30 minutes was a maximum time to do this, although it meant some sacrifices as there were some images that revealed more the longer you watched.'

Andy Cowton, who has worked on most of Bush's films since 1992, designed the mysterious and rather ominous soundtrack. 'Andy made the track out of found and junk sound, and this track is so important in giving this haunting sense of a society which has somehow lost the way and is struggling to find it again.

During the production of *Rumour of True Things*, Bush wrote an outline for an adaptation of Samuel Coleridge's long poem 'The Rime of the Ancient Mariner' called *The Albatross*. 'I was definitely looking ahead to what I should do when I finished *Rumour* and it seemed commercially sensible to try another scratched film. I'd been away from scratching by now for at least a year so I was missing it a little. I also had two small children and working at home on an ordered project seemed quite a nice prospect for the next couple of years (*Rumour* was requiring me to chase to all ends of the country.). I had written an outline of the project and sent it to Colin Rose at the BBC. A few weeks later I met Colin at the Cinanima festival in Portugal and he asked what I was planning next – I told him it was on his desk – within a month he had read it and agreed to fund it. This was unusual for the BBC who normally only did series or longer "Christmas Specials". Eventually I found three other funders to put in money which made it by far the biggest budget film I ever made.'

For *Albatross* Bush used live-action footage with actors and a combination of Doré's engravings and engravings from 19th century illustrated books and magazines. He then engraved on both. 'Doré had illustrated the "Ancient Mariner" and I used some of his work, particularly the images of the Ancient Mariner himself, together with engravings that were commonplace in the newspapers and books of the time'. To make the engravings move, Bush used hand-held camera movements, cut outs, and three short, drawn frame by frame, animation sequences.

Watching *The Albatross* is like reading a book by moonlight on a boat. The sharp black and white contrasts combined with a vibrant scratch effect give the film a dreamy, ethereal atmosphere. The film follows a mysterious and crazy old drunk who runs into three men on their way to a wedding party. He rambles on about a curse that has befallen him because he killed an albatross. The viewer sees things that may or may not be there and hears the haunting words of a potential madman that may or may not be true. Nothing is certain. 'The question is', adds Bush, 'does the mariner have a message that is useful to the wedding guest or not? He might not be a guy you want to spend time with but is he one with something important to say that will change your life or is he just softening you up before he asks for some money?'

The dash of colour that offers temporary relief from the film's noir atmosphere all came from film stock. 'The colours come from the tri-pack layers in colour film stock, magenta, yellow and cyan. As you scratch deeper you go through these colours till you hit white. *Flik-Flak*

Fortunately there happens to be two different types of film stock in which the colours are arranged differently. The two basic colours I could get were dominantly blue, or dominantly green. But to get two more colours – the reddish purples and yellow oranges, I scratched a negative image in ordinary film stock and had them print it as if it were negative.'

Bush structured the film like an illustrated book. The spoken text is never heard over the illustrations. There is only music and sound. 'I felt the way we understand text and the way we read pictures is so different that I didn't want them to clash. To have the Ancient Mariner constantly present as a narrator periodically interrupting the flow of his own story is a device that Coleridge used. I put the audience exactly where the Wedding Guest is in the poem.' Bush also selected thirty of the verses that tell the main story very directly and with fewer of the antiquated words or digressions of the original. In this way, the Mariner could be an old guy you could meet today on the street.

Aside from the disappointing *Secret Love* (2002), which was commissioned by Welsh Television, Bush has moved away from scratch animation towards single frame animation; most notably *Furniture Poetry* (1999), *Dr. Jekyll and Mr. Hyde* (2001), and *Pas de Deux de Deux* (2001).

Furniture Poetry is a playful philosophical piece inspired by a Ludwig Wittgenstein quotation: 'What prevents me from supposing that this table either vanishes or alters its shape when no one is observing it and then when someone looks at it again changes back? But one feels like saying – who is going to suppose such a thing?' Bush contributes to the question by manipulating tables, chairs, and various domestic objects into a frenzied and comical dance. The result is a relatively simple film that satisfies both eggheads and children. 'I would have quite happily made a version of the film without the Wittgenstein quotation and I think it makes some people nervous as it sounds more profound than either I or Wittgenstein meant – he was of course being playful himself at this point.'

Children, in particular, are captivated and amused by Bush's choreography. 'I like *Furniture Poetry*', adds Bush, 'because it is a film that seems to give a lot of people of all ages, including the youngest children, happiness. People have written long after to tell me how moved they were by *The Albatross* but you don't get an immediate reaction like you do with laughter.'

Furniture Poetry is an important bridge between Bush's scratch films and his single frame works. The fascination with perception and everyday objects in *Still Life* continues in *Furniture Poetry*;

however the single frame technique adds a new dimension, an *The Albatross* unsettling and fractured choreography that shatters the whole into constantly shifting fragments that merge and disband simultaneously. In *Dr. Jeckyll and Mr. Hyde*, for example, two people play Dr. Jeckyll. Their bodies change continuously throughout the film. The concept fits perfectly into the schizophrenic theme of the original story, however, Bush adds his comic philosopher touch by having all the characters flicker. The technique is masterfully utilized in the film's final moments. As Jekyll stands before his accusers denying that he is Hyde, his two faces dance before us like the dying movements of a slot machine.

In the strange and funny Pas *de Deux de Deux*, a performance of Swan Lake is transformed from a graceful, smooth, ballet into a mechanical, awkward, and ugly routine. 'All the physical inconveniences of dance that ballet does so well to hide are visible in this film, except the blisters, the smell of sweat, and the rash caused by the tutus', says Bush. 'It was commissioned for a programme of experimental dance films and after its première many of the people involved told me that they loved the music which they could suddenly enjoy again and find moving, because the film had kind of de-kitsched the ballet for them.'

For *Jeckyll* and *Pas De Deux*, Bush had the actors re-stage scenes from existing film versions. For *Dr. Jeckyll*, Bush re-staged scenes

219

Pas de deux de deux from Victor Fleming's 1941 film version with Spencer Tracy and Ingrid Bergman. 'I used the Victor Fleming version because the key scenes – Jekyll drinking the potion that will turn him into Hyde and the wonderful scene at the end where he cannot stop himself changing identity – were both possible to restage using this new technique.' For *Pas De Deux*, Bush used a Russian version of Swan Lake from 1946. 'I had to search a long time for a ballet I could use. It had to be without camera movements and without the dancers being off the ground too long because I couldn't replicate these in single frame. The film identically copies the original. That's how it works. The actors see themselves superimposed on the original footage, frame by frame.'

Bush's success with his own films eventually led to a few commercial gigs. In 2000, he and Phil Mulloy began a series for Channel 4 called *Flik-Flak*. 'With all my films', says Bush, 'there have been economic pressures which have resulted in one film being made rather than another. *Flik-Flak* is a result of a particular strong economic pressure at that time.' This bizarre and cynical series features a stream of characters (who look like extras from the Pac Man video game) who spout meaningless and often stupid things to no one in particular. 'Phil and I are friends and we admire each other's work', says Bush. 'There was a 5-part, three minute slot available on Channel 4, and we decided to start from scratch (putting aside our own particular specialities) and try and devise a series for it. We wrote them together and I animated one, Phil the other.' Only two 3-minute episodes were made.

After making *The Albatross*, Bush was invited to join the commercial studio, Picasso Pictures. Although Bush would stay with Picasso for seven years, he only worked one year. 'However it was an extremely lucrative year', adds Bush. First, he made a 'hugely expensive' commercial based on the look of *The Albatross* for Japan's National Panasonic. Later that year, Bush was hired to do a commercial (*Room 2*) for a chain of Scottish furniture stores. 'The agency people were very chuffed at finding [Norman] McLaren's *Begone Dull Care* and wanted a version of this for the commercial. I showed them *Furniture Poetry* and suggested we combined the two ideas using pixilation of some of the shop's products. I did a couple of days pixilation in front of the camera and then got a group of people – Barbel Neubauer, Lucy Lee and an ex-student of mine, Rima Patel, to bleach, paint, draw etc. on the film for as long as we had money for. Then we presented all this stuff to an editor (poor guy) to piece together with the sound.' And, true enough, the end result is an upbeat, toe-tapping commercial that blends the rhythm of Oscar Peterson's score for *Begone Dull Care* with Bush's own *Furniture Poetry*.

Rumour of True Things

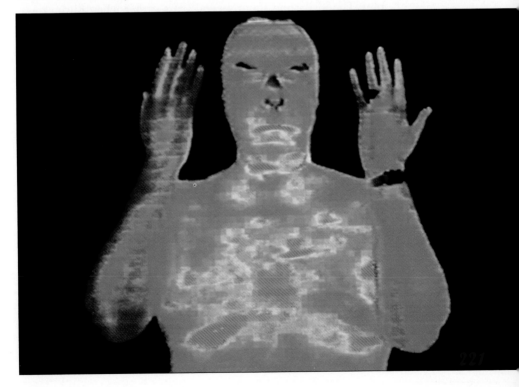

227

In the late 1990s, much of the funding for independent animators dried up. Channel 4, the biggest supporter of independent animation, turned more towards TV productions. The change didn't seem to affect Paul Bush's output. Before 2000, Bush made five animation films and since that time, he's produced at least eight works. 'I've continued to receive funding but more indirectly than before. *Secret Love* was funded by Welsh television and I currently have a 3-year fellowship from NESTA (National Endowment for Science Technology and the Arts) for development of my work, primarily in feature films. During this time I've managed to make a couple of films on the side but now I'm obliged to use DV and I've sold my super-16 camera. Bush has also continued to supplement his income with teaching. After teaching one day a week for six years on the visual arts course at Goldsmith's College and doing intermittent work at the National Film and Television School, Bush now teaches a nine-week winter course at the HGK Luzern in Switzerland. 'I don't like the length of travel and time taken away from my own work but it's a special place at the moment with very strong teaching staff [including German animator, Gerd Gockell and noted critic/historian, Otto Alder].'

Recently, Bush has been experimenting with time-lapse photography. The idea came about several years earlier when Bush experimented with a few scenes involving people while making *Furniture Poetry*. 'I filmed some people sitting and standing really still while the objects moved. These were guys who played living statues for money in the street and they really looked still. You couldn't see them move with the naked eye, but the camera showed them moving about like crazy. When I saw how much the body moved in time-lapse it became the basis for the later work like *Busby Berkeley's Tribute to Mae West*, *Shinjuku Samurai* [time lapse portraits of twenty-six Tokyo citizens] and another film I've been working on for two years called *Time Travellers*.'

Busby Berkeley's Tribute to Mae West (2002), in particular, stands out. For just over a minute – with no soundtrack – a penis flaps about on a split screen. 'This was not the kind of film you can get funded', says Bush. 'It came about because of the time lapse films I was taking of the human body and this seemed to be an interesting area to investigate – more action-packed at any rate. I had the simple idea to shoot a penis in profile as it became erect, then limp and then erect again. Speeded up through time lapse photography it looks like a needle on a dial moving up and down.'

Busby Berkeley's Tribute to Mae West is one of the funniest and most uncomfortable films seen on the animation circuit in some time. The discomfort seems to stem from a combination of the film's silence and the rare appearance of male genitalia. If the film had been made with a woman's breasts or vagina, the film might not be as uncomfortable because we are so accustomed to seeing the female body sexualized. 'I have been extremely embarrassed by this work on numerous occasions', says Bush, 'but there was no stopping its run through the festival circuit'.

It shouldn't be surprising that a guy who never really intended to be an animator in the first place doesn't really follow an agenda or a strict set of rules. 'I never learned animation and have no techniques worth mentioning or even passing on to anyone else. Therefore I don't feel there is an area that is not open to explore. Ideas lead from one to another. I don't want to continue to make the same film again once I've achieved a result I'm satisfied with. I have ideas, I do tests and sometimes they lead to dead ends. It was a lot of work and testing and dead ends before I got from *Furniture Poetry* to *Jekyll and Hyde* although I always thought I could somehow get there in the end.'

Paul Bush is part scavenger, part inventor. Nothing is out of bounds and everything is worth trying. This is what makes Bush's works so welcoming; you never know what you're in for but you know it'll be smart, funny, provocative and unique. In the insecure world of animation too many animators stop pushing themselves once they find a comfortable style; they set up shop in the house of art, content with talking to themselves. Bush refuses to be pigeonholed or stagnant. He continues to push himself by rummaging through the junkyard of possibilities so that he can find new ways of expressing ideas about life and how we live it.

Filmography of Paul Bush

1994	*His Comedy*
1995	*Still Life with Small Cup*
1996	*The Rumour of True Things*
1998	*The Albatross*
1999	*Furniture Poetry*
2000	*Flik-Flak* (with Phil Mulloy)
2001	*Pas de Deux de Deux*
2001	*Dr. Jeckyll and Mr. Hyde*
2002	*Busby Berkeley's Tribute to Mae West*
2002	*Secret Love*
2003	*Geisha Grooming* (with Lisa Milroy)
2004	*While Darwin Sleeps*
2004	*Shinjuku Samurai*
–	*The Time Travellers* (in progress)

Chapter 28

Bathing in the Sunlight of Dennis Tupicoff (2005)

Sure, before dying, Socrates said all that stuff about how foolish we are to fear something we know nothing about, but hey, that doesn't make me feel any better about death. Besides, I *do* know that death will mean no breath, no love, no kisses, no hate, no wanks, no heartbreak, no pleasure; there's no nothing. Fuck the poets. Fuck the preachers. Death ain't beautiful. It's as ugly as split-open roadkill. If there is any good thing about death it's that the fucker is unbiased. It gets all of us in the end: the assholes and the angels.

Dennis Tupicoff doesn't like death either. He's afraid of it and, based on his animation films, obsesses on it. While most people call animation, 'the illusion of life', Tupicoff's films could easily be called 'the reality of death'. His films *Dance of Death*, *The Darra Dogs*, *His Mother's Voice*, and *Into the Dark* all deal with the grim corner we're all going to pass by one not-so-fine day. And while there is beauty in Tupicoff's narration and pictures, he doesn't paint

Into the Dark

Dennis Tupicoff

pretty pictures of death. Death, for Tupicoff, is harrowing, personal, baffling, and painful – at least for the living. 'Death spills into everything I write', says the Australian animator. 'If I displayed a similar attachment to the (of course psychologically related) subject of sex, I would be regarded with more suspicion – though come to think of it I'd probably be more prosperous.'

Darra, Australia isn't quite hell, but it's certainly not among Australia's desirable destinations. This industrial suburb of Brisbane houses mostly factory workers and tradesmen. Into the sixties it shared the soil with a sewage dump, along with army and immigrant camps. By the time, Dennis Tupicoff was born in Darra in 1951, his family's roots there were deep. His father and uncle worked as foremen for a Darra cement company before establishing Darra Welding Works, a steel fabrication business. The company eventually expanded to two sites and about forty employees (including Tupicoff's mother who took care of the accounts). 'Neither of my parents went to school beyond early high school', remembers Tupicoff. 'They were proud to be of the independent working class – owned their own home etc – but they were quite ambitious that we (three sons) should be better educated'.

Tupicoff was the first person in his family to attend university. He 'acquired rather aimlessly a liberal arts degree (majoring in history and politics)'. After graduation, the now 6'10" Tupicoff worked as an assistant archives researcher at the Queensland State Archives in Brisbane, before embarking on a tour of Europe in 1972 and then training as a teacher in 1973.

This was not a particularly good time in Tupicoff's life. One of his older brothers died in a motorbike accident and a couple of his close friends also died in motorbike and car accidents around the same time. Meanwhile, teaching turned out to be a disaster that lasted less than three months. 'My brother died in mid-1973; one friend in early 1971 and an earlier one in probably 1969. It did come at a pretty low time for me: I was (re) training for a new job as a primary school teacher, and I'd just got over hepatitis and was generally pretty miserable.'

It wasn't Tupicoff's first encounter with death: 'I suppose I hadn't come across much untimely/premature death until that period in my life. Though I had plenty of thoughts about mortality as a child – shooting birds, what is nothing?' The loss of his brother hit Tupicoff particularly hard because they were a close family and his brother left behind a wife and small son. His brother's death was also not instantaneous. He died from complications of a broken leg. 'He took a couple of weeks to die and each of us said goodbye to him as a line of medical staff waited to dismantle the gear and lay his body out.'

By now, Tupicoff had developed an interest in film: 'I had been doing B&W photography for some years and had shot quite a bit of footage and shot/edited a narrative live-action Super 8 film'. After his teaching career flopped, Tupicoff went to New Zealand, working at various 'menial jobs'. In New Zealand, Tupicoff heard a song by John Prine called, 'Please Don't Bury Me'. 'I have no idea where this thought came from but I thought [the song] would make a good animated film.' Unlike many animators, Tupicoff was not born with the proverbial 'pencil in his hand':

> 'My parents would often say in amazement: "You never drew as a kid". I used to doodle in the margins of my university lecture notes, and I did do some drawing at art school, but really my impulse to draw came out of wanting to make films, to tell stories. And if they were to be animated films, who else would animate them?'

Tupicoff returned to Australia and decided to teach himself how to make animation. 'I found a new art school that had some film equipment, bought *Technique of Film Animation* and set to work', says Tupicoff. 'I got some tips from Max Bannah – who was the only animator I could find in Brisbane.' With further assistance from the Australian Film Commission Tupicoff finished the short film, *Please Don't Bury Me* (which I have not seen) in 1976.

In 1977, Tupicoff enrolled at a 'real' film school: the Swinburne Film and Television School (now called the VCA Film and Television School) in Melbourne where he made two films: *My Big Chance* (1977) and *Changes* (1978). After leaving Swinburne, Tupicoff opened a one-man animation production company. '[I was] trying to make a living out of animation, doing whatever work people were willing to give me.' It was during this period that Tupicoff began work on *Dance of Death* (1983), the first film to bring Tupicoff international attention.

Like Chris Hinton's later animation film, *Watching TV* (1994), *Dance of Death* is a satire of the use of death and violence on Television. A young girl watches endless images of death and violence. The images are so fast, dehumanized and distant that the girl (and her family, who sit back unconcerned) becomes immune. They are just images from some far-off world. Tupicoff drives the point home through a game show called *Dance of Death* where people are randomly chosen to meet their maker. TV and life eventually merge when the girl and her family receive a call from the host of the show saying that they've been randomly chosen to bite the dust next.

Dance of Death is the most lightweight of Tupicoff's work. The drawings and tone are closer to cartoons than to Tupicoff's later, darker films. 'After doing a lot of gags for a children's TV programme, I realized that I had a facility for ultra-short and ultra-cheap animated sight-gags. At first – probably as a reaction to the TV work – I just set out to do as many as I could that weren't for kids – choosing violence rather than sex – and chose the best ones.' During this process, the *Dance of Death* story emerged.

As for the decidedly 'cartoon' drawing style, Tupicoff admits, 'I'm not a cartoonist with any sort of original style. The film leans heavily on the graphic styles of others, whose work I had absorbed thoroughly by then – particularly that of Tomi Ungerer.'

Dance of Death was shown in competition at international festivals and it was awarded a jury prize at France's Annecy International Animation Festival, and the best non-feature animation at the 1983 Australian Film Industry awards.

Tupicoff didn't make another personal animation film for ten years. After *Dance of Death*, he spent the rest of the eighties working on various commissioned projects, ranging from TV commercials and title sequences to making films about teeth. 'I wrote various drafts and developed a (mainly live-action) feature film which attracted a producer and went to the financial market in 1987 or 1989, but couldn't get financed.' And what was the subject of the feature film? Well, of course, death, skeletons, the after-life and country western music. In 1990, Tupicoff also wrote, produced and directed, *The Bear,* a mostly live-action film about an animator who is taken over by one of his characters.

During this period, Tupicoff wasn't just producing films. He and his partner, Louise, also created two daughters, Zelda (1985) and Anna (1991). In fact, Zelda inadvertently provided the inspiration for Tupicoff's next film when she asked her father for a dog. His response was the film, *The Darra Dogs* (1993), a collection of memories about the dogs of Tupicoff's Darra childhood. The stories in *The Darra Dogs* came out of an evening with a group of friends. 'In trying to explain to a group of friends why I reacted so strongly [to my daughter's request], all those memories came gushing out as my palms sweated and my body shook.' But *The Darra Dogs* isn't your typical sanitized and cheerful nostalgic piece about a man's happy memories of traveling through the fields with his oh-so-cute puppy dog. *The Darra Dogs* is a harrowing memoir that deals with the pain of loss and death. As much as Tupicoff loved dogs as a boy, he says in the film's voice over: 'the trouble was they kept dying'. When Tupicoff thinks of the dogs from his childhood, 'memories of terror and death that keep coming back

His Mother's Voice

Family and Friends

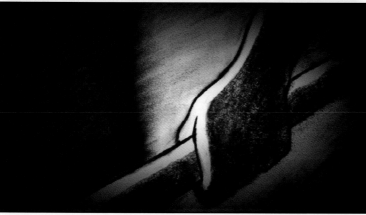

The Darra Dogs

to me'. The film is filled with distressing stories of dogs disappearing, being hit by cars, and, most gruesomely, being shot and beaten. 'In my head', says Tupicoff, 'they were each fully formed as little movies: all the individual storyboards and images were roughed out in a day or two.

Tupicoff's soft, warm, and pained voice-over heightens the film's emotional impact and gives the film its deeply personal resonance. '[My] emotions were so powerful after all those years and [I wanted] to re-create the emotions that I felt.' Often, animators rely too heavily on their soundtracks because they don't have enough faith in the power of their images, but Tupicoff is a rare example in animation of an animator whose emotionally-packed narrations complement and never overwhelm the images. 'There's nothing wrong with words', says Tupicoff, 'most of us use them, after all. Some people even use them well. There is good talk, and there are certainly poor pictures. I get irritated with films that seem to have taken a vow of silence (for whatever reason) and are reduced to a dumb-show accompanied by toots and whistles and lots of significant gestures.'

Visually, Tupicoff lures the viewer into the world of the film with a cool, clean and simple colour palette. He then uses shadows to give the film a darker, menacing overtone. Initially I thought that Tupicoff had rotoscoped the movements of the dogs, but in fact they were all drawn and animated. 'I initially intended to make the film using rotoscope but rejected the technique. I thought that somehow their accuracy would be compromised. Of course, this led to practical problems and I had never animated a four-legged animal before, so I had to go into training before I started.'

Oh, by the way, Tupicoff's daughter never got a dog.

In 1995, Matthew Easdale was shot and killed by a homeowner when, according to newspaper reports, 'he apparently broke into the wrong house in search of people who had assaulted his friends and damaged a car'. A few weeks later his mother, Kathy, gave an interview on Australian radio. One of the many Australians tuned in was Tupicoff: 'I heard this interview at lunchtime in our kitchen. It is an extremely powerful piece of audio that had other listeners pulling their cars over because their eyes were blinded by tears. It has always struck me as a six-and-a-half minute song of lamentation, disguised as a narrative monologue.'

His Mother's Voice (1997) is based on this six-minute interview with Kathy Easdale. The film is divided into two parts. In the first section, Tupicoff uses the familiar thick lines and a flat color scheme of *Darra Dogs* – this time rotoscoped with actors – to re-create, from Kathy Easdale's perspective, the evening her son died. We follow her from the moment she first learns that something has happened to Matthew, to the moment she and her other son learn that Matthew has died. In the second part, Tupicoff uses the same monologue, actors and technique, but now shows us – using charcoal drawings and no music – the world around the Easdale home during the time of the interview. The camera begins and ends with Kathy's face. In between we see Matthew's room, their street, the yard.

In the film we never see the shooting nor are we ever told how Matthew was killed. 'As a filmmaker, I was not interested mainly in why or how Matthew was killed. For me, and for his mother, he might have been drowned or killed in a car crash. It's her story and her voice that are so affecting.'

The intensity and precision of Easdale's monologue enables the viewer to step into her mind and feel her conflicting feelings. As she recounts the evening, her voice travels through a variety of emotions from confusion to hope and finally, utter despair. Although she obviously knows the outcome of her story, it's as if she thinks that by re-telling the story she might bring about a different ending. Her pain is multi-layered; a fusion of past and present. While she is remembering this tragic night (part one), that process of memory confirms in the present (part two) that the events were real, that her son is never coming back. In this second part, Tupicoff's shots emphasize the absence and quiet in and around the house. There is a sense that something is missing or lost. In re-creating the physical interview and life around the house at that moment, Tupicoff also shows us that life is still going on. This tragic, heart-wrenching monologue becomes both death and life.

Tupicoff followed *His Mother's Voice* with a rather unusual film called *The Heat, The Humidity* (1999). This black and white comedy-mystery tells the story of an escaped armed robber who flees to Australia. Upon arriving, he struggles with the Australian heat only to be told continually (the only dialogue in the film) that, 'It's not the heat, it's the humidity'. Even in jest, though, Tupicoff can't escape death. The robber eventually evaporates from the intense heat, sorry, I meant, humidity. It's certainly not a standout film, but like *Dance of Death*, it shows that Tupicoff does have a funny bone, albeit a black one. 'This was my response to a call for submissions by SBS, the network in Australia that has given most support for animation', says Tupicoff. 'I liked the idea of making a voice-over from just one phrase – and that phrase carries an oddly comic punch for Australians who live in the tropics. I wanted to make a funny and simple film in B&W. Though it has a few good moments, it's not as funny as it needed to be.'

In 2001, Tupicoff returned to personal territory with, *Into The Dark*, a story about a dying man who remembers his fear of death as a child. The film was again made for SBS, this time as part of an anthology called 'Home Movies' which called for scripts that were of a personal nature. The dying man was based on Tupicoff's father who had died a few years earlier. What is interesting, though, is that the boy we see in the past is actually based on Tupicoff's own childhood memories. 'In imagining his experience of death, I was imagining my own, combined with what I can remember of my thoughts from childhood about death and nothingness.' The film opens in the past. A young boy shoots a young bird. Thinking he'll feel triumph, he instead feels guilt. He begins to wonder about what it means to be nothing. As he lies in the bath he 'wants to feel nothing, to be free'. Suddenly, the solemn, beautiful and languid scene transforms into a dirty, chaotic world. We are on a stretcher in a hospital. A man is gasping for breath.

Like *His Mother's Voice*, Tupicoff again uses two drawing styles to differentiate between past and present. A dark, sketchy charcoal style represents the chaotic uncertainty of the present while Tupicoff's distinct flat colour style is used to recreate the past. While Tupicoff's voice guides us, there is less reliance on narration than in *Darra Dogs* or *His Mother's Voice*. Having said that, with *Into The Dark*, Tupicoff doesn't seem able to trust the power of his images to convey the necessary emotions. Instead he uses a photograph of himself as a child at the beginning and end of the film to help situate the viewer, and relies on a heavy, foreboding piano accompaniment. Both are unnecessary and come close to pushing the film into melodrama. Fortunately, Tupicoff's unflinching honesty and his positioning of the viewer with the eyes of the boy and man, prevents the film from entering schmaltzy territory. This subjective experience shifts death – and even life – from an anonymous and distant experience to something inevitable and universal. Because of the power of Tupicoff's memories and voice, *Into The Dark* remains a moving, intelligent film that unites life and mortality, man and boy, and, most powerfully, father and son.

Throughout his career, Tupicoff has also worked in live-action and documentary. His most recent film is a documentary called *Taringa 4068: Our Place and Time*, which looks at life and death in an Australian suburb through the eyes of several generations of one family. He has also spent the last two decades developing two live-action feature films. 'Both films deal with death in a very direct way', says Tupicoff. 'In fact, Death is one of the main characters in each film.' The films, though, remain unproduced. 'Perhaps life– as expressed by the inscrutable workings of the film funding process – is trying to tell me something', adds Tupicoff.

The Darra Dogs

After twenty years of making animation films, Tupicoff is not even convinced that he's an animator: 'Perhaps the truth is that, as a rather shy young man at the end of his tether, I just fell into it. I was interested in filmmaking, could read and write, could draw a bit and found I had the patience to persist in this odd activity called animation. Perhaps, one way or another, I've been trying to do live-action – disguised as animation – ever since.'

Either way, this is the road that has been paved. Despite the serendipitous roots, Tupicoff has become firmly established and recognized in the international animation world. His films are routinely shown at festivals and they provoke strong emotions and thoughts from viewers and critics. Given the intensely personal nature of his work, have these films helped Tupicoff come to terms with his life, and death? 'Making these films has helped me to understand things in the past', says Tupicoff. 'And perhaps even to remember them at all: at one point as a young man I remembered nothing of my whole childhood.'

Tupicoff makes no apologies for his death obsession: 'Our awareness of our fate is one of the few things that make us uniquely human. And, yes, it really is part of life, and so we can laugh at it and still be scared of it and sad about it. I certainly don't have a program or any particular axe to grind. I just seem to see things from the dark side. Or perhaps it's the other way around: maybe I'm just looking down into the darkness of my shadow, dazzled by the sunlight in which I'm bathed!'

Filmography (selected) of Dennis Tupicoff

1976	*Please Don't Bury Me*
1977	*My Big Chance*
1978	*Changes*
1983	*Dance of Death*
1993	*The Darra Dogs*
1997	*His Mother's Voice*
1999	*The Heat, The Humidity*
2001	*Into the Dark*

Chapter 29

Gianluigi Toccafondo's
Puppet Consortia Denied
(2005)

Pinocchio

Running around going nowhere in particular. Sometimes we're not even moving. Just sitting there-here-where racing around for something, anything that gives a fix on it all, a sense of who we are and just what it is we're supposed to be doing here. Dog chasing tail. We never get to where we're going 'cause we don't know where it is. Then again if you don't know where you're going, you can't get lost. Are we even supposed to be going anywhere? It's all about the chase, ain't it? It's not the beginning or the end; the moments in-between give life its essence. Besides, we're never quite as we were, are, or will be. Identity is always changing. Sure, some bits and pieces of habit linger longer than others. That's a good thing. Or is it? If the world around us is always changing, with new situations confronting us, then to remain stagnant and unchanged is to die, ain't it? But is the world changing or is it all just a re-hash of what once was. Ecclesiastes told us that there is no new thing under the sun. But Heraclitus charges that the sun is new again each day. Even if we are changing are we living through something new or just running through the same maze?

The animations of Italian animator, Guianluigi Toccafondo don't necessarily ask these existential be-all/end-all questions, but they certainly inspire them. Toccafondo's inspired mix of painting, cinema and animation creates a world of uncertainty and the illusion of possibility. Like *Pinocchio*, a story that touches all of Toccafondo's films, his characters are feckless creatures, constantly on the run from things and persons unknown. The fools think they're free to do as they please, unaware that their destinies are being determined for them by the shadows of those they cannot see.

Toccafondo's destiny began in San Marino in 1965. His father was a painter and ceramist. His mother was an elementary school teacher. The family lived in a small provincial village that was crowded with tourists during the summer and deserted come winter. Toccafondo's father had a particularly strong influence on the young boy. 'I started to draw when I was 2 or 3 years old', says *The Criminal*

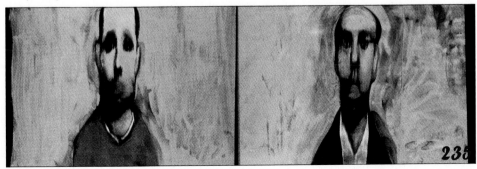

235

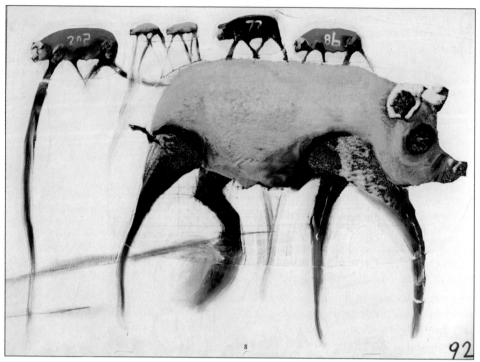

La Pista Toccafondo. 'In my home there were a lot of art books. My father has always given me the instruments to draw, to paint and to work with clay. I spent entire days in the laboratory with him.' The ceramics laboratory was a sensual experience for the boy: 'the smell of the humidity and the earth near the furnace, the cooking, the colour spread on the terracotta and re-baked is oxidized and always vibrates'.

While Toccafondo's father often made vases and other finished pieces, young Gianluigi was fascinated by middle stage of the ceramic process. 'The potters start from a piece of clay and they begin to turn the lathe until that piece takes a form. In the beginning there is nothing. At the end is a vase standing alone. But what occurred between the piece of clay and the final result was an incredible work with a thousand successive phases during which the form changed continuously. Passing through these forms was much more interesting than the final result itself.' Toccafondo's father often left pieces unfinished. These often crooked, disfigured objects mesmerized Gianluigi and had an enormous influence on his films 'These incomplete pieces became forms on which you could imagine lots of things, most of the time magnificent. Maybe this I why I have never believed in an idea or subject, or a conclusive story; I'm always more interested in development and transformation of movement. I spent my childhood in the middle of these forms changing continuously. I think all the work done by my father is at the origin of my personal way to work.'

Toccafondo studied at National Institute of Arts of Urbino. 'It was an eye-opening experience for me', remembers Toccafondo. 'There were a lot of foreign students and excellent teachers. A painter named Professor Ricci taught the animation course and he really taught me to paint moving objects.' Using black and white 16mm film, Toccafondo did his first animation experiments at Urbino.

After graduation, he started work at a commercial production house called, Mixfilm. 'I learned everything there', says Toccafondo. 'The studio's designers, Giancarlo Carloni, Giovanni Mulazzani and Tomislav Spikic were generous with their experience. They taught me a great deal and produced my first short-films.' In Mixfilm studio, Toccafondo began to mix painting and cinema. 'In the studio, I made photocopies and drew with the aid of photos. There was a moviola, the frames, and shooting with film. In my own studio, there were cloths for painting, clay and wax, so I joined the two worlds.'

With MixFilm, Toccafondo made his first short films, *La Coda* (1989), *Boxe* (1990) and *La Pista* (1991). All three films are playful *Pinocchio*

237

experiments that take existing film footage and playfully manipulate it. The result is at once surreal and comic.

Toccafondo's debut film, *La Coda* – translates as 'The Tail' – uses footage from various Buster Keaton films and manipulates them by painting over the scenes, slowing the speed down, reversing the footage. In most of his films, Keaton is seen fleeing from someone or something. In *La Coda*, Keaton is at the mercy of Toccafondo who toys and torments Keaton throughout the film. In the end, Keaton escapes a pig-shaped house when his umbrella suddenly turns into a propeller and he whirls away into the sky.

There is also a strong element of choreography in *La Coda*. In Toccafondo's world, Keaton is transformed from a stuntman into a dancer. 'I made drawings to study the movements of Buster Keaton', says Toccafondo. 'I photographed the frames from TV. Then I enlarged them and painted on them. I rented a little studio where I went to work in the evening and there I made experiments. I reconstructed the incomplete parts of photos, I lengthened Keaton's arms, legs, nose and ears and other similar jokes.'

While the 20-second piece, *Boxe*, turns a boxing match into a silly, harmless mash of colour and shapes, *La Pista* (The Dance Floor, co-directed by Simona Mulazzani) uses scenes from a Fred Astaire

La Piccola Russia

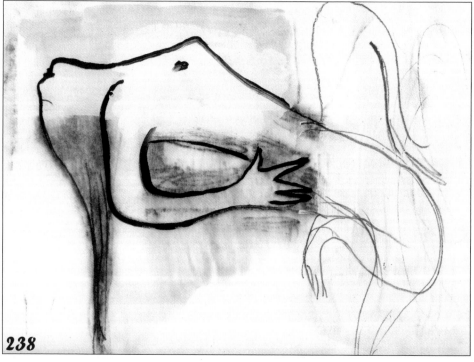

and Ginger Rogers film (mixed with animals!). As Fred and Ginger dance, their faces and bodies are stretched, distorted and painted over to the rhythm of a tango. Under Toccafondo's hand, the performers become superhuman, their limbs elastic. The duo have full control over their bodies and can even fly with ease. At the end, Fred and Ginger are replaced by a horde of pigs that march around with ridiculously long legs.

On the surface, Toccafondo seems to make the impossible possible, but in a deeper sense, he is really showing us the common nature of us all. For all our thinking, imagining, self-awareness, we are ultimately at the mercy of our bodies.

La Pista del Maiale (1992) – which translates, roughly, as The Dance of the Pig, is a strange experimental piece that follows the last moments of a pig before it is slaughtered. Set inside what appears to be a cold, white room where pigs meet their fate, Toccafondo takes this haven of death and transforms it, momentarily, into a celebration and remembrance of the pig, and life. The blank white walls come alive like cave drawings, a black and white drawing of the tail end of a pig appears. The animal is desperately trying to escape from the room. Stretching its body to a magnificent length, the pig manages to break free. The pig is alive, its colour returns. All is well. Then there is darkness again. The colour fades and the pig is being pulled back along the walls of the room. The images darken. The music heightens. Blackness sweeps through the frames. The walls begin to close in. In an instant, the pig is gone. All that remains are its broken remains scattered on an anonymous table. It is the fate of the pigs. It is the fate of us all.

Toccafondo spent five months in Paris working on his next film, *Le Criminel*. 'It was the first time I succeeded to do a short film without the interruption of commercials projects.' In *Le Criminel*, Toccafondo shifts from silent comedy and musicals to the film noir and gangster genres for inspiration. The film opens with dead bodies on the streets. An investigation follows. Mug shots and fingerprints flash across the screen. The camera follows suspects through the dark, shadowy city streets. More murders take place. Armed shadows skulk in the darkness. Death lurks. At long last, a culprit is found, perhaps. The frozen face is distorted, indistinguishable from those that came before. At once a playful tribute to Hollywood film noir, *Le Criminel* is also an exploration of identity and mortality. Do we all live life as criminals, worrying about the fate that awaits us all in the shadows?

For a man who loves to control and manipulate his characters like puppets, it's no surprise to hear that Toccafondo is drawn to the story of Pinocchio. 'Since I started animating, I have always thought of *Pinocchio*. He's in all my short films. I had always wanted to do a film and in the beginning had very clear ideas. Unfortunately, it's been a film that I cursed more than others I made. I never managed to finish it until the producers finally forced me to complete it after three years of work.'

Toccafondo's interpretation is quite different from the saccharine adaptation of Walt Disney. Toccafondo restores the darker elements of the original story (e.g. the cricket's death) and also injects the story with the madcap playfulness of silent comedies. In fact, underneath Toccafondo's painted Pinocchio, we can see snippets of footage from the films of Buster Keaton. It's a fitting fusion as silent comedians like Keaton, Laurel and Hardy, and Charlie Chaplin are all boys at heart. They are curious, ignorant man-boys still awed, surprised and horrified by the world around them. They constantly struggle to escape the soul-killing clutches of the structured, mysterious, and often harmful, world of adults. Toccafondo compresses the story into a manic, breathless six-minute dream. Like Keaton, Pinocchio runs about frantically trying to flee from one menacing figure after another. The viewer is given no sense of a beginning or end. We are simply tossed into the nightmare of another. Toccafondo is more interested in Pinocchio's journey and the process of transformation rather than the actual metamorphosis itself. The serendipitous beauty of movement and colour splashes onto every frame. Shapes and colours dance, duck, and dive across the screen to the accompaniment of Mario Mariani's frenetic Nino Rota-inspired score.

Fittingly, the ending is ambiguous. Is Pinocchio dead or asleep? Was this a dream? Is he a boy or a puppet? Does it matter? Toccafondo's story is a celebration of childhood's manic moments of horror, wonder and discovery.

In 2000, Toccafondo was one of six young Italian directors commissioned to make a film to celebrate the 25th anniversary of the death of the great Italian filmmaker/poet, Pier Paulo Pasolini. Each director had to take as their starting point one of Pasolini's films, stories or characters. Toccafondo's contribution, *Essere Morti o Essere Vivi è la stessa cosa* (Being Dead and Alive is the Same Thing, 2000) takes sentences from Pasolini's early poems along with a series of images from Pasolini's films. 'I put *La terra vista dalla Luna* and his sketches all together with Totò, Ninetto and Silvana Mangano ...' Toccafondo told Italian journalist Cristiana Paternò in 2001. 'I saw *Accattone*, *Mamma Roma*, *La ricotta*, Cosa sono le nuvole again. I was inspired by the Friulian poems of Pasolini that already then contained scenes from many of the films Pasolini would go on to make. I was inspired by the Chapel of the Scrovegni in Padua. I consider Pasolini to be the Giotto of his day.'

The film begins with a man jumping to his death from a bridge. As he dies, we are taken through a fresco of his life before the dark angel of death arrives to take the young man away. When they arrive in the heaven (?) above, the angel then transforms the man into an ape. The ape runs off on a new journey.

United Arrows commercial

Being Dead and Alive is the Same Thing is much more than a tribute to Pasolini. Using fragments of poems, along with images from Pasolini's films of dancing, living, and dying, Toccafondo transforms Pasolini's art into a provocative meditation on Pasolini's life and the inescapable bond between *all* life and death. Pasolini's life and death become our own.

Toccafondo's most recent film, *La Picolla Russia* (Little Russia, 2004), is set in an Italian village near the Adriatic Sea. 'The title comes from the nickname of the village where my grandfather lived (that name was used for the areas, villages and popular quarters that admired the Soviet system).' The story traces the life of a young boy who grows up to be a murderer. In the beginning, we follow a young boy and his parents. We see them eat, dance, and enjoy life. They seem happy. One day the boy sees his father kill a rabbit. Later, the mother cooks the rabbit for dinner. The event traumatizes him. His parents struggle to console him. Time passes. The boy's passions turn to girls, and then women. Although he dreams

241

of love and marriage, the portly boy is alone and soon spends his time at strip clubs watching women do their half-hearted come-hither-and-fuck me dances. Soon he is swimming in a sea of paid passion, sucking, licking and fucking any and all who take cash. It's never enough, though. He remains alone, unloved; his passions unfulfilled. The world is not as it should be. He is not as he should be. Tormented by his salacious desires he soon murders a prostitute. After dumping her body in the sea, he returns home, where he first slaughters his father like a rabbit, and then decapitates his mother (whose head becomes the moon). With the money he steals from his father, he finds another prostitute and makes love to her. Finally – in a shot that resembles the final shot of *Pinocchio* and the earlier shot of the disconsolate boy struggling to comprehend the murder of the rabbit – we see the man sitting with his head down on a table in some anonymous seaside hotel. Is it all a dream, a terrible nightmare of another world, another time? Is he dead? No, the man is soon surrounded by police and taken away. A gentle meditation of childhood and community turns into a sinister and violent psychological gore film.

While *La Picolla Russia* is arguably Toccafondo's most narrative driven film, each image stands alone like a painting or a photograph in a scrapbook. 'It wasn't born as a film', says Toccafondo about the film's origins. 'It should have been a picture-book of sorts.' Like Michèle Cournoyer's brilliant animation, *The Hat*, greys, whites, and blacks distort and swallow the photographed images in *La Picolla Russia*, giving the film both a cloudy, dour ambiance while reflecting the menace of doom and chaos that litters the protagonist's confused mind.

La Picolla Russia is a document of the passions of a man who is born, lives, loves and kills. Toccafondo does not judge. It doesn't matter really. What is done is done.

Toccafondo has also made a number of commissioned films including i.d.'s, commercials and credit sequences. Among the highlights are the poetic commercials, *More Cinema, More Europa* (1992), *Woman Finding Love* (for Levis' Jeans, 1993), *United Arrows* (1998), *La Biennale Di Venezia* (a trailer for the 1999 Venice Film Festival), *Italia Taglia* (2001), a tribute to Italian cinema; *La Sposa* (1998), an erotic sequence from a French live-action feature film, *Le Monde à l'envers; and Sipario Ducale* (1999), made to promote a local arts festival in the Italian province of Pesaro-Urbino. Toccafondo, and collaborator, Massimo Salvucci, turn this commissioned work into a strange, beautiful and personal journey through the various regions where the festival is held. 'We have shot all the places where this event takes place, then we have edited all the material and, finally, I drew on it. It was one of the first experiments where we mixed real images with drawings, many of which are made directly with computer.'

Having grown up in the region, the film became a journey through the landscapes of Toccafondo's past. 'It's a journey that allowed me to uncover the lands where I was born and raised: between the *francesco di giorgio martini's* fortresses and Adriatic sea.' Like the festival, the film is a celebration of people, of life. As the old woman beautifully says (the only dialogue in the film) at the end to Toccafondo: '... when the season starts, here there are ice-creams, *piadine* [a sort of local bread]... and all sorts of good things'.

In summarizing his work, Toccafondo says, 'Cinema is my starting point. I make photos from film-clips, I xerox them on paper and then paint on them, transforming the original subject. Finally I make the shots with the 35mm film and they become cinema again.' Like Dr. Frankenstein, Toccafondo takes scraps from an old world and breathes new life into them.

This frantic, fragmented nature of Toccafondo's world becomes an apt reflection of a life that is not only fleeting, but also filled with seemingly random and innocuous moments. Everything seems to flash by us with no order, no meaning or logic. We have little opportunity to catch our breath and take it all in. Yet, paradoxically, these are the moments that count, that continually define, create and challenge us. With each of these moments, life begins anew, carrying traces and hints of what came before. As we were, we are, and are not.

Filmography of Gianluigi Toccafondo

1989	*La Coda*
1990	*Boxe*
1991	*La Pista*
1992	*La Pista Del Maiale*
1992	*More Cinema, More Europe* (commercial)
1993	*Criminel*
1993	*Woman Finding Love* (commercial)
1998	*United Arrows* (commercial)
1998	*La Sposa* (film sequence)
1999	*Sipario Ducale*
1999	*Pinnochio*
2000	*Being Dead or Alive is the Same Thing*
2001	*Italia Taglia* (TV promo)
2004	*La Piccola Russia*

Chapter 30

Sullivan's Travels (2005)

Family Sounds
(drawing)

Three troubled and unhappy individuals living in a dour, industrial American town. Themes of dysfunctional families, Catholicism, Social services, and alcoholism. *Consuming Spirits* isn't your typical animation film, and creator Chris Sullivan isn't your average animator.

If animation has an answer to the great writer, Hubert Selby Jr. (author of such fine novels as *Last Exit To Brooklyn, Requiem for a Dream, The Room*) it's Chicago animator, Chris Sullivan. Like Selby, Sullivan shows us the world, as it is, not how we imagine it to be. A world that is neither heroic or beautiful, nor exceptionally ugly or evil. This is not your typical animation world of animals, dick jokes, or abstract non-figurative symbolic blah blah blahs about wallowing artists. Sullivan's working class characters struggle daily against poverty, abuse, death, madness, want and despair. But Sullivan is no preacher or social activist. His blunt, bare and unpretentious films aim, not to shock, but to engage us, to simply show us a world that most of us deny living in.

Born in 1960, Sullivan was one of eleven children in a catholic family from Pittsburgh. 'Being smart and liberal in thinking was important in my family', says Sullivan. His parents were politically active through the Catholic Church and the civil rights movement. Sullivan's dad worked with the United Steel Workers union.

Tragedy struck the family early and often. In 1955, Sullivan's older sister, Franny was killed after being hit by a car. In 1968, Sullivan's brother Brian died of leukemia. The following year, his father died under mysterious circumstances. 'My father officially died, I assumed, from alcoholism [his heavy drinking started after Franny died], but in later years I found out he was actually beaten by some thugs, and was also taking medication for seizures.'

Raising nine children alone proved to be an exceptional challenge for Sullivan's mother. 'My Mother was a bit of an observer, though

a dynamo in her own right', notes Sullivan. 'She was often cooking to keep us all alive, and was very intellectually and spiritually intense. Sometimes my Mother handled things well, other times she didn't. She and my father spent some time in mental health facilities. During one of those times, I lived with another family.'

Chris Sullivan

'My childhood was actually full of fun and pleasure', says Sullivan, 'but my house began to fall apart in terms of cleanliness, to the point that the social service intervention became a big part of my life. A woman named Miss Bainim came to our house and helped my mother clean. It was very humiliating for my Mother, and I remember feeling very vulnerable.'

During the sixties and seventies, social workers intervened and split the family up for periods for time. 'My two older brothers Tony and Nick', remembers Sullivan, 'lived with my Aunt Bertha for several years, and my Brother Nick stayed there throughout his highschool years. My sister Suzy went to live with a family named the McMackins.'

One of three siblings with Bachelors of Fine Arts degrees, Sullivan always thought of himself as an artist. After high school he went to art school at Carnegie Mellon University to study painting and ceramics. A school crush led Sullivan to take an animation class at the school. In the class, Sullivan made a super-8 animation film called *Tea* (1979). This story about a man making tea is drawn in a very jagged style using only black ink on white paper. The use of distorted, exaggerated perspectives gives this normally bland act an hallucinogenic quality. Students loved the film. 'When I showed it at a student super-8 get-together, it got this huge response. I was also in a poetry class, where a reading also made me realize this idea of audience. Audience is an unavoidable part of media art and literature and I really liked that.'

Sullivan soon found that writing was becoming increasingly important to him and that animation 'was a new world that offered

Endomitriosis
(drawing)

246

The Beholder

something that my paintings and ceramics did not'. He also realized that he was at the wrong school for such desires and transferred to the Minneapolis College of Art and Design.

In Minneapolis, Sullivan made the films, *Lessons* (1980), and *Ain't Misbehavin* (1981). In *Lessons*, a boy gets in trouble at school when his teacher catches him making drawings in class. After he continues

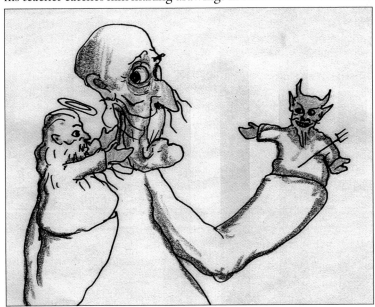

Landscape with the Fall of Icarus

Master of Ceremonies

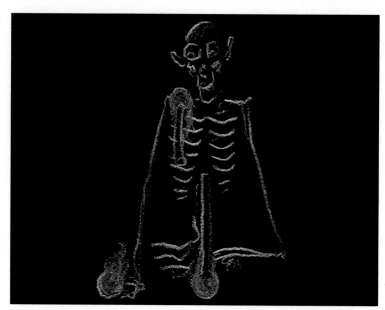

to muck about in the class, the teacher loses her temper and chases the boy around the classroom with a paddle. The scared boy eventually escapes the classroom and runs home through the woods. Sullivan's scrappy, raw style has the feel of a child's drawing. The pictures of the children are gently drawn using light crayon colours, while the teacher – who is seen through the eyes of the boy – is depicted more harsh and abstractly with red and black markers. Her fragmented, jittery image shakes and rattles menacingly throughout the classroom, creating a nightmarish and sadistic atmosphere.

In *Aint Misbehavin*, the mind of a man becomes a battlefield of overlapping images and voices. As he spends the day in his house doing an assortment of domestic jobs: cooking, eating, reading, writing, and bathing, images of war and death enter the man's mind. Is it a day in the life of a schizophrenic or a snapshot of a state we all know? All of us live through different realities simultaneously. When you're riding a bus, streets, houses, cars and people pass by, but often we don't see these things because we're 'seeing' another reality in our heads (e.g. thinking about unfinished work, groceries, listening to an mp3 player.) In a span of seconds, we pass through different spaces. When we see the protagonist in *Aint Misbehavin'* walk through a room filled with other people who all resemble him, is he really insane or are we simply seeing a truth that we all know is within us?

'I think we all feel the absurdity of our lives sometimes', says

Sullivan. 'I have characters who have blinders. They cannot see it all because it is too beautiful, or too painful, or too unattainable. I sometimes cry at movies. I think it is because the emotions in the movie are emotions I have had once, but can't seem to locate now, and I cry for their loss. In my life, my blinders keep me from constantly seeing this loss.'

After graduating in 1983, Sullivan made *The Beholder* (1983). On a city street, a man rants about god, the devil, and repentance. Nearby, people sit in a crowded restaurant. Detached from those around them, they eat, mumble, and fantasize without any passion or engagement. A waitress apathetically recites the specials. Two men literally pass through each other near the toilets. These people have shelter and food, but they aren't alive. The restaurant almost becomes a security blanket, a place to hide from their crazy, mundane and trapped existences. As Sullivan cuts back and forth – without judgement – between the man and the restaurant people, you begin to see that there is little to distinguish them. In fact, the preacher, for all his ramblings and drooling, is at least engaged and passionate about the world. He's the only one who seems to be living a life he wants.

In *Master of Ceremonies* (1987), a house burns to the ground and the occupants perish. As the dying transform into spirits, the voices of the house resonate. Before they head to wherever it is spirits go, death decides to put on a nice little vaudeville show to cheer up the recently dead.

As the fire rages through the house, the family's efforts to escape are futile. Doors, walls, objects stand in the way. As they frantically try to break free, voices from the past are heard throughout the house. Only in death does the family finally break free of themselves and all they carried with them.

On one level *Master of Ceremonies* is a film about the cruelty of death. Death doesn't care. It takes what it wants, when it wants. On another, this is a film about the death of the past, about how life moves on with or without us. Only in death do we truly silence ourselves.

In Pieter Bruegel's painting, *Landscape with the Fall of Icarus*, the fall of the god, Icarus, passes unnoticed on earth. The farmers continue to work the land and the boats sail on. As William Carlos Williams later wrote in his poem of the same name, a once mighty god becomes 'a splash quite unnoticed'.

Inspired by the Bruegel painting, Sullivan spent five years making *Landscape with the Fall of Icarus* (1992). In Sullivan's version, Icarus becomes Ray, an aging preacher whose congregation is dwindling as fast as his sanity. As Ray's condition deteriorates, society fails to notice or care. In the end, Ray finds solace in a bar singing hymns about 'weaving footprints through the snow'. Around him are figures from the nightmares that have tormented him. They no longer bother him here. He is at peace. The bar becomes a new church for Ray, a sanctuary. When Ray leaves the bar in the film's final shot, he has become invisible except for his footprints. Outside of his safe haven he becomes that 'splash quite unnoticed'.

The decline of the Ray's church is less about a loss of spirituality than it is about a society turning away from itself. 'I think of the emptying church', says Sullivan, 'as an emptying inner city, being emptied of normal familial moments of peace and love. I don't think of this as a something politically placed on people, I think of it as a breakdown of love, both abstract love and real warmth.'

Lydia the Tattooed girl
(drawing)

Since 1996, Sullivan has been working on an independent animation feature. Considering the time and expense that goes into making animation short films, why on earth would an animator like Sullivan want to make an independently produced feature animation film? 'Most of my favourite films are features. John Cassavettes, Terrence Davies, and Todd Haynes, are people I love', says Sullivan. 'The film kind of turned into a feature, through the years. If I could go in a time machine, I would make something a little bit more manageable, but my interest remains in feature productions.

Having only part one of *Consuming Spirits* (the film will be completed by the mid-2005), it's difficult to discuss the film in great detail. *Consuming Spirits* focuses primarily on three characters: Earl, Jen, and Victor. All three work at the local newspaper. Outside of work, Earl hosts a late night radio show on gardening; Jen takes care of her foul-mouthed mother; when Victor isn't dating Jen, he's out drinking while driving down rural roads.

The film is loosely based on Sullivan's childhood and hometown. 'I start with autobiographical moments, but it is a fiction. One of the main fictions is that I come from an 11 children family, and the two families in this film have 1 and 2 children respectively. This

Untitled drawing

51

was for deeper character development, but also for pragmatic reasons of animating too many characters.'

Consuming Spirits takes place in the past and present. The past is told using sketchy, ink-on-white, drawn animation, while the present is depicted with cut-out and model animation. 'My interest in using cut-outs', says Sullivan, 'came out of an interest in having real time in my work. With drawing there are the cycles and holds, but it is difficult to maintain variance. I like the possibility of animating someone fidgeting for a whole minute. I was also interested in a full colour palette, that I could get with cut-outs. There is still a magic with the drawing that cut-outs cannot duplicate, but I traded off some things for others. The models were a later decision that I actually like a lot. I enjoy that they are both (an) illusory and obvious model train village at the same time.' The cut-out and model techniques also give the film a heavy, lumbering atmosphere. The town is dark, gloomy and stagnant, littered with dead trees. The characters are awkward, plain and frail. They look as though they might fall apart in an instant.

As with Sullivan's previous films, the characters here are neither good nor bad. They are confused, myopic and haunted people, struggling through life until something happens to shake them from their waking sleep. 'I often have sudden things happen to my characters because that is the way life is to me', says Sullivan. 'There is very little build-up to the real life changing events of one's life. You are walking down the street and you wake up in a hospital, having been struck by a car. You are playing with your kids on the lawn and you have a heart attack. You go to the doctor for a hangnail, and are diagnosed with cancer. By the same token, you take a random class while in college, and fall in love. You walk in the woods, and see a deer right in front of you. You read a sentence, and your heart is lifted or broken.'

In all of Sullivan's films, religion (death, angels, church, preachers, nuns, Jesus statues) envelops the characters and landscape. In part one of *Consuming Spirits*, Earl cares for an injured nun and Jen is sent to a church to take pictures. While there, a nun, perhaps sensing Jen's unhappiness, subtly suggests that she also consider becoming a nun.

'I am not religious', says Sullivan, 'but I am not sarcastic about other people's belief systems. I am very secular. Issues of God are more interesting to me sociologically than spiritually, I am some-times saddened, but not too concerned about dying and disappear-ing into a void of nothingness.' Hope for characters like the street preacher in *Beholder* and Ray in *Landscape*, only seems to come through religious faith. In the end, even religion fails them: Ray winds up half-mad in a bar; the street preacher lives as an outcast on the fringes of society. Sullivan, surprisingly, remains optimistic. 'I do have hope, but I think the world will get darker before it gets lighter.'

Given the time spent on *Consuming Spirits*, it's no wonder that Sullivan remains frustrated with animation. 'The big question for me in relationship to animation is its slow gestation period, this will always be an issue for me. I am in many ways a writer first, and most of my ideas come from writing. Animation is a difficult way of manifesting these ideas. I might write two pages in a day that will then take a year to animate. The images are always chasing the ideas, and, to be honest, last year's idea.'

Chris Sullivan is truly an unsung animator. Despite making some of the most honest, potent and thoughtful animated films, he remains a somewhat marginalized figure even within the animation festival community (where most animation shorts are screened). Outside of a few festivals, Sullivan's work has been ignored.

The animation festival circuit (with a few exceptions) tends to be too easily swayed by lightweight films that are well crafted but have little to say. Films that promote peace and harmony and all things good and nice, sugar and spice, also tend to be more highly valued than their darker, dysfunctional siblings. Sullivan's films are perhaps too raw, real and ugly for the animation aesthete.

'In terms of being slightly marginalized', says Sullivan who currently lives in Chicago with his wife Susan Abelson, and their daughters Carmen and Silvia, and teaches animation at the School of Art Institute in Chicago. 'I do feel that many of my animation heroes – Frederic Back, Paul Driessen, Priit Pärn, Wendy Tilby, Yuri Norstein, and The Quay Brothers – have films that are simply, more beautiful than mine. I find their work very inspiring, and perhaps I just have to make better work. I am up for the challenge'.

Are *we*?

Filmography of Chris Sullivan

1979	Tea
1980	Lessons
1981	Ain't Misbehavin
1983	The Beholder
1987	Master of Ceremonies
1988	Rume's
1992	Landscape with the Fall of Icarus
1996–	
2005	Consuming Spirits

Chapter 31

Ruth Lingford: Old Halo Coffins Layered (2005)

Death and the Mother

I n her beautiful, poignant film adaptation of Philip Larkin's poem, *The Old Fools*, British animator, Ruth Lingford ruminates on aging and our inevitable erosion. Larkin wrote the poem while his mother lay dying. Lingford made the film while her father was ailing. I watched the film while my grandparents were dying.

> *My grandmother's Alzheimer's got so bad that we had to put her in a nursing home in 1997. The move devastated my grandfather. They were in their 56th year of marriage. You rarely saw them apart. For the first time since 1941, he was alone. He initially tried to limit his visits to the home, but before long he was making the half hour drive almost daily. He'd help feed her, bring movies and music for the residents, and continually care for her. We understood, but it was heartbreaking to see him unable to carve out what remained of his life with the rest of his family. He took little interest in anything but her. In 2003, tired of long lonely winters and sleepless nightmares, he announced that he was selling the house and moving to the nursing home. I found it heartbreaking. I grew up in their home. It was my only real home. Now it was being taken away. I sensed that there was something my grandfather was keeping from us. Sure he was sad, tired and lonely without my grandmother, but he had family around him. Why on earth would he move to a nursing home? Unless …*

Ruth Lingford was born in London in 1953. She grew up in the London suburb of Muswell Hill. 'I had a mainly happy sort of childhood. I was a bright child with a strong moral sense.' She was, though, plagued by insecurities. 'I was a terribly messy child and would make a mess with paint and crayons. I was also fat and was subjected to a certain amount of teasing, especially from my older sister.' Lingford was also routinely haunted by nightmares. 'I can clearly remember a witch that lived in the lampshade over my bed and would come out and torment me every night.'

Ruth Lingford

'Puberty', remembers Lingford, 'hit me like a strong wind'. She went from a bright and loving girl to a demon daughter. Growing up in the late '60s, Lingford embraced the generation of excess and experimentation. 'This was the late '60s, post-pill and pre-feminism, and it was considered rather impolite not to sleep with anyone who asked. Sitting round smoking dope, the boys would hold forth with their

255

stoned philosophical theories, while chicks were expected to be silent, sexually available, and make the tea.'

During this time, Lingford struggled to find a place for herself. She took an Art Foundation course in Brighton, but when her drawing failed to impress anyone, she dropped out and opted for a Psychology degree at Brunel University. Her stay at Brunel was brief. 'A bad marihuana habit meant that I rarely succeeded in finding any lectures or tutorials, or in staying awake through any that I did find.' Lingford was eventually given the boot from Brunel.

Life wasn't all bad. Before she left Brunel, Lingford met her future husband, John, 'a small whiskery nugget of goodness who has doggedly stayed married to me all this time'.

Lingford soon found a job working as an Occupational Therapy Aide at Friern Hospital, a psychiatric facility. The job was to have a monumental effect on her life and films. 'Friern Hospital, now converted into luxury flats, was a huge Victorian institution, famous for having the longest corridors in Europe', remembers Lingford. 'It took a while to identify the source of the distinctive smell that permeated the place. Gradually I identified its components. There was long-cooked cabbage, and piss. But the third element came from the patients' habit of collecting cigarette ends, rolling the damp fragments of tobacco up in newspaper, and smoking them until their fingers burned into orange and black blisters.'

Lingford also discovered that patient abuse and neglect was all too

Sea in the Blood

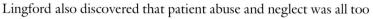

common: 'I was shocked by some of the cruelty I saw on the "back wards" – an old bent man with large ears made to "dance, monkey!" by the young male nurses. But my immature idealism was probably no more effective in making the patients' lives any better. Still, the job accorded with my image of myself as a "really nice person".' After a few more years at the hospital, Lingford took a three-year training course and, in 1979, became a qualified Occupational Therapist. The same year, she and John had their first child, George (a second, Abigail, was born in 1982). 'While the kids were small, I worked part-time as an Occupational Therapist, mostly with elderly physically and mentally ill people. I loved having the children, and quite enjoyed the work, but gradually it dawned on me that I wasn't really as nice a person as all that. Meanwhile, I went with a friend to some daytime life drawing and painting classes, mainly because there was a crèche where we could leave our children. The teacher of the class, Jack Piesse, was a handsome, charismatic, and gifted teacher. My work improved and began to become more interesting and important to me.'

> A few months after he moved to the nursing home, my grandfather died in an Ottawa hospital. He didn't want to go this way. He moved to the home to die beside my grandmother. He died alone inside the anonymous hospital walls at 6:30am. An hour later I was staring down at the only real father I ever knew. Now he was the first dead man I ever knew.
>
> He sure had a lot of nose hair.

Considering Lingford's unique background, it's no surprise that her parents lived a rather distinctive and stimulating life. 'My dad [Jack Selford]', says Lingford, 'was a Jewish boy from the East End of London, who irritated his family by joining the Communist Party and marrying two non-Jewish women. My mother [Alison MacLeod] was from the impoverished upper classes and irritated her family by joining the Communist party and marrying a black man and a Jew.' (Though to put this in context, her aunt, the writer Rebecca West, was a trailblazer in the family scandal department, having H.G. Wells' lovechild, and affairs with Lord Beaverbrook, Charlie Chaplin, and others too numerous to mention).

Both of Lingford's parents were heavily involved in communism. Her father wrote plays for a Communist theatre in London, while her mom wrote for the Daily Worker newspaper. She worked there until 1956, when she decided to leave the Communist Party (as did Jack) following the Soviet army's brutality against a Hungarian uprising, and Khrushchev's public rejection of Joseph Stalin. Their faith in communism betrayed, Jack and Alison saw their world radically altered. 'My parents', says Lingford, 'were confronted by the crumbling of all the things they believed in. This involved losing their jobs, many of their friends and the whole structure of their lives. So I grew up with a distrust of big ideas.'

Jack, who had trained as a teacher after World War II, returned to teaching. Mcleod found work, oddly enough, with financial papers like The Times Business News and Euromoney. She also wrote six historical novels, and a book about leaving the Communist Party called *The Death of Uncle Joe*.

> *My grandfather wrote once. A few days after his death I drove out to the nursing home with my cousins. Inside a drawer in my grandparent's room, I found a birthday card for grandma. It was from grandpa. He was not an affectionate man. He did not show emotion. He just acted. Even then he never really seemed to be enjoying himself. However, inside this card he wrote: 'To my darling wife. I miss you. I need you. I love you. You are everything to me.' It was heartbreaking stuff. He probably never said anything like this to her before. He never felt he had to. Life would go on. There would always be tomorrow.*
>
> *Her faculties are long gone. She will never read this card. She will never know.*
>
> *I will bury the card with her when she goes.*

Maybe Ruth was a nice person after all. In 1987, an elderly neighbour breathed his last breath and left Lingford £10,000. 'This was quite unexpected, as he had spent his time, when I knew him, wrapped in a pissy blanket, and when I did his shopping he

Crumble

wouldn't let me buy him teabags, as he felt them to be a gross extravagance.' Lingford used the money to enroll in a Fine Art course at Middlesex Polytechnic. It was to change the course of her life. 'I painted, drew, made prints, bent bits of wire, chipped bits of rock... Then, in my second year, I found an old Standard 8 movie camera on a second hand stall for £5. My first idea was to record the building-up of a painting. I had been oil painting, and was frustrated by the way the layers would be lost as the painting was built up. So I tried that, and found I had only used up about 10 frames of film. So I used up the rest with lots of experiments – drawing from Muybridge photos, pushing sugar about, just drawing.'

When she finally projected her Super 8 experiment, Lingford was mesmerized. 'The really magic thing about animation, I soon decided, was its ability to transform one thing into another via sensuous, sinuous movements of line. I started by working in a straight-ahead, stream-of-consciousness way, drawing and tracing and seeing what happened.' Lingford now knew what she wanted to do when she grew up.

> My grandma made sacrifices to raise a family of four and, later, a grandchild (me). She loved to whistle with the backyard birds. Sometimes she spoke of her love of music. As Alzheimer's was devouring her, wartime music would, momentarily, call her back to us. What did she give up to raise a family? Was she satisfied with staying at home in the country while my grandpa went to work? I sometimes think she didn't live the life she wanted. But maybe he didn't either.

An important influence on Lingford during the Middlesex days was her Art History professor, Peter Webb. Webb also authored the controversial book, *The Erotic Arts* (1975), which addressed issues of repression, sexuality and censorship, and encouraged artists to explore darker and more complex visual material without fear of repercussions. Stimulated by Webb's ideas and encouragement, Lingford and her classmates made work that explored the darker recesses of their sexuality. For Lingford's first film, *Whole Lotta Love* (1989), she took the raging uninhibited sexuality of Led Zeppelin's famous song and re-situated in the new era of AIDS. Her second film at Middlesex, *Sea in the Blood* (1990) addresses issues of fertility and motherhood.

'Animation', says Lingford, 'seemed to be a good way of exploring interesting and difficult things. It took a long time to do, but it seemed to catch people's attention in a way that I could only dream of as a painter or sculptor. People actually seemed to *want* to watch it!

259

Oh, and as for Peter Webb, his uninhibited ways – which included molesting boys and collecting child pornography – landed him in jail.

After graduating from Middlesex in 1990, Lingford attended the prestigious Royal College of Art (RCA) to do her Masters. She made two films at RCA: *Baggage* (1992) and *Crumble* (1992). Drawing on her experience working with the elderly, *Crumble* looks at the crumbling lives of the wrinkled, decaying souls in a nursing home. Using a simple coloured pencil on paper technique, Lingford takes us inside the minds of those suffering from dementia to try and comprehend what these eroding people see. In *Baggage*, a woman fucks a man she meets at a party. Afterwards she is haunted by images of her fertility. Everywhere she turns, she sees fetuses. In her apartment elevator, a giant fetus jumps at her and tries to smother her. In the end, the disconsolate, paranoid woman transforms into both fetus and mother, and feeds off herself.

'Both films got good feedback at the graduation show and did the rounds at animation festivals', says Lingford, 'but getting paid work was not so easy. I had a rather interesting job for Dorling Kindersley for a while, animating medical diagrams, and this gave me a hint of the possibilities of animation. In the process of animating the working of the heart valves, it became clear to me that my previous understanding of the process, gained through diagrams, was completely wrong, and the process could only really be communicated using movement.'

On some Sundays I visit the nursing home and feed my grand-

mother. To still my discomfort, I think back to when she fed me as a baby. It makes me feel good. I am caring for her, I think, as she once did for me.

After failing to get a job working on chintzy TV animation productions, Lingford got word that her application for a grant from Animate! (a project run by the Arts Council of England and Channel 4 to fund short experimental animation films) to do a film called, *What She Wants* (1994), had been approved.

As a woman walks through the landscape of the city, she is bombarded by images of sexuality that skulk behind advertisements, products (a purse becomes a vagina) and infrastructures (the subway tunnel as sexual metaphor). Inspired by the paintings of Goya and Eugene Delacroix, and the *History of Sexuality* books by French thinker Michel Foucault, *What She Wants* explores the connections between desire, sexuality and capitalism, and how the language of advertising and business creates, infiltrates and exploits our internal fantasies.

Without the support of a college, Lingford had no access to cameras or other equipment. What she did have though, was a home computer. 'I did some experiments to see whether I could use our home computer for animation. This was a very basic Amiga, and I found I could do about eight frames, using a basic programme called Deluxe Paint. Having got the grant money, I could buy a bigger model, and the film was made on about 20 floppy discs.'

Lingford's next project, *Death and the Mother* (1997) was developed as part of an Animator in Residence project devised by London's Museum of the Moving Image. This unique and rather bizarre residency had the animator working inside a room, in full view of the museum's visitors. The animator, in essence, became an exhibit. 'Taking into account that I would be working as a museum exhibit with children watching', says Lingford, 'I thought I'd better come up with a safer topic for a film than the sexual aberrations that had made up my work so far. I thought a fairy tale would be safe, and opened the collected works of Hans Christian Andersen at random. The story I found there, *The Story of a Mother*, was more shocking and disturbing than anything I had dealt with so far, but the story virus had got into my bloodstream and that was the film I had to make.'

Inspired by German expressionist woodcuts, Lingford's black and white film is a harrowing story about the death of a child. Disguised as an old man, death approaches a house. Inside, a mother sits, holding her sick girl. Death lures the woman out, snatches the child from her and flees. The mother gives chase and eventually finds death. When she begs for her child's return, death gently responds

The Old Fools
(three images)

by revealing the sad and painful life her daughter would otherwise live. The heartbroken mother painfully acknowledges that this life would be much worse than death and agrees to let go of her daughter. Told without words, Lingford's woodcut style gives the film a haunting, expressionistic tone that beautifully complements this soul-shaking tale of a fate much worse than death.

Death and the Mother put Lingford on the international animation map. The film was shown worldwide and captured a number of awards, including a graphic award at the 1997 Annecy festival and a special prize from the jury of the 1997 Cartoon d'Or.

> *I keep hoping my grandmother will die. She sits there absent and unaware. She recognizes nothing, no one; a drooling zombie who sleeps, eats and shits. Most of her children hardly visit. They want it to go away. They want to live in the memories of who she once was. This is no way to live.*

'Pleasures of War', says Lingford about her next film, 'came out of an idea of Clare Kitson (at Channel 4) and Dick Arnall (of Animate!) to put writers and animators together. I was given a blind date with Sara Maitland, a novelist and theologian.' Drawing their inspiration from the biblical story of Judith and Holofernes, Lingford and Maitland create a raunchy tale about an heroic woman who sacrifices herself to save her people. After an army led by General Holofernes invades the town of Bethelia, the widow Judith approaches the general's tent as an ambassador. After seducing the general with a little wine and sex, Judith sticks a sword up Holofernes' rump before using it to decapitate him. 'We were interested in the links between war and sex, eros and thanatos [Greek meaning, respectively, 'love' and 'death'], and in female violence', adds Lingford. 'In psychology, there is a phenomenon known as 'risky shifts' whereby a group will make a decision riskier than any individual member would make alone. Thus, the sex and decapitation scene became more and more extreme as we riffed on it together.' (When asked where the sword up the ass scene came from, Lingford says with a grin, 'it's from my marriage'.)

Once more using a woodcut style, the heavy contrast between bleached whites with black is accompanied by a touch of yellow and a brilliant bold red that gives the film a stark, sensuous brutality. Live-action footage of war occasionally stains the background, giving the film a timeless, universal context.

And here we come, at last, to *The Old Fools* (2002), Philip Larkin's ode to death and decay, and Ruth Lingford's most calm and gentle film. As the images shift from footage of elderly people to icons of their fading existence, Lingford's mixture of live-action footage and drawn animation is bathed in a warm sea of soothing blues. In one

263

scene, images of dentures, pills, glasses, slippers and other 'tools of the trade' appear as a deck of cards in a game of memory. Only now, memory is no longer just a game, it is a failing fight for life.

Larkin's poem is a moving, pained plea that evokes our schizoid emotions towards old age and mortality. His words are sarcastic and scared ('What do they think has happened, the old fools/To make them like this?'), yet also warm and sympathetic ('Perhaps being old is having lighted rooms/Inside your head, and people in them, acting'). Bob Geldof's reading of the poem is a masterpiece of restraint. His voice is warm and hypnotic. It soothes us as we are led towards oblivion. The unutterable is uttered. Death was never more peaceful.

Lingford's inspired choice of material is also the cause of the film's main weakness: the text and voice are so powerful that they often overwhelm the images. There are times when the voice and text are so enrapturing that your eyes close as the words seize your imagination. That's okay for an audio book, but not for a film.

'Some criticism I've had for this film', adds Lingford, 'which I think has some truth, is that it is too much an illustration of the poem. I do think it might have been more successful as a film if I had edited the text, and taken it somewhere more extreme, visually, but I felt a responsibility both to the poem and to my father's image.'

To pay the bills that animation films never can, Lingford teaches at the Royal College of Art and the National Film and Television school (she also has a year's teaching gig at Harvard in September 2005.) She has also worked on a couple of commercial projects. Lingford was the principal animator on *Silence* (1998), a concentration camp memoir and *An Eye for an Eye* (2001), a mind-blowing music video about the spread of ideology (co-directed with Shynola) for the band, Unkle.

Since making her debut animation in 1989, Ruth Lingford has put together a modest yet acclaimed body of work. Unlike many animators, Lingford has no recognizable visual voice. She has worked with a variety of media ranging from computers and live-action, to drawn animation and photographs. With the exception of *Pleasures of War* and *Death and the Mother*, she does not repeat herself. In terms of content, her last three independent films have been adaptations of existing texts. So why is it that you can still pinpoint Ruth Lingford's work in a crowd? Perhaps being a late bloomer in animation was a blessing. While many enter animation still struggling to come to terms with the strange hair that grows between their legs, Lingford began with, more or less, a stronger sense of who she was and what she wanted to say. As a result, the material rarely overshadows Lingford's voice. She has taken poems, fairytales and biblical stories and made them her own by using the core of those sources to pose difficult and personal questions about sexuality, desire, death, aging, violence, and identity. Lingford's films makes us squirm, so that we might think. She makes us think to make her, and us, better. As my grandma, and every grandma before her, once said: 'if it don't kill you, it'll make ya stronger'.

> In January, I went to visit my grandfather's grave. It's in this small village outside of the town. The cemetery is small and isolated surrounded only by trees. It was unplowed so I had to park the car near the highway and walk from the road. His grave is way at the back. The grave is unmarked because the family decided that it was best to wait for my grandmother (although that gal keeps on ticking). I have a general idea where he's buried but I'm not 100 per cent certain ... anyway ... so here I am standing in arctic conditions ... with no one around ... it's completely silent ... and I just start talking to my grandfather out loud ... and of course ... while I'm doing this I start conversing with myself out loud ... asking myself why I'm doing this. I ask myself, 'shit ... if he can hear me so can the others here ... so I say hello to them ... and then figure ... well ... if they CAN hear me ... then they likely know all that's going on in the world and don't need me to spell it out ... besides... if they're spirits ... they probably ain't here anyway ... this goes on for about 10 minutes ... and then I say bye and walk back to the car. I sit a bit and wonder what the fuck was that all about.'

'We shall find out.'

Filmography of Ruth Lingford

1989	Whole Lot of Love
1990	Sea in The Blood
1992	Crumble
1992	Baggage
1994	What She Wants
1997	Death and the Mother
1998	Pleasures of War
2002	The Old Fools
2004	Unkle: Eye for an Eye

265